The Book of

SAMPFORD COURTENAY
with Honeychurch

The History of a Rural Community

BY STEPHANIE POUYA

HALSGROVE

First published in Great Britain in 2003

*This book is dedicated to the people of
Sampford Courtenay and Honeychurch,
past, present and future.*

British Library Cataloguing-in-Publication Data
A CIP record for this title is available from the British Library

ISBN 1 84114 249 2

HALSGROVE

Halsgrove House
Lower Moor Way
Tiverton, Devon EX16 6SS
Tel: 01884 243242
Fax: 01884 243325
email: sales@halsgrove.com
website: www.halsgrove.com

Frontispiece photograph: *John E. Hawkins of Solland with a Red Devon bullock, 1922.*

Printed and bound by CPI Bath Press, Bath.

*Whilst every care has been taken to ensure the accuracy of the
information contained in this book, the author and publisher disclaim responsibility
for any mistakes which may have been inadvertently included.*

CONTENTS

Above: *Chevrolet with hay sweep at Sampford Chapple, 1930s. Left to right, back row: Courtenay Johns, Bill Paddon; front row: George Horn, Eva Paddon (née Arscott), James Fewings Arscott junr, Ellen Arscott.*

Right: *Charles Reddaway trimming hedge banks, 1940s.*

Below: *Bank Cottage and Little Hilly Cottage, c.1910. The boy in the centre of the picture has not been identified.*

ACKNOWLEDGEMENTS

With special thanks for their support and interest to:

Les Beer, Mary Cleverdon, the late Bert Coates, Valerie Hawking, John Hawkins, Myrtle Hunkin, Jack Jervoise, Freddie Johns, Barbara and Bob Johnson, Lilian Loosemore, Rosemary Lowe, Ann Miles, Don Miles (especially for his contribution of more than 50 photographs), John Morris, Margaret Murray, Doris and Len Piper, Marion Pratt, Marguerite Pye (postcards collected by the late Norman Pye), Audrey and Phil Reddaway, John Reddaway, Jose and Stewart Reddaway, Peter and Shirley Reddaway, Robert Reddaway (Reddaway Farm), Irene Sampson, Mavis Sleeman, Ralph Squire, Lorna Weeks, Marilyn Weeks and not least to my partner John Askew for his help and forbearance over the last two years.

With grateful thanks also to:

Pat Cockwill, Kate Dean, George Dennis, Rosie Dunn, George Gardner, Ann and Peter Green, Doris Guy, Sandra Harper, John Hawking, Joyce Hershey, John Hodge (Shores), Pauline Houben, Irene Morris, Ruth O'Byrne, John Pearson, Bert Piper, Betty and Sam Robertson, Mary Rowell, Clarice Sampson, Jean Shields, Pat Squire, Penny Stanley, Mike Steward, Denise and Stan Stimson, Christine Stoneman, Elspeth Veale, Hugh Webb, Margaret Weeks and Charles Westlake.

May Queen Rose Hawking with attendants Pauline Reddaway and David Piper, Rosemary Cleverdon and Patricia Shead, 1962. [Western Times]

Canon Arthur Squance 'skittling for a pig', church fête at the old rectory, 1950s.

Hawkins' family cycling trip to Dartmoor, 1919.

Eleanor Hawkins at Solland, c.1915.

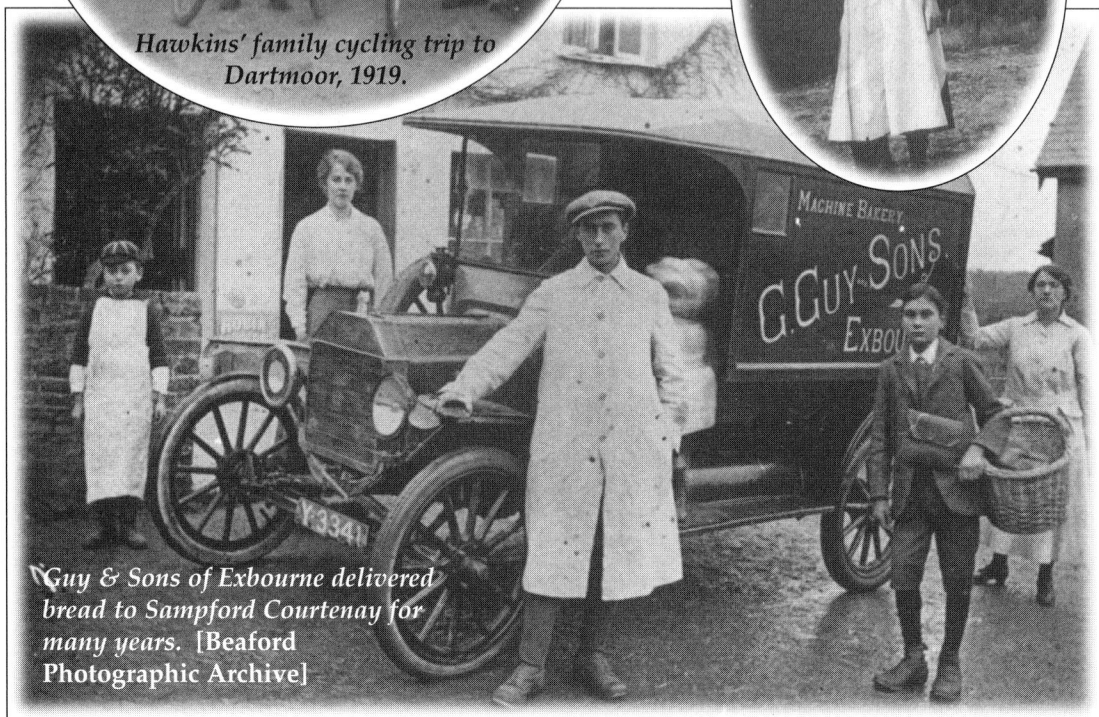

Guy & Sons of Exbourne delivered bread to Sampford Courtenay for many years. [Beaford Photographic Archive]

INTRODUCTION

I first saw Sampford Courtenay and Honeychurch on a wet, grey afternoon in November 1994. We had extended our house-hunting expeditions into Mid Devon and, even in the rain, we immediately fell in love with Frankland, one of the sixteenth-century farmhouses in the parish. Following our move to the area in the fine summer of 1995, we soon became aware of the many attractions of the surrounding countryside. Living in an old house, I was curious about the previous inhabitants. I did some initial research which led to a desire to know more of the parish as a whole. The only existing history was a brief account written in 1957 by Revd Fulford Williams and I had to refer to original sources for most of the pre-twentieth-century information. The decision to attempt this book has led, over the past two years, to my spending many absorbing and amusing hours browsing through the old records and talking to local residents. There is a wealth of information available, particularly on the manorial history held by the lords of the manor, King's College, Cambridge, much of which I have, as yet, been unable to examine. I hope that in the following pages I have selected the most interesting facts and the most entertaining anecdotes. Inevitably, faced with blurred memories and differing versions of facts and events, I will have made some errors and, having to restrict my narrative to a manageable number of pages, I have had to make many omissions; for both I apologise.

This book would not have been possible without the support and guidance of the many people who have helped me with the loan of photographs and other memorabilia, recollections of events and anecdotes and answers to my endless questions. I am grateful also for financial assistance from the Village Hall Management Committee and from the Awards for All Lottery Grants Scheme.

Stephanie Pouya, March 2003.

Sampford Courtenay School, c.1900 – Rebecca Cooper (see pages 169–172) is pictured in the fourth row, seventh from the left. Note the laced boots with steel-capped toes and heels.

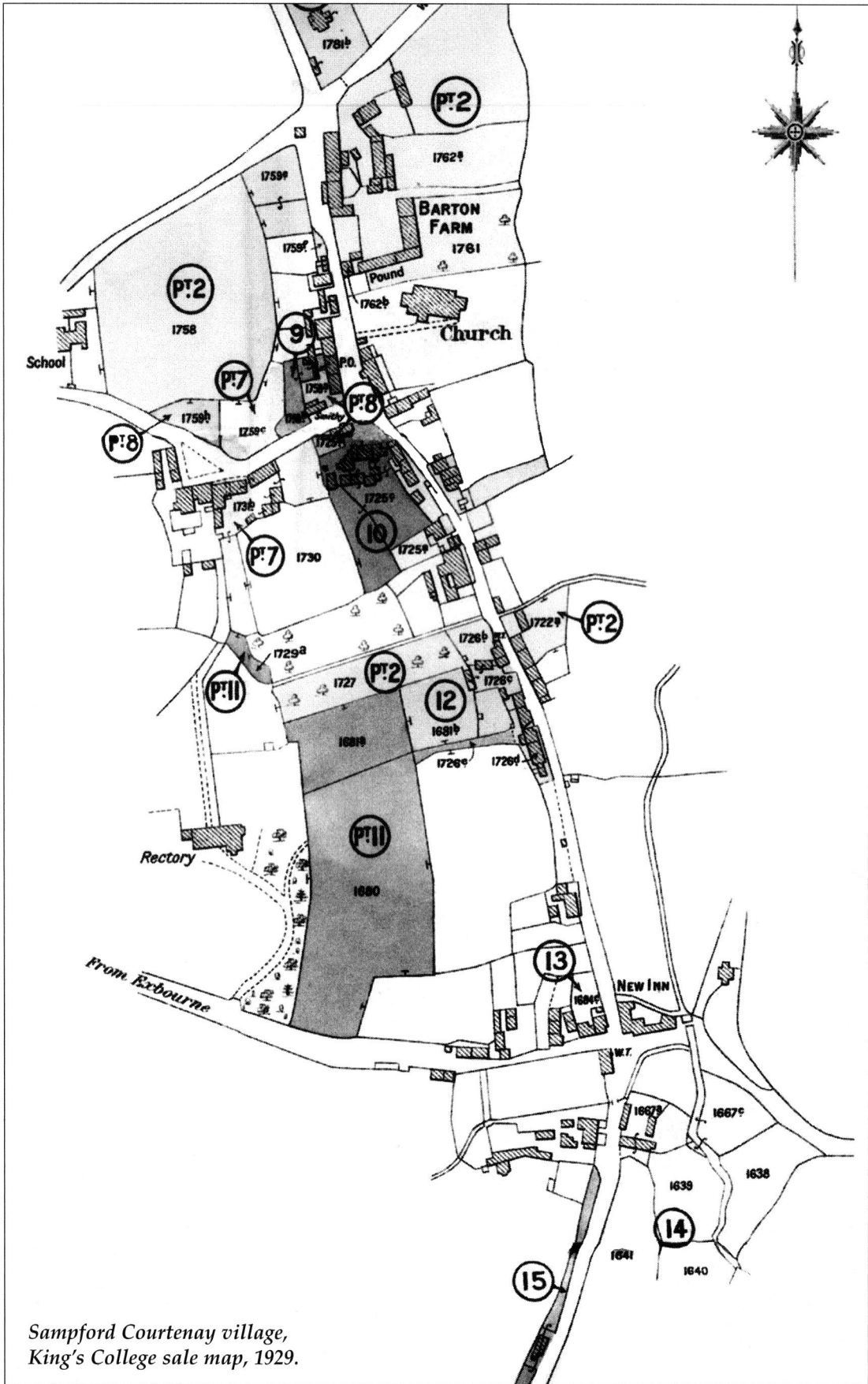

Sampford Courtenay village,
King's College sale map, 1929.

Chapter One

THE EARLY YEARS

How often have I loiter'd o'er thy green,
Where humble happiness endear'd each scene!
How often have I paused on every charm,
The shelter'd cot, the cultivated farm,
The never-failing brook, the busy mill,
The decent church that topt the neighbouring hill.
From 'The Deserted Village' by Oliver Goldsmith, 1770.

Sampford Courtenay is situated in the very centre of Devon and is an attractive rural parish, lying between the River Okement to the west and the River Taw to the east. The hamlet of Honeychurch forms the northern boundary, whilst the southern boundary follows the northern fringes of Dartmoor. A southern spur of the old parish, which was in existence until 1987, stretched to the foothills of the moors at Sticklepath. From the high point of Honeychurch, the southernmost part of the parish can be seen, some five miles distant, with the large expanse of Cosdon Beacon and the high peaks of Yes Tor and High Willhays forming an impressive backdrop. The landscape comprises undulating hills and valleys with numerous winding, steep-sided lanes criss-crossing between the isolated farms and hamlets. The small village is situated towards the north of the parish and is one of the prettiest in Mid Devon, described by the historian W.G. Hoskins as 'cheerful, neat and clean with much whitewashed cob and good thatching.' In the centre of the village are the imposing fifteenth-century Church of St

Andrew and Church House, where the Prayer Book Rebellion began in 1549. In many ways the parish, the village and the hamlets, particularly Honeychurch with its twelfth-century church and original Domesday farms, have changed little over the centuries.

There have been several alterations to the parish boundaries in the last 100 years or so. Following the Local Government Act of 1894, Honeychurch was joined to Sampford Courtenay for civil purposes. In 1927 the two parishes were united ecclesiastically, with Sticklepath separating to join Belstone. In 1987, following a review by the Boundary Commission and the construction of the new A30 trunk road, Sticklepath detached from Sampford Courtenay to form a separate civil parish. There were also some minor transfers of land from Bondleigh to Honeychurch in 1884 and the mid-twentieth century. Sampford Courtenay now covers a total area of 3,350 hectares (8,275 acres) but with a relatively small population of 528 people (year 2000 figures). Sticklepath comprises 166 hectares with a population

Looking south to Cosdon Beacon from the north of the parish, 1996.

of 421. The combined population of Sampford Courtenay (including Sticklepath) and Honeychurch in 1801 was 1,026 and, therefore, has changed little in 200 years.

Sampford Courtenay is one of the few places in Devon west of Exeter with a definite link with Roman Britain. In 1952 a Roman road running westwards from Exeter was discovered on the line of the boundary between North and South Tawton parishes. A Roman station was established at Nemetostatio (North Tawton) – the site is just east of the River Taw, not far from Falcadon Farm, which is on the western bank of the river in Sampford Courtenay. A fort has been identified at Okehampton (possibly a new location for the North Tawton garrison) so the Romans must have continued their course westwards through Sampford Courtenay parish. A main Celtic trackway or fosseway from Tongue End to Beacon Cross has also been traced. The road from Okehampton via Appledore Hill and Beacon Cross to Newland Bridge was the main road from west to east in medieval times. The origins of the naming of Beacon Cross probably date back to the end of the Roman period when a network of fire beacons on the high points of the countryside was used to give warning of seaborne attack. Beacons formed part of the Saxon defence against the Vikings and were prepared at times of invasion scares such as in 1588 against the Armada and in the early 1800s against Napoleon.

The Saxons are thought to have entered Devon in the seventh century and their land unit of the 'manor' as the holding of a single lord, and the grouping of manors into hundreds, was gradually established. Sampford Courtenay is unusual amongst large Devon parishes in that it consists of one manor which, under the later Saxon kings, acquired its own church. The present parish (together with Sticklepath) is constituted by the original manor, with lands later cultivated in the surrounding 'waste' and added to it. The hundred is that of Black Torrington. There must have been a reason, now lost, for the inclusion of Sampford Courtenay with a distant hundred centre rather than the much nearer one of North Tawton.

The Saxons favoured an 'open-field' system of farming, where very large fields around the village were divided into numerous narrow strips, each one cultivated by a different farmer. Nineteenth-century maps reveal evidence of a possible strip system north of Green Hill. Most open fields disappeared very early in the South West, probably in the thirteenth and fourteenth centuries, to be replaced by the small fields with high hedge banks still much in evidence today.

Following the Norman Conquest of 1066, most of England passed quickly into the hands of William the Conqueror. The Domesday Book, a survey of his kingdom completed in 1086, recorded 'Norman' as holding 'Sanfort' before 1066 under Edward the Confessor. 'Sanfort' progressed to 'Sanford', 'Sandfort', 'Saunforde Curtenay' by 1242, and finally, to Sampford Courtenay by 1274. The name probably originates from the 'sandy ford' crossing a tributary of the Hole Brook at the main approach to the village, with 'Courtenay' added following the acquisition of the manor by that family. In 1086 Baldwin (de Brionne) held 'Sanfort'. It paid geld (tax) for two and a half hides – a hide was the amount of land which could be ploughed annually by a team of eight oxen, usually around 120 acres. There was land for 40 ploughs and, in demesne (land reserved for the lord's benefit), one hide with four ploughs and eight serfs. There were 40 villeins (who worked on the lord's lands in return for their tenements) and 30 bordars (smallholders) with 20 ploughs and one and a half hides. There were 60 acres of meadow, 40 acres of woodland, and pasture two leagues long and one league wide – a league or 'leuga' was traditionally a mile and a half, but possibly shorter. There were: one cob (packhorse), 28 cattle, 200 sheep and 40 goats. It was worth £12, formerly £9 when Baldwin received it. Domesday does not record details of families, but the total population of Sampford Courtenay at this time can be estimated to have been around 300.

Walter held 'Honechercha' (Honeychurch) from Baldwin. Alwin Black held it before him. It paid tax for half a hide. There was land for five ploughs and, in demesne, two ploughs, four slaves and one virgate of land – a virgate was about one quarter of a hide, notionally 30 acres. There were four villeins with one plough and one virgate of land, four acres of meadow, ten acres of pasture and two acres of underwood, 30 cattle, eight pigs, 42 sheep and 19 goats. Its value was 30s. (15s. when Walter acquired it).

The Book of Fees, or 'Testa de Nevill', in 1242 contained details of land holdings and feudal tenancies for Exchequer purposes. Sampford Courtenay and Honeychurch were part of Okehampton Honour, with various sub-manors held for knight's fees. A knight's fee was a feudal obligation to provide military service to the Crown in the form of a knight with his retainers for 40 days each year. Knight service was often commuted to the payment of a fine and was abolished in 1660. The sub-manors were:

Durneford [Dornaford] *held, with three others outside the parish, by John de Molis for two and a half knight's fees.*

Lewidecote [Lydcott], *Cockescumb* [Corscombe], *Westcote* [Westacott in Honeychurch], *and Rokevurth* [probably Rowtry in Honeychurch] *all held by Richard Cadyo for one knight's fee.*

Harpeford [Halford] *together with Radeweye* [Reddaway] *held by Richard Fitz Ralph and Galfrid de Radeweye for one half of a knight's fee.*

Wytheleghe [Willey] *held by Drogo de Teynton for one twentieth of a knight's fee.*

Hunichurche [Honeychurch] *held for one knight's fee by William de Legh, Walter de Mumlaunde and Adam and Margery de Hunichurche.*

The expansion of the manor of Sampford Courtenay by cultivation of the waste is a lost process but is partly revealed by the dates when the farms first appeared in various records, although the origins of many must have been much earlier, possibly dating from pre-Saxon times. The following details of the farms of Sampford Courtenay and Honeychurch are extracted from the *Transactions of the Devonshire Association*, 1957, and the *Place Names of Devon*, 1931.

Agistment: Agisterment – a Norman legal term for the letting of grazing land [Assize 1306].

Appledore: Apeldorneford – probably 'appletree ford' [Subsidy Roll 1330].

Beaumead: Boghemede – the 'curved meadow' [Assize 1306].

Beer: The home of John atte Beare [Subsidy Roll 1330].

Beerhill: Bearehill – Beare meaning 'wood' [Rental Roll Edward VI].

Brook: Broke [Rental Roll Edward VI].

Cliston: Clerkeston – the 'clerk's land' [Subsidy Roll 1333].

Coldacott: Caldecote – the 'cold cottage' [Assize 1238].

Coombe: Combe – the 'hollow' [Edward VI Rental].

Corscombe: Cockescumb – the 'cock's valley' [1242].

Dornaford: Durneford – the 'secret or hidden ford' [1242].

Frankland: Franklond – perhaps 'Franca's land' [Edward VI Rental 1549].

Fullaford: Foleford – the 'dirty ford' [Inquisition Post Mortem 1378].

Halford: Herpeford or Herpford – the ford by the 'herepaeo', 'herepath' or 'army path' [1242].

Hatherton: Hatherdon – the 'heath land' [Assize 1418].

Hayrish: Hayrish juxta Tawe – the 'stubble land' [Fine Recovery 1637].

Honeycott: Honycott [Edward VI Rental 1549].

Incott: Yundecote – 'further cot(e)' or 'beyond the cot(e)' [Subsidy Roll 1330].

Langabeer: Langbeare – the 'long wood' [Edward VI Rental 1549].

Langmead: Langemede – the 'long meadow' [Assize 1238].

Lydcott: Lewidecot or Ludecote – probably originates from an Old English name 'Leofgyp's cot(e)' [1242].

Oxenpark: [Fine Recovery 1637].

Pitt: Pithayes – the 'farm in the hollow' [Fine Recovery 1616].

Ratcombe: Radcombe – the 'red valley' [Edward VI Rental 1549].

Reddaway: Radeweye – the 'red way or track' [Assize 1238].

Rowden: Rughedon – the 'rough hill' [Assize 1244].

Rowtry: Routrewe – the 'rough tree' [Assize 1283].

Slade: Slaed – meaning 'valley' [Fine Recovery 1592] *but the existing farmstead is older (mid-fifteenth-century).*

Solland: Sanlond – the 'sandy land' [Subsidy Roll 1330].

Trecott: Trycote – the 'cottages by the tree' [Assize 1296].

Underdown: Underdowne [Assize Edward III].

Ventown: Fennetowne – the 'fenny land' [Edward VI Rental 1549].

Westacott: Westcote – the 'cottage in the west' [1242].

Willey: Wythelgh [sic], *Wygelege, Wyghelegh or Wytelegh, probably 'Wiga's leah' a personal name* [1242].

Withybrook: Wythibrok juxta Saunford Curtenay [Assize 1291].

Wood: [Edward VI Rental].

Yondhill: Yundehill – 'beyond the hill' [Edward VI Rental 1549].

The Okehampton Honour, which included Sampford Courtenay and Honeychurch, passed from Baldwin de Brionne firstly to his son Richard and then to his daughter Adeliza. She died in 1142; the barony subsequently passed through the female line and was eventually inherited by Hawise, Baldwin's great-great-granddaughter. In 1173 Hawise married Reginald de Courtenay and the title of Baron of Okehampton passed to Courtenay in right of his wife.

The Courtenays

The Courtenay family, who take their name from a small town to the south of Paris, crossed from France to England with Eleanor, daughter and sole heir of William Duke of Aquitaine, on her marriage to King Henry II in 1152. Reginald de Courtenay immediately established himself in Devon by his marriage to Hawise. Robert, the son of Reginald and Hawise, inherited the Barony of Okehampton on the death of his father in 1194 and married Mary, daughter of William de Vernon (de Redvers), the 5th Earl of Devon, whose father, Baldwin de Redvers, was the son of Baldwin's son Richard. Baldwin de Redvers had been created 1st Earl of Devon in 1141. The earldom passed to the Courtenays after they were judged the legitimate heirs on the demise of the de Redvers/de Vernon family.

Robert died in 1242 and the Barony of Okehampton passed to John, three Hughs, Edward (the 10th Earl of Devon), another Hugh and to Thomas in 1422. Thomas, the 12th Earl, was eight years old and became a ward of the King. John Copelstone and Nicholas Radford were appointed stewards of the Courtenay inheritance in Devon during the minority of the young earl. Thomas made a good marriage in 1431 to Margaret Beaufort, the granddaughter of John of Gaunt, which allied him to the Lancastrian cause. He was a haughty man and did much to provoke lawlessness and violence in Devon. Thomas died in 1459 and his three sons all met violent ends during the Wars of the Roses – Thomas, the 13th Earl, beheaded at York after the Battle of Towton in 1461, Henry beheaded at Salisbury in 1467 and John, the 15th Earl, killed in the Battle of Tewkesbury in 1471. All were unmarried. The elder line of the Courtenays thus became extinct or out of favour and Edward IV granted the lands and honours of the Earls of Devon to Humphrey, Lord Stafford, who was the 14th Earl in 1470 for three months, then briefly to John Courtenay, followed by John Nevill, Earl of Northumberland, who was killed in 1471, then to George, Duke of Clarence (King Edward's brother), who was executed in 1478, and finally to John, Lord Dynham.

After the Battle of Bosworth in 1485, Lord Dynham was dispossessed and Henry VII restored the estates to Edward, the grandson of Hugh Courtenay (this Hugh was the brother of Edward the 10th Earl). Edward, the 16th Earl, died in 1509 and was succeeded by his son William, who married Katherine Plantagenet, daughter of Edward IV. The marriage was to prove somewhat disastrous, for the connection with the House of York led Henry VII to imprison William for fear he might conspire against him. When Henry VIII came to the throne, William was pardoned but he died in 1511 before his formal investiture as Earl of Devon could take place. King Henry granted all the estates of the earldom of Devon to William's widow, Lady Katherine, for her life.

William and Katherine's second son Henry, born in 1501, was restored in blood in 1512 so that he was able to take the title of the 18th Earl of Devon. Through his mother, Henry was cousin to King Henry VIII; the two young cousins were at first great friends and the King created Henry Courtenay Marquis of Exeter in 1525. The Marquis was immensely popular in the South West, not only because of his ancestral position but also for his personal charm. An ancient document gives an interesting description of him:

The Marquis of Exeter, 36 [years of age]*, lusty and strong of power, specially beloved, diseased often with the gout and next unto the Crown of any one within England.*

His subsequent disfavour with the King was largely due to his nearness to the throne, but was increased by his close friendship with the Pole family, who were also of Yorkist blood. At this time King Henry's obvious intention to marry Anne Boleyn was beginning to make him unpopular and it was rumoured in the South West that Henry Courtenay would 'wear the garland' some day. These rumours were reported to the King and in 1538 the Marquis and Lord Montague, one of the Poles, were arrested and indicted as traitors. It is quite certain that they had committed no crime; the trial was a farce, but a guilty verdict was inevitable and Courtenay and Montague were executed on Tower Hill on 9 December 1538. Courtenay's execution caused bitter resentment against the King in the South West and may well have been one of the causes of the Prayer Book Rebellion a few years later.

King Henry extended his animosity to Henry Courtenay's 12-year-old son Edward, whom he deprived of all hereditary rights and imprisoned in the Tower. The Courtenay estates reverted to the Crown. Henry Courtenay had been by far the greatest landowner in south-western England, with property in Devon, Cornwall, Somerset and Dorset besides other lands in Berkshire, Buckinghamshire and Hampshire. In Devon alone the rental yielded over £1,320 per year, including Sampford Courtenay manor valued at £28.7s.4d., the advowson at £26.13s.4d. and Sticklepath advowson at £2. Sampford Courtenay was granted to Thomas Clynton and the advowson given to Queen Catherine Howard and, on her execution, to Catherine Parr. Edward Courtenay remained in captivity for the next 15 years until released by Queen Mary and restored

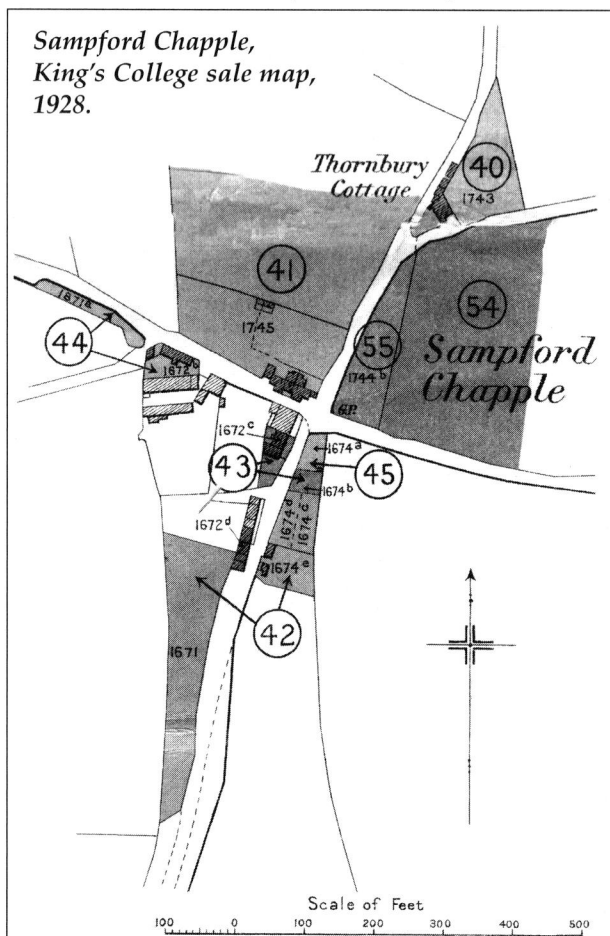

Sampford Chapple, King's College sale map, 1928.

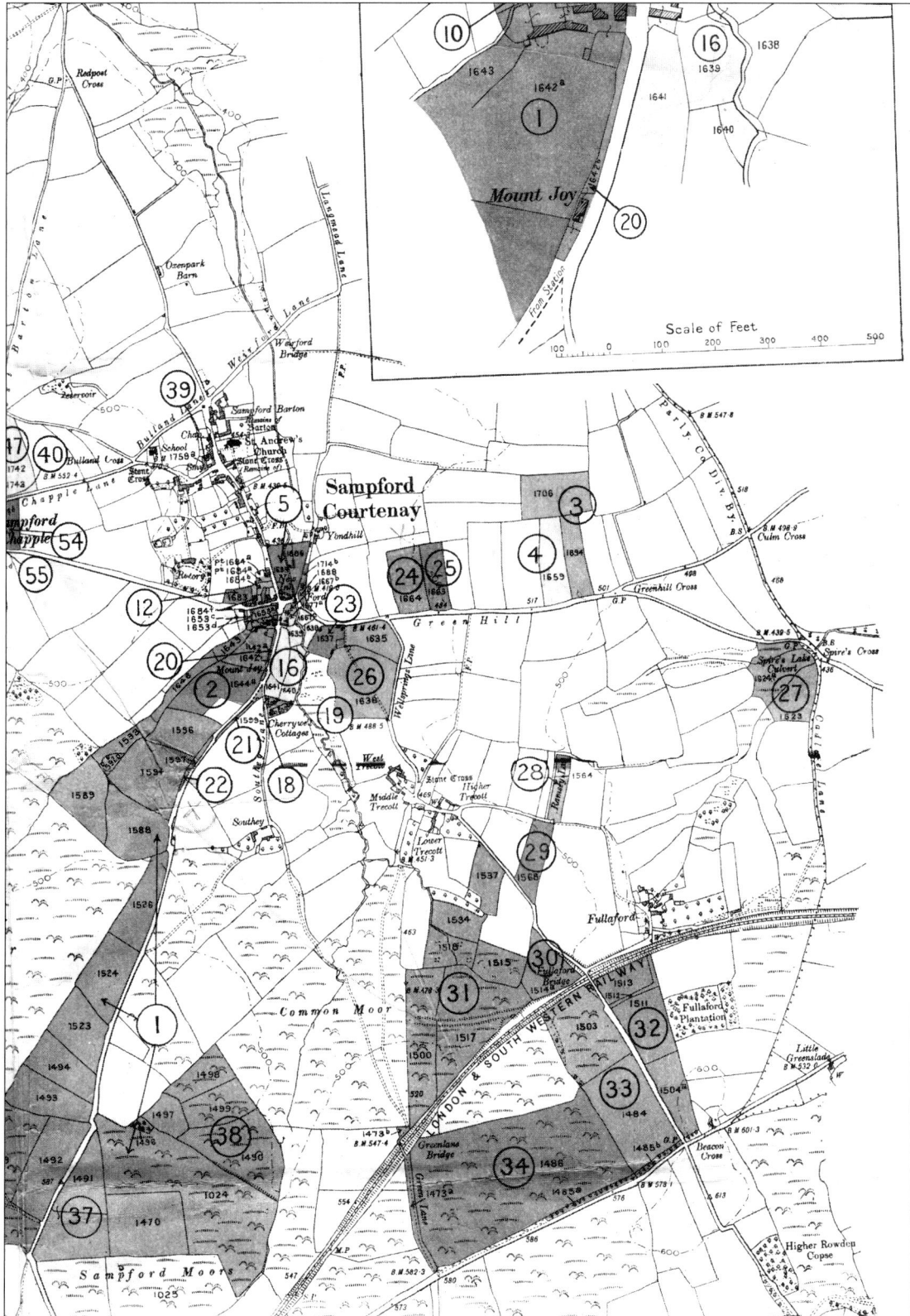

Sampford Courtenay – King's College sale map, 1928.

as Earl of Devon in 1553. The Queen was looking for a husband and did not find the prospect of Edward sharing her throne unfavourable. Unfortunately for the young Courtenay, he preferred Princess Elizabeth and a request to transfer his affections to her younger sister did not meet with Mary's approval. Offended, she placed her scorned hand in that of Philip of Spain. This unpopular marriage provoked many, particularly in the South West, to favour a union between Elizabeth and Courtenay and the establishment of the young couple on the throne. Revolts followed, from which Elizabeth dissociated herself, for she had no liking for him. In 1556, when travelling in Italy, Edward Courtenay, still unmarried, died in Padua; there was some suspicion of poison.

Thus ended the male line of the elder house of Courtenay; Edward's possessions, including the dormant claim to the Barony of Okehampton, passed to the descendants of the four sisters of his great-grandfather Edward, the 16th Earl of Devon. The manor of Sampford Courtenay passed from Thomas Clynton to his daughter Winifred Lady St John, with reversion after her death to Thomas Sackville, Lord Buckhurst. In 1569 Lord Buckhurst covenanted to convey to Queen Elizabeth the lordship and manor of Sampford Courtenay and the advowson of the church (which Sir John Paulet, Lord St John and Lady Winifred his wife held for the life of the said lady) in exchange for the manor of Witham in Sussex held by King's College, Cambridge. By deed enrolled in Chancery, dated 12 January 1570, Lord Buckhurst granted the manor and the advowson to the Queen and on 4 March she re-granted them to the Provost and Scholars of King's College. Lord Buckhurst granted a yearly rent of £28 to the college for the life of Lady Winifred and it was not until 23 December 1601 that the college finally took possession. King's College remain lords of the manor to the present day, although they sold the farms and cottages in the 1920s.

The Prayer Book Rebellion, 1549

The most notable event in Sampford Courtenay's history is its participation in the Western Rebellion of 1549. What is so intriguing is why the people of a tranquil country parish were so resolute against changes to the format of their religious observance, that they were willing to risk their lives in what they must have realised was a hopeless cause against the might of the King's armies. The quotes included in the following description of the events, unless otherwise stated, are those of John Hooker, a contemporary historian living in Exeter.

The Reformation of the Catholic Church began under Henry VIII with the Dissolution of the Monasteries. In the 1530s all those in Devon were swept away and their lands passed into the hands of the King, who immediately either sold them to the local gentry or granted them to loyal supporters. The largest receiver of monastic lands in Devon, including the greater part of Tavistock Abbey, was John Russell, who had begun life as a Dorset squire, had risen high in the service of the King and did much of his unpleasant work. Whilst Henry had broken with Rome, he did not introduce any radical or extensive changes to church services. His Six Articles of Religion, passed by Parliament in 1539, had under his instruction to remain in force until his son Edward came of age. In the unessential parts of the Mass English had replaced Latin, but such alterations were largely ignored in remoter parts of the kingdom, where the ritual in parish churches still retained its ancient splendour, brightening the dull, daily routine and drab surroundings of the poorer people. However, following the succession of Edward VI in 1547, Archbishop Cranmer set out a programme of more radical reform, which abolished 'papistical superstitions and abuses'. A visitation of the whole kingdom was ordered to enforce a series of injunctions which required the destruction of all images and cancelled all fast and feast days, condemned any form of recitation of the Rosary and forbade the burning of all lights apart from two on the altar. All processions, both inside and outside the church, were to cease. The Chantries Act forbade all chantry chapels where private masses were said for the repose of the souls of the dead. During 1548 commissioners toured the country to ensure that these new rulings were being carried out. Within a matter of months, the people were deprived of the

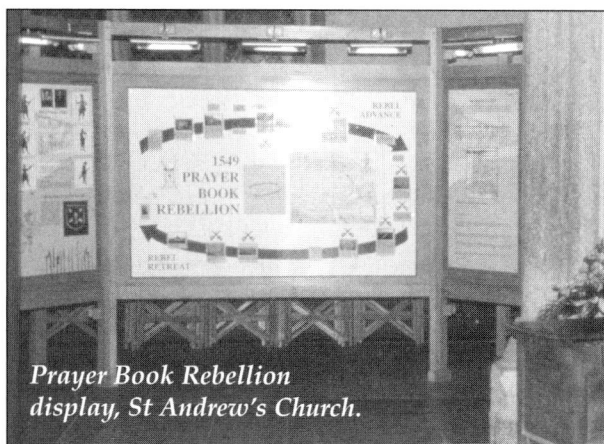

Prayer Book Rebellion display, St Andrew's Church.

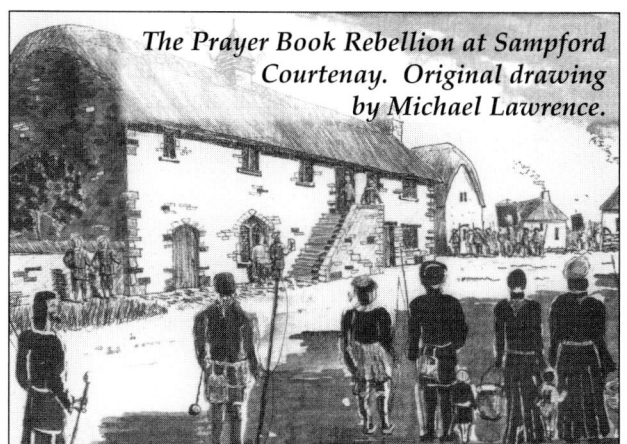

The Prayer Book Rebellion at Sampford Courtenay. Original drawing by Michael Lawrence.

Church House, Sampford Courtenay, c.1980.

ancient symbols of their faith which had been familiar to them from childhood.

The visitation to Cornwall provoked riots which were swiftly and brutally dealt with by the King's men and left a smouldering resentment throughout the South West. Meanwhile, Cranmer was busy preparing his new Prayer Book, which translated all church services from Latin into English, eliminated much of the ancient ritual and removed most of the feast days from the calendar. The book was passed by Parliament in January 1549 and in March received royal assent. The new service was to be introduced in all churches on Whit Sunday and there were hefty punishments for clerics refusing to use the book. Cranmer's translation was to be appreciated in the centuries to follow, but the common people of the time were suspicious; for them the old Latin was the surest safeguard of orthodoxy. In Cornwall members of the gentry, including Humphrey Arundell and John Wynslade, joined priests and commoners in opposition to the proposed new practices and within a short space of time some 6,000 rebels, with Arundell as their general, had assembled at Bodmin. The rebels claimed continued loyalty to the King, but felt that it was their right to take up arms to persuade him to change his mind in the best interests of the people. Their demands were set out in eight Articles. In the meantime, a disturbance in the next county was to increase the alarm of the Privy Council and Protector Somerset, the King's uncle.

In Sampford Courtenay on Whit Sunday, 9 June, the village and the church were unusually crowded; everyone wondered whether the rector, William Harper, would abandon his richly embroidered vestments and use the new form of service. Exactly why the people of Sampford Courtenay were so opposed to the new English service is uncertain but Harper may well have been an agitator. He had been presented to the living by Catherine Parr and previously had been her Clerk of the Closet, a position of some importance. After Henry VIII's death it seems likely that Harper, by then nearing 70, took refuge in a remote country parish, as he was out of sympathy with the changes at Court. When the priest entered the chancel, the congregation were stunned for Father Harper had left off his fine vestments and he used the new English version of the Prayer Book, abiding by the new order of service. The service ended and the people issued from the church complaining angrily of the loss of their gorgeous ceremonial.

When Monday came, a larger and more hostile crowd assembled, many attracted by the Whitsun Ale festivities at Church House. As the priest approached the church, Thomas Underhill, a tailor, and William Segar, a labourer, barred his way and demanded to know what service he meant to say. 'In obedience to the law set forth I must say the new service,' answered Father Harper. 'That you will not!' he was told, 'We will have all such laws and ordinances touching Christian religion as were appointed by King Henry... until the King's Majesty that now is reaches the age of 24 years.' The crowd applauded and the priest, his resolve shaken, 'yielded to their wills and forthwith clothed himself in his old popish attire and sayeth mass and all such services as in times past accustomed.' Having listened reverently to the old service, the triumphant crowd came out of the church to enjoy the Whitsun celebrations or listen to inflammatory speeches. News of events at Sampford Courtenay spread quickly to neighbouring parishes 'as a cloud carried by a violent wind and as a thunder clap sounding through the whole country.'

The local Justices rushed to the scene to maintain the King's peace. Hearing of their approach, the ring-leaders consulted together and were 'so addicted and wholly bent on their follies that they fully resolved themselves willingly to maintain what naughtily they had begun.' Some discussion took place but, unwilling to use force or possibly because they were sympathetic with the rioters, the Justices departed:

... without anything done at all... The commoners having now their wills were set upon a pin that the game was theirs and they had won the garland before they had run the race!

It was at this point that William Hellyons, a franklin from a nearby parish, intervened, urging the mob to renounce their rebellion, but he only antagonised them further. He was taken prisoner and carried to Church House, where:

... he so earnestly reproved them of an evil success, that they fell in a rage with him and, not only with evil words reviled him, but also as he was going out of the church house and going down the stairs, one of them named Lithibridge [Lethbridge] with a bill struck him in the neck, and immediately notwithstanding his pitiful requests and lamentations, a number of the rest fell upon him and slew him and cut him in small pieces.

This was the first blood shed in the rebellion. There was now no going back and the rioters decided to join the Cornish rebels, who were by then advancing to London to press their demands.

On 11 June, the little company of Sampford Courtenay men joined the march east. Banners were unfurled, including that of the Five Wounds of Christ borne aloft during the Pilgrimage of Grace some years earlier and which had become the popular symbol of the Catholic faith. Behind the banner was carried the pyx, which traditionally hung over the altar and contained the sacra-ment. It is estimated that between 2,000 and 3,000 men had followed Arundell. When news of the rising reached London, Protector Somerset authorised two members of the Devon gentry, Sir Peter Carew and his uncle Sir Gawen, to do all that they could to persuade every man to return quietly to his home. In accordance with this instruction, on about 21 June a little company under Sir

Badge of the Five Wounds

Banner of the Five Wounds.

Peter's command set out from Exeter towards Crediton. Meanwhile, the rebels had barricaded the highway at Crediton and two barns adjacent to the road had been pierced with 'loops and holes' and men 'well appointed with bows and arrows and other weapons' had been positioned within. When the Carews arrived, the rebels refused to talk to them. Sir Peter charged the rampart and, in the struggle and confusion, the barns were set on fire and the defenders driven out. However, when Carew's men entered Crediton the town was deserted and the Government forces, with no enemy to encounter and insufficient men to hold the town, returned to Exeter having achieved nothing. The peasantry were far from paci-fied; the burning of the barns had inflamed them even further and, with the Banner of the Five Wounds before them, the procession of Devon and Cornish farmers and labourers marched on to Exeter.

By this time, fearing that affairs in the West were becoming much more serious, Somerset had appointed Lord John Russell, the Privy Seal, to head an army to suppress the rebellion. Lord Russell was President of the Council of the West, with jurisdiction over Devon, Cornwall, Dorset and Somerset, and an experienced commander. He was the obvious choice to restore peace. Towards the end of June, he left London and soon established a base at Honiton with a small group of professional soldiers. The rebels had now reached Exeter and the men from Devon joined their Cornish colleagues to send a manifesto to the Privy Council in the form of fresh Articles signed by the chief captains Humphrey Arundell, John Bury, John Sloman, Thomas Underhill and William Segar – the last three Sampford Courtenay men. The manifesto demanded a restoration of all the old customs and rituals, each article preceded by 'Item, we will have'. The rebels asked for: the sacrament again to hang over the high altar; curates to minister the sacrament of baptism on weekdays as well as on Sundays; holy bread and water every Sunday; palms and ashes at the times accustomed; images to be set up again in every church; the re-establish-ment of chantries; and the restoration of the two principal monasteries in each county. They also stated:

Item, we will not receive the new service because it is but like a Christmas game, but we will have our old service of Matins, Mass, Evensong and procession in Latin, as it was before.

The rebels tried to persuade the people of Exeter to support their cause. Many leading citizens had Catholic beliefs and sympathies, but decided their duty lay in obedience to the King, so they refused the rebels entry into the city. The gates were shut, but not before many sympathisers had left to join the rebel army. So began, on 2 July, a siege which lasted six weeks. The rebel forces, which had increased to several thousands, encircled the city. However, Arundell's army was not equipped to undertake the siege of a large city and was mainly reduced to firing small-calibre cannons, positioned on high ground outside the North Gate, and sniping from houses outside the city walls. In retaliation, the defenders made sallies from the city to demolish the closest houses.

Russell arrived at Honiton on the day the siege began, but his army numbered little more than 100 men and he had to wait for reinforcements before proceeding to Exeter. The Carews joined him with a contingent raised from Dorset and, on about 21 July, 150 Italian arquebusiers under Spinola arrived (an arquebus was a type of handgun), followed by about 1,000 German lanzknechts under Lord Grey de Wilton on 3 August and Sir William Herbert with 1,000 Welshmen on 6 August. The royal forces eventually numbered around 4,000. Arundell was keen to strike before Russell's reinforcements arrived and, in the last week of July, leaving a small force around Exeter, advanced as far as Fenny Bridges near Honiton. Russell decided to attack and, after a fierce battle, was the victor. Some 300 rebels were killed beyond the bridges in Blood Meadow.

The situation in Exeter was becoming desperate; the inhabitants were short of food and ready to surrender. On 3 August Mayor Blackaller was about to cut his way out when Russell, joined by Grey's lanzknechts, began his march to the city. Russell camped for the night at Carey's windmill on Aylesbeare Common. Under cover of darkness, Arundell launched a surprise attack but the rebels were driven back and suffered many casualties. The rebel commanders summoned help and a force said to number 6,000 men was assembled. Although the rebels possessed an advantage in terms of numbers, the royal troops were trained professionals with superior equipment. On the morning of 4 August, there was a battle at Clyst St Mary. Russell's men set every house in the village on fire; the insurgents, driven out of the houses, made a brave resistance, fighting to the death in most cases. About 1,000 men were slain and many taken prisoner. The royal army continued to advance, but Grey thought he saw the glint of armour to his rear and, to prepare for what he believed might be an attack, Russell ordered all 900 prisoners to be slaughtered. That night, Russell's men camped on Clyst Heath. On hearing of the massacre, a large contingent of rebel forces entrenched themselves on the lower slopes of the heath. Russell attacked at dawn the next day. The rebels fought fiercely:

Valiantly and stoutly they stood to their tackle, and would not give over as long as life or limb lasted, yet in the end they were all overthrown and few or none left alive.

Russell then marched to Exeter where the remains of the rebel forces, realising they were defeated, had raised their camps and retreated silently towards the west. Before midnight, the camps were empty. Early on the morning of 6 August, Russell was outside the South Gate of the city and the mayor and his officials came out to welcome him. The royal troops spent ten days in Exeter and the dreadful reckoning began. Gallows were set up and among those hanged was Robert Welsh, the vicar of St Thomas, who was strung up 'in his popish apparel' at the top of his church tower. By all accounts, his corpse remained there until the reign of Mary (1553–58).

While Russell was occupied in Exeter, the rebels were quietly reorganising what remained of their forces near Sampford Courtenay. They were encamped and entrenched on high ground to the east of the village. Russell heard the news on 16 August and set off immediately with an army made larger by the arrival of the Welshmen under Sir William Herbert. After camping at Crediton overnight, Grey and Herbert were sent forward the next morning with a large division of the army, while Russell was to bring up the rear. There was a skirmish in the lanes at the 'Wardons' (War Downs) in North Tawton parish, in which Maunders, a Sampford Courtenay shoemaker, was captured. One of the fields there is still known as 'Blood Acre'. The royal troops then approached the rebel camp from two directions and attacked with such violence that the rebels were pushed back upon Sampford Courtenay village. Although a counter-attack was made on the rear of the royal army by a contingent under Humphrey Arundell and a battle raged for an hour, the rebels were forced down into the village streets, where they made a last desperate stand:

They would not yield to no persuasions nor did, but most manfully did abide the fight and never gave over until that both in the town and in the field they were all for the most part taken or slain.

Between 500 and 600 men were killed, among them Thomas Underhill, the Sampford Courtenay tailor who had become one of the chief captains, and, in the pursuit of those that fled, another 700. Arundell escaped to Okehampton, where he made a further stand, but was captured at Launceston on 19 August. Others fled into Somerset but were overwhelmed by the end of August. Four of the rebel leaders, including Humphrey Arundell, were tried at Westminster in November and, in January 1550, hanged, drawn and quartered at Tyburn. Another 1,000 rebels were captured and executed under martial law without trial.

Bulland Cross (Cross No. 1).

Trecott Cross (Cross No. 2).

Cherrywell Cross (Cross No. 3).

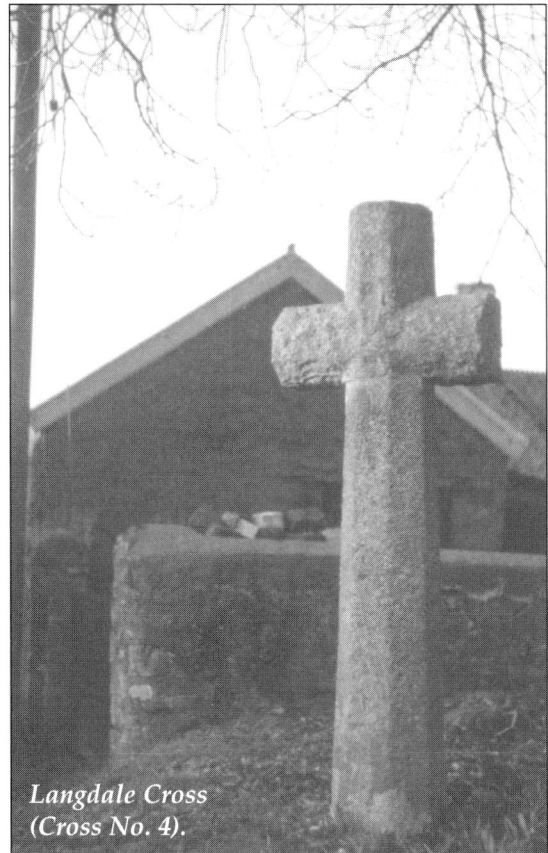

Langdale Cross (Cross No. 4).

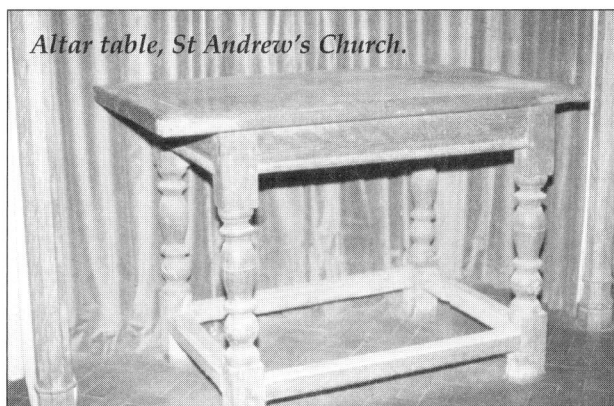

Altar table, St Andrew's Church.

The Stone Crosses

There are several stone crosses in and around the village of Sampford Courtenay. They are constructed of 'moorstone' (granite weathered on Dartmoor for thousands of years) and date from the fourteenth or fifteenth century. The churchyard cross is small and of rectangular section, chamfered below the arms and set on a large octagonal pedestal of two steps. Judging by their positions, the four wayside crosses appear to have protected the ancient approaches to the village. Wayside crosses mostly survived the Reformation, but were allowed to remain on sufferance only. In 1645 an Ordinance was passed for the removal of all crosses in or upon all churches, chapels and other open spaces, but the remote parts of the country such as Devon escaped much of the destruction. The wayside crosses are as follows:

Cross No. 1 is situated at Bulland Cross, near the Village Hall, at the fork of the old road leading to Exbourne and the lane to Cliston hamlet. The road was probably the original western exit of the village. This cross, which is of octagonal shape, is the only one to have survived intact. It has a small recess at the back of the shaft, which was possibly used as a niche for an image.

Cross No. 2 is situated in Trecott hamlet, probably still in its original position on the road which formed the southern access to the village from South Tawton and Dartmoor. The shaft is roughly square at the base but chamfered into an octagon above. The upper portion which has split down the centre has been secured with an iron band. It is attached to the shaft with iron clamps at a point where it has broken across, a short distance below the arms. According to E.A. Rawlence of Rawlence & Squarey (the King's College land agents), in an article written about the crosses in around 1928, tradition hands down the following account of the damage and repair. At the time when Robert Hern farmed West Trecott (mid-nineteenth century) a nearby oak tree was cut down and fell upon the cross, leaving it in a badly damaged condition. From the day of this accident, Hern was dogged with persistent bad luck – his cows and sheep cast their young and his crops failed. One day, as he was wandering over his land, a sudden inspiration came to him. Rawlence writes:

At the end of 1549, Cranmer published a pamphlet in answer to the Articles of the rebels in which he made a scathing attack on 'the ignorant men of Devon and Cornwall' who had died for their faith. In 1550 an Act directed that all popish books were to be destroyed. Any person found to possess such books, or any images taken from any church or chapel, was to be prosecuted. Orders were given for all altars in churches to be removed and replaced by 'the Lord's board after the form of an honest table decently covered.' The altar table currently situated in the north chapel of Sampford Courtenay Church is probably the one introduced following this Act. All resistance to change in religion was effectively quashed. A second prayer book, introduced by Cranmer in 1552 and which simplified worship even further (with some additional changes made by Elizabeth in 1559) remained substantially the Prayer Book of the Church of England. The suppression of the rebellion, known locally as the 'commotion time', signalled the decline of religious devotion among the people of Devon and Cornwall. After the passage of a few years, it was replaced by decent conformism, religious inactivity and widespread disinterest.

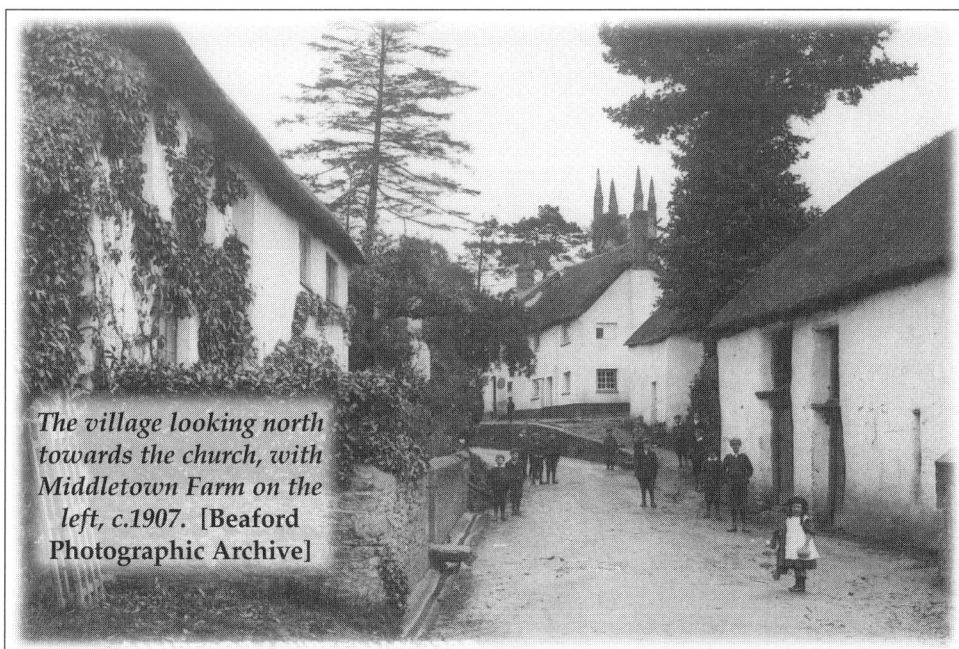

The village looking north towards the church, with Middletown Farm on the left, c.1907. [Beaford Photographic Archive]

Outside the New Inn, 1890. [Robert Burnard]

Above: *Westbury Cottage and Fir Cottage, c.1930.*

He stopped suddenly, and doffing his hat and scratching his head, as Devonshire farmers do on important occasions, he ejaculated aloud 'Dall'd if I don't believe it is that 'ere old cross!'.

No time was lost in putting matters right. The village blacksmith had soon constructed iron bands and clamps, and the cross was reassembled and set up in its place again. There it has remained to this day; the iron bands still bear the farmer's initials 'R.H.'. Rawlence relates: 'From that day the luck at West Trecott changed; the stock became prolific and Mother earth yielded her increase.'

But the dangers that beset the old cross were not yet ended. A rumour came to Farmer Hern's ears that a local builder was going to apply to the lords of the manor to erect cottages on the piece of wasteland where the cross stood. This probably would have meant the destruction of the cross and a return of his bad luck. Before the lords came down to hold their next court, he extended the orchard that existed behind the cross, to completely enclose the triangle, and planted the site with apple trees. This appeared to work as the arrangement continued well into the twentieth century. The old cross, rather ignominiously, was used as the falling post for the orchard gate and a ring of hoop-iron was welded around its stem to slip over the head of the gate to keep it shut. The gate and the orchard have now disappeared and the cross again stands on a separate piece of wasteland.

Cross No. 3 is situated near Cherrywell Cottages, on the angle between Station Road and the lane leading to Southey Farm. This lane originally continued south across Common Moor and joined the main Crediton to Okehampton Road at Withybrook Cross. The cross disappeared from view for many centuries. Where it once stood a cottage called Lower Mount Ivy was built, probably in the

seventeenth century, the old cross being unceremoniously appropriated for use as one of the jambs of the large open hearth, whilst the head was built into the back of the chimney. The cross came to light in 1900, when the copyhold of the cottage reverted to King's College and the building, being so old and dilapidated, was pulled down. The cross, which is also of octagonal section, was repaired by the college and reinstated on its original site.

Cross No. 4 suffered a similar experience. It is now sited near Langdale on the junction of the road from Sampford Courtenay to Honeychurch and Weirford Lane, which is probably where it originally stood, marking the northern exit of the village. The shaft was discovered in the 1920s. Rawlence reported that it was being used to support the oak bressumer (lintel) beam of a large fireplace in an old copyhold farm which had fallen into the hands of the college. The chimney had to be pulled down as it was insecure. It is not clear to which building he was referring. North Barton farmhouse had disappeared before 1885 and South Barton did not fall into the college's hands at this time. A small cottage, called Little Albury, still existed in the 1920s at the bottom of Bulland Lane, and according to local memory the shaft of the cross came from here. The building has now disappeared. The shaft, originally octagonal, was in good order but about two inches of the back had been hacked off along its length to give a flat surface on one face. The head had been broken off at its juncture with the shaft and has never been found. A new head was constructed and the cross installed on its present site, presumably at the expense of the college.

A fifth cross possibly existed on the eastern approach to the village at Green Hill Cross. In recent years the head of a cross, similar to the other four, was discovered in a field in North Tawton where soil and rubble, removed from Green Hill Cross during road widening in the 1970s, had been deposited. Unfortunately, the shaft has not been discovered.

Chapter Two

SAMPFORD COURTENAY CHURCH, CHURCH HOUSE AND CHAPELS

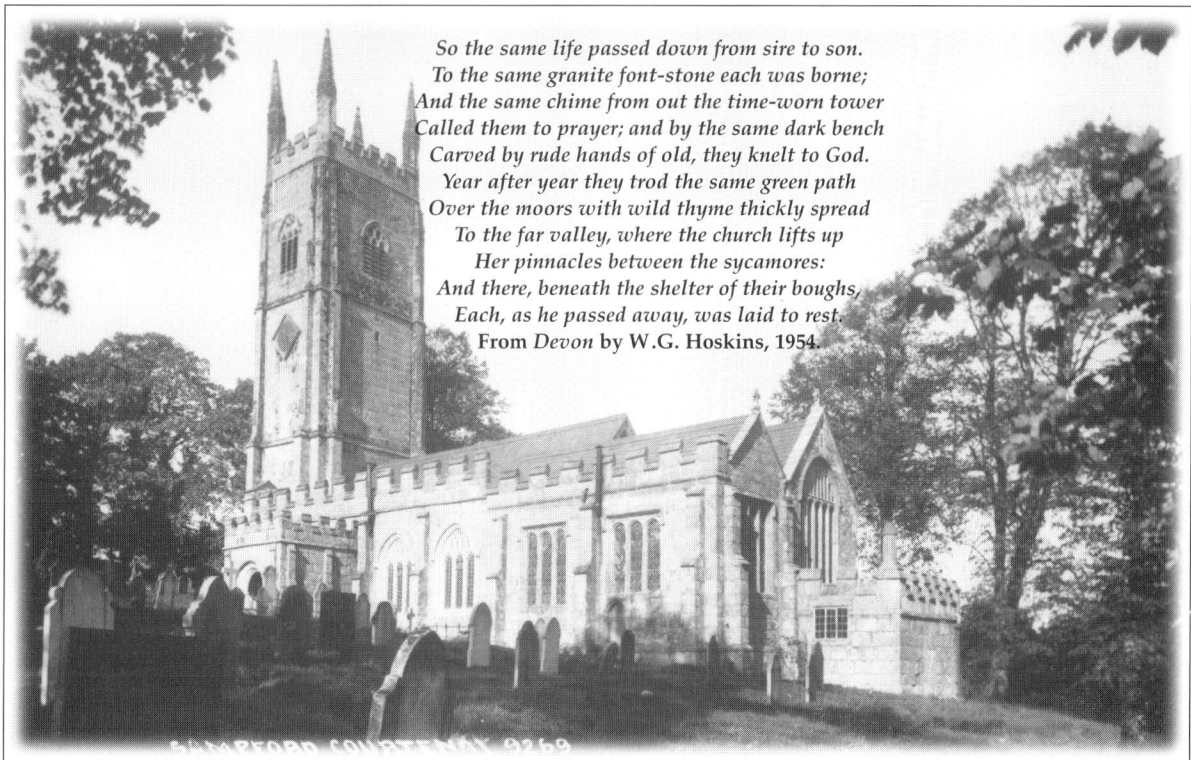

*So the same life passed down from sire to son.
To the same granite font-stone each was borne;
And the same chime from out the time-worn tower
Called them to prayer; and by the same dark bench
Carved by rude hands of old, they knelt to God.
Year after year they trod the same green path
Over the moors with wild thyme thickly spread
To the far valley, where the church lifts up
Her pinnacles between the sycamores:
And there, beneath the shelter of their boughs,
Each, as he passed away, was laid to rest.*
From *Devon* by W.G. Hoskins, 1954.

St Andrew's Church, c.1915.

The Church

There would have been a cross in Sampford Courtenay churchyard, although not the present one, which is late medieval, before any church was built. It would have been erected to be the centre of the Christian burial-ground. Later, when a site for the church had to be found, the north side of the hallowed ground would have been chosen in order to keep the graves clustered around the cross in the sunshine.

The present church dates from around 1450, but would have replaced a Norman structure of which only the foundations remain. The font is now the earliest feature of the church, c.1100, and made of rare Purbeck marble with a fluted tabletop basin. The original marble shafts have not survived and it is now set upon a plain octagonal granite shaft. The dedication of the church to Saint Andrew the Fisherman was common for a church built near a stream. The fifteenth century was a time of prosperity for Devon and funds for building the church probably came from the profits of the woollen-cloth industry. The tower, south aisle and porch are built of granite ashlar whilst the north aisle and chancel are of stone rubble. This suggests two different building dates, as does the differing form of the two arcades. On the north side there are five bays of granite piers. The four west bays of the south arcade are of dove-grey polyphant stone from Cornwall, although the two bays beyond the screen are granite. The main features of the building are very similar to those of many West Country churches of the Perpendicular period, although unusually here the chancel roof is at a lower level than the nave. Also, at the east end there is a projecting vestry, a very uncommon feature in Devonshire churches. The tower, described as 'one of the most majestic in Devonshire', is three-stage embattled with buttresses and large crocketted pinnacles. Tradition has it that, when the architect who built the tower of Okehampton Church saw that of Sampford Courtenay, he threw himself down from his own tower in envy and despair. There are fine wagon-roofs throughout, apart from that of the south aisle which is flat. There is a wealth of carving and an excellent variety of bosses, including a sow and seven piglets, an earl and countess (said to be of the Courtenay family), a wheel of three one-eared rabbits (the tinners' rabbits), the Courtenay arms and three 'green men'. Some small pieces of fifteenth-century stained glass survive. The parish chest was made from a single hollowed-out block of oak, probably placed in the chancel to receive the communion alms as directed in the first English Prayer Book of 1549.

Until 1830 an oak rood-screen, apparently a very fine one, spanned the entire church, but in 1831 the rector, George Richards, who then held the office of rural dean, ordered its removal. The entry in the rural dean's visitation book was as follows: 'The screen to be removed altogether or placed farther back.' No more is heard of it; it was doubtless the simpler plan to remove it altogether. Tradition maintains that the screen was burnt. During the 1899 restoration, when removing a panel from one of the box pews, it was discovered that a small part of the screen had been allowed to remain in its original position, in order that the pulpit, moved to its 'more commodious situation', might have it as an invisible support. The rood-loft doorway and stair survive.

The present altar stands on an ancient granite altar slab which was found built into the walls of the old rectory when the house was pulled down in 1870. It remained lying in the rectory grounds until it was transferred to the church in 1899, to serve as the base of the new altar. The five crosses are quite discernible on the stone. It is thought that its original placing in the rectory dated back to 1397 when Bishop Stafford granted a 'licence to celebrate divine service in a domestic chapel or oratory' to John Passenham, the rector of Sampford Courtenay and Eleanor his sister. Another altar stone is used as one of the jambs of an old fireplace at Great Cliston; this too may have come from a private chapel.

A 1553 inventory recorded four bells in the tower. The present six bells were cast by Pennington in 1770; the tenor bell was recast and the bells rehung in an oak frame by Stokes in 1905 and rehung again in 1970 by Arthur Fidler of Bow.

In 1814 a 'singers' gallery' was constructed at the west end of the church at a total cost of £77. Money was raised for such projects, as well as for the regular

Above: *St Andrew's Church before the 1898/9 restoration. Note the pulpit with sounding-board, gallery and box pews.*

St. Andrews, Sampford Courtenay

Left: *Roof bosses, St Andrew's Church: two 'green men', a sow with piglets and the three rabbits.*

maintenance of the church fabric, by rates imposed on landowners in the parish. The levying of church rates invariably caused problems. In 1860 William Brealey went before the magistrates, claiming too high an assessment for 'Irish' (Hayrish). He lost his plea and had to pay two years' arrears, amounting to 6s.11½d. Unfortunately, the costs incurred by the parish in connection with the case amounted to 10s.! Church rates were abolished in 1868. In 1826 Archdeacon Froude, on a visitation to the church, insisted that the seating should be renewed. He suggested that undecayed parts of the existing seats be used for the free sittings for the poor and new seats allocated 'according to the station of the inhabitants, having respect to the number of their families and the amount of their contributions to the church rates.' A faculty petition was sent to the Bishop of Exeter by the rector, William Beauchamp, claiming that the existing seating was in a very dilapidated state. A plan for new seating was put forward, 'with care being taken to provide proper free seating for the accommodation of the poor under and in the gallery to the number of about 150' and 'with some inconvenience' for another 25 to 30 persons in four long seats in the body of the church. The rest of the seating was to be in the form of closed box pews. Approval was granted and the work carried out during 1827–28 at a cost of £235.

In 1831, at Revd George Richards' suggestion, the old pulpit, which was in a very shabby and infirm state, was replaced with one of mahogany. This must have been second-hand, being of eighteenth-century design, and cost £15. The cost of labour and materials, which was 'considerably more than £5', was met by Richards. The pulpit was restored on an oak base in 1899 and the old octagonal sounding-board, discovered in 1915 by Revd Burnaby in a heap of rubbish, eventually became the table near the church door. In 1831, Richards also organised the removal of the rood-screen 'for the better accommodation of the congregation'. In 1833 it was agreed that 'the pillars, several being got considerably out of perpendicular, shall be spand [sic] and supported with iron.' The work was completed at a cost of £6.19s.6d.

By the end of the nineteenth century, the church fabric had deteriorated considerably, possibly partly due to the cessation of church rates. In 1894 the rural dean reported that the church needed entire restoration and in 1896 related:

It is very sad to walk about this noble fabric and tell of its desolations. An earnest effort is being made for its restoration and surely all who dwell in the neighbourhood will willingly do their utmost to help the rector and the parishioners in their arduous task.

The *Church Builder* of 1898 recorded that Sampford Courtenay Church:

Has unhappily suffered much from neglect, from wanton injury, and from the low notion of worship prevalent at the beginning of this century. To these various causes we must attribute the present unsafe condition of the roof and arcades, the seating with high box pews, the mutilation of the beautiful polyphant columns to get a little extra space for these pews, and the loss of all the tracery from three large windows in the south aisle.

However, by the end of 1894 the new rector, Revd Thomas Little, had arranged for a London architect, George Fellowes-Prynne, to provide an estimate for the extensive restoration work required; this initially was £1,970. Little appealed to King's College:

The College is the only owner upon whom the parish has any considerable claim... The parishioners would welcome the restoration of their church if the means is forthcoming to do it and also they would themselves give their mite towards it...

The college promised a donation of £400. In November 1895 an appeal was launched and over the next two or three years £1,600 was raised, although the estimated cost had risen to £2,500. In March 1898 a faculty petition was submitted, comprising proposals to remove the gallery, reseat the church, construct a new organ chamber, renew the roof of the nave and the three windows in the south aisle, reposition the pulpit and font, construct new surface drains around the western end of the church, recast the tenor bell and rehang all the bells and construct a chapel at the east end of the south aisle for week-day services. The new seating arrangements would give 335 sittings, compared with the 331 current at that time, temporarily to be provided by good-quality chairs to replace the 'present unsightly and uncomfortable deal box pews'.

The restoration work began in the summer of 1898, with W. Wiffen of Holsworthy as the building contractor. The old schoolroom in Church House was used as a temporary place of worship. On 10 June Little wrote to Charles Grant, the bursar of King's College: 'The work of demolition has been going on for the last ten days... the foreman says he has never seen a roof in so unsafe a condition.'

On 3 March 1899 another letter reported:

They are making good progress with the church, but the fund is practically making none. I have no faith whatever in the diocese giving us anything. Portman [Little's curate] and I between us have sent over 100 letters in the last ten days and the whole of the response is 5s.

However, more money was raised and the majority of the projects were completed. Both the columns

Restoration of St Andrew's Church, 1898.

placed in what was called 'the country' or, in other words, the bare earth. The box pews were removed and chairs 'temporarily' substituted; it was intended eventually to fix modern open pews throughout the church. The *Exeter Diocesan Gazette* of July 1903 described the chairs as being 'according to the architect's special design and stained green. These have been much admired, and have been the subject of inquiry from many visitors since.' Over 100 years later, Fellowes-Prynne's temporary chairs are still in situ! The panels of the old pews were utilised as a dado around the walls, painted dark green to match the chairs. The roofs were entirely reconstructed, the old bosses and carving carefully preserved and incorporated in the new work, and the 'unsightly' gallery removed. The floor was re-laid with wood blocks and the font repositioned. The grand reopening ceremony of the church, at which the Bishop of Bristol officiated, took place on 25 July 1899. The restoration fund was still in debt by £500; this was eventually paid off, King's College contributing a further £100. The final cost was £2,563.10s.7d.

In 1901, on the second anniversary of the reopening, a new lych-gate was dedicated by the Bishop of Exeter. The gate, in common with the 1899 restoration, was designed by Fellowes-Prynne and constructed by Wiffen. It was built of oak and granite and erected in memory of Queen Victoria and 'in thanksgiving for her great and good reign'. The 1899 restoration did not include the necessary work on the bells and, by 1904, Little was again sending begging letters to King's College. A letter from him to the provost read:

and walls of the nave, which were out of the perpendicular, were taken down and rebuilt on firmer foundations. Apparently, there were previously no foundations to the columns, which were

St Andrew's Church with Fellowes-Prynne's chairs.

Subject of our church bells, the ringing of which we now consider it necessary to discontinue until they are put in order. Sum required will not be less than £200. Mr W. Lethbridge [of Willey] will give £10 and he says: 'if I can get King's College to give you £25, I will make my donation up to the same amount'. Hope you will take up the challenge.

A couple of chaser letters to the college followed and a possible third provoked a note from the provost to the bursar: 'What answer ought I to send to the enclosed? *[no enclosure]* What are we to do about T.W. Little and his bells?' Presumably the funds were realised, as the tenor bell was recast and the bells rehung in 1905.

In 1922, during Revd Burnaby's time, a new pipe-organ, built by Cartwright & Son, London, was installed. In 1923 the small, surviving fragments of red and green painted oak from the old rood-screen were incorporated into a restoration of a portion of the screen, forming part of the organ case. The estimated cost of the work was between £750 and £800. The doors of the screen were donated by Thirzena Manuell in memory of her husband William, who was the village schoolmaster and church organist from 1876 to 1893, and of her son Harold, who from his youth was a church chorister and organist. During Canon Squance's incumbency, in the late 1950s, the roof timbers were treated for attack by death-watch beetle and parts of the roof drainage system renewed. Canon Squance's initials can be found on one of the replacement bronze downpipes near the church porch and, on another, the initials of the Southcombes of Wood Farm, whose bequest of just over £1,000 enabled the work to be completed. During the cold winter of 1963, the church boiler iced up. Revd Bickerton recorded in his diary:

Hoping that some sections may be in working order. Phil Reddaway and Bert Piper at work with Mr Ash [the local builder and churchwarden] giving instructions. Alas the rear section completely blown out and the three other sections leaking – so no chance of salvage. So we must change from coke to oil. The young men of today don't like looking after these old coke boilers as the old men did.

An automatic oil boiler was installed at a cost of £463. At the time of writing, repair of the lead roof over the southern part of the church has become urgent and pointing on the south wall and part of the tower needs attention. The estimated cost of the necessary work is about £60,000 and various projects are in hand to raise the money.

During the nineteenth century, the money raised from the church rates was used for a variety of purposes other than the maintenance of the church. Sticklepath Chapel of Ease, too, was regularly maintained. By the 1830s the ancient cob building had

Sticklepath Church, 1940.

become ruinous and Revd Richards described it as 'a place not fit for the decent performance of divine service in a Christian land.' Some repairs were carried out but, in 1875, the old chapel was pulled down and, at a cost of £700, a new stone building erected. Other more unusual expenses include payment in 1725 for killing 95 hedgehogs and two otters and the following:

1809 – To 19 bottles of wine for the sacraments
£4.18s.0d.
To beer for the ringers £1.0s.0d.

1811 – To strings for the bass viol and violins
£1.0s.0d.

1816 – To part payment for a flute (with Mr John Legge)
£1.0s.0d.

By the 1840s these instruments had ceased to be used.

1819 – To the expence of the Dean Rulers meeting. (This was a bacon and egg dinner, no notice of his coming having been received.) 10s.0d.

1830 – To Thomas Jackman for a new pair of stocks
£1.0s.0d.
To John Heathman to ironwork and nails for the new stocks 6s.1d.

1845/6 – To T. Tamlin tin case for map and lock for ditto 10s.0d. [For the tithe map, still in use.]
To J. Heathman for iron and fixing map case
2s.6d.

The Bell-ringers

Successive generations of the Reddaway family have featured strongly in Sampford Courtenay's team of bell-ringers. Henry Reddaway was a bell-ringer, as were his sons Ern (who was captain of the tower and gravedigger for over half a century) and Will. Ern's son Phil was a bell-ringer for 63 years. Jack Reddaway from Honeychurch and his father William were also part of the team in the early-twentieth century. The 2003 team includes Chris Clayton (captain), Joe

Right: *Bell-ringers' Dinner, c.1960.*
Left to right, standing: *Phil Reddaway,*
Will Reddaway, John Horn, Clifford Short,
Ivan Hodge, Fred Scoble, Jack Seaward,
Jim Seaward, John Boles, Ern Reddaway,
Courtenay Ash; **seated:** *Courtenay Johns,*
Henry Johns.

Below right: *Bell-ringers, Millennium Eve,*
1999. **Left to right:** *Chips Rivett,*
David Pope, Gary Stoneman, Joe Stoneman,
Karen Squire, Raymond and Ben Squire,
Linda Pope, Sheila Cartwright,
Chris Clayton, Jane Field, John Dickinson.

Main picture: *Will and Ern*
Reddaway, aged 80 and 83,
Sampford Courtenay
churchyard, 1983.

Stoneman (vice-captain) and his children Gary and Nicola, Chips Rivett, Raymond Squire and his wife Karen, John Dickinson, Malcolm Craig and Mike Flanagan. The bell-ringers regularly take part in local ringing competitions and hold an annual dinner and a summer outing.

The Parsonage House

It is not known if Glebe House near the church, or a former property on the same site, was ever occupied by the local priest. It would appear that the parsonage stood on Rectory Hill, at Culverhayes, from at least the fourteenth century when John Passenham held the Sampford Courtenay living and applied for his oratory. Some time later, possibly in the sixteenth century, the house (or part of the house) was rebuilt and the altar stone incorporated into the wall. An early-seventeenth-century terrier of the glebe lands, which then totalled 72 acres, described the site of the parsonage thus: 'The Culverhaye and Homstalle, some eighte acres, bounded with the King's highe waye uppon the southe.' A terrier in 1679 described other properties within the glebe:

A small house and garden near the bottom of hill next to the highway [Sunnyside, formerly Rectory Cottage] and another tenement on the side of the churchyard south the church with a garden, joyning to another smaller tenement south [the first Glebe House and the second Green Cottage].

Above: *The old rectory (now Culverhayes), Sampford Courtenay.*

Right: *Blessing of the new rectory by the Bishop of Exeter, March 1959. Left to right, back row: Archie Watts, Gwen Watts, Miss Toogood, Pearl King, Edna King, Emily Gubb, ?; front row: Rosemary Cleverdon, Margaret King, Robert King, Canon Arthur Squance, Gertrude Huntley, Mary Cleverdon, ?, Bishop Mortimer, Mary Squance.*

A 1727 terrier, when William Donne was rector, gave an interesting description of the old parsonage, which:

Contains from north to south, a large kitchin with an oven and new furnace, floor'd with old lime-ashes, ceil'd anew. Next a dary [dairy] with a new brick floor, a large old parlour, ceil'd of old, but lately floor'd with daleb [deal boards]. A closet with an old floor of boards and an old ceiling. From east to west, a new little parlour, wainscot'd and floor'd with dale b., ceil'd, sash'd... Out of the kitchin a new staircase of dale boards and wainscott'd. Next a narrow buttery, then a large hall; both with very old earth floors, but neither ceil'd... Lastly a cellar not ceil'd, but pav'd and parted with a wall.

Above stairs, from north to south, the kitchin chamber is floor'd with very old oaken boards and patcht ill since, not ceil'd to the thatching, but repair'd lately in the walls and boards of the windows. The old parlour chamber is floor'd with very old oaken boards and patcht ill since, ceil'd not well but the south end has been rebuilt with bricks and new windows have been struck out with frames and seats. The study has a new east wall and chimney of bricks, is covered with helling stones and ceil'd anew. From east to west, the little parlour chamber has a tolerable old floor of boards, ceiling and windows, but is hung anew with

blue stuff [and] *has a small closet floor'd and ceil'd alike. The next chamber is floor'd with very old oaken boards, not ceil'd at all. The hall chamber alike. The cellar chamber is floor'd anew, not ceil'd but the windows of the three last have been repaired.*

The house from north to south is built with stones, smal and greater, cover'd with reed, from east to west built with cobb, supported on both sides with stone buttresses and rough cast towards the south end, cover'd with reed.

The terrier also described the various outbuildings, which included linhays, a hay house and a threshing or tithe barn and gave details of the church plate, including 'a new sylver paten for communion, stamped with five stamps... it cost [in] 1724, £3.18s.6d.'

In 1866 Revd Theed submitted plans to the bishop for the rebuilding of the parsonage, reporting the existing house to be 'in a decayed and dilapidated condition [and requiring] to be pulled down and rebuilt.' The new house was designed by Henry Lloyd of Bristol and was a much grander building, comprising below ground a wine cellar, beer cellar, larder and dairy, on the ground floor a water-closet, scullery, cook's pantry, butler's pantry, kitchen, servants' hall, pantry and storeroom to one side of the house and a library, entrance lobby, hall and staircase, dining-room and drawing-room to the other side. Upstairs were seven bedrooms, three dressing-rooms and a water-closet. The cost of the work was estimated at £1,850. The new parsonage was constructed south of the old building in 1870; the oaken timbers from the old house were saved and used in the servants' quarters, new pine being used in the main rooms. The upstairs water-closet had a 200-gallon cistern, filled from the rainwater gutters, and a pull handle, although the servants had to make do with an earth closet. In 1959 a modern smaller house, built to the east of the nineteenth-century property, became the rectory and the older house passed into private hands. In 1995 the newer rectory was sold by the diocese, the incumbent now residing at North Tawton.

The Rectors

A man he was to all the country dear,
And passing rich with forty pounds a year;
Remote from towns he ran his godly race,
Nor e'er had changed, nor wish'd to change his place.
From 'The Deserted Village' by Oliver Goldsmith, 1770.

The first recorded rector of Sampford Courtenay was Alan de Nimet in 1290, and the first presented by King's College was Roger Gostwyck in 1609. Gostwyck had been to Eton, was a fellow of King's College and a theological writer. He died in 1645 and was buried in the chancel. On his tombstone were inscribed the following lines:

You that seeke wonders
Lo a wonder heere
I that was soil'd by sin
By Christ am cleere
My sin is His
His righteosnes is mine
He tooke my shame
That I by Him might shine.

William Beauchamp, who was in office from 1797 until his death in 1827, gave the church the oil painting of 'Our Saviour on the Cross' which hangs in the north-west corner of the nave.

George Richards, rector from 1829 to 1859, was responsible for the removal of the rood-screen, but this type of 'modernisation' was common practice in the nineteenth century. Richards was fairly rich; in 1842 the commuted tithes totalled £650 a year and he also had the income from 85 acres of glebe land. In 1851 the parsonage household consisted of the rector, his wife and five children plus a governess, valet, cook, nurse and housemaid. Probably a gardener and/or other servant(s) lived at Rectory Cottage. In the *Diary of Ann Palmer* (see Chapter Eleven), Richards commented on the spiritual state of his parish:

It must be confessed with grief, that Christianity here could boast but of few triumphs, and that ignorance, superstition and hostility to the gospel were lamentably exhibited.

His parishioners, however, held him in higher esteem than he them, for his memorial in the church reads:

From his fatherly kindness,
Christian charity and zeal
In the ministry of the gospel,
Beloved by all who knew him:
Affectionately remembered
By the flock he faithfully served.

Edward Theed followed Richards and he was rector for 35 years. He was in his forties when he took office and previously had been vice-provost of King's College, in Cambridge. By dispensation from the bishop, Theed also held the living of Honeychurch, with a net annual income of about £89, from 1875 until his death aged 80 in 1893. In common with his predecessors, he was responsible for Sticklepath Chapel, although his duties there were, for the most part, covered by a curate. Theed was the first chairman of the School Board, which was established in 1874, and he made regular visits to the school throughout his incumbency. He gave an annual 'tea treat' for the schoolchildren, held in the rectory grounds. The *Exeter Flying Post* of 3 August 1864 included an amusing account of one such celebration:

On the afternoon of Thursday last the Rector of Sampford Courtenay (the Rev. Mr Theed) entertained the school children of his own and Honeychurch parishes with the annual tea in his lawn; the otherwise beautiful appearance of which was heightened by decorations and banners bearing mottoes of various kinds, as 'Feed my lambs', 'God save the Queen', 'Pity the poor heathen' etc., etc. The rich waited on the poor with admirable and endearing condescension and pleasantry. After the scholars had done justice with the various good things before them, and the rector had returned thanks, the juveniles betook themselves to the various games and healthful amusements that their fancies preferred in the most unbridled way. Some of the seedy members of the party mixed themselves up in their gymnastic exercises freely, living as it were some of the light-hearted hours of early life over again...

The next rector, from September 1894, was Thomas Little, who was in his early thirties. Honeychurch was given up; for some reason a new rector had already been appointed to the living in October 1893. During Little's term as rector, and that of his successor, there were protracted negotiations with Belstone in connection with the Sticklepath living. The proposal was to annex Sticklepath to Belstone, give up the tithe on the southern part of the parish, and take on instead the endowments of Honeychurch. Unfortunately, Little and Charles Grant, the bursar of King's College, could not reach an agreement with Revd Lucas, the patron of Belstone, on the amount of tithe to be surrendered and the sale value of the relative part of the advowson. Little, too, was on the School Board and he and his wife took a great interest in the children. He was a regular correspondent with Grant and their letters provide much factual information as well as many interesting anecdotes. Little transferred to St Marychurch in 1906.

William Surtees, who succeeded Little, had graduated from King's College, but was the first non-Etonian since 1609. The possible annexation of Sticklepath to Belstone remained unresolved; in 1905 the Honeychurch living fell vacant and at first Surtees resisted the proposal that he should take it on. However, in January 1908 informal arrangements were made for Sticklepath and South Zeal to be worked together by an assistant curate and Surtees took on Honeychurch. The official annexations of

Sticklepath to Belstone and Honeychurch to Sampford Courtenay did not take place until 1927; the subject is covered more fully in the next chapter. Surtees resigned in 1911, he was later to be Archdeacon of Exeter, 1925–30, and Bishop of Crediton in 1930.

Henry Burnaby was instituted in 1912 and was the first rector who had not graduated from King's College since the latter had become lords of the manor. Burnaby's long reign covered the two world wars and he was to see many changes in the parish. During his incumbency, on 28 June 1927, Honeychurch was finally annexed to Sampford Courtenay for ecclesiastical purposes, but it was not until 1930 that Burnaby assumed full duties there. He was a school manager and his wife, who was a trained nurse, was often called upon to administer first aid to the children. Burnaby was the last of the 'squarsons'; there are varying accounts of him employing between eight and 14 servants. John Reddaway remembers him as a 'country gentleman, who'd tell the old tale pretty good.' Irene Sampson recalls his stories, especially about the First World War: 'We used to say "It's one of Mr Burnaby's stories, you can believe it or not!".' Burnaby served as an Army chaplain in France during this war and as a captain of the Home Guard in the second conflict. He took part in many village activities; he was in the cricket club and played whist and billiards at the reading-room. He was a great friend to young John Reddaway, who had had polio as a small child, and regularly took him in his car to the orthopaedic clinic in Okehampton. Irene Sampson recalls that, although her family were Methodists, whenever any of them were ill Burnaby would always visit them at Solland.

Canon and Mrs Squance, 1954.

Freddie Johns remembers:

Parson Burnaby getting a group of children [including Freddie] with knives and mats, to weed the cobbles in front of the church rooms and up the path from the church to the lych-gate. Seven or eight of us did it.

The children were paid, which provided useful pocket money. Mrs Burnaby and her daughters always did the church flowers and they had a tame rook which would accompany them. Revd Burnaby died in December 1946.

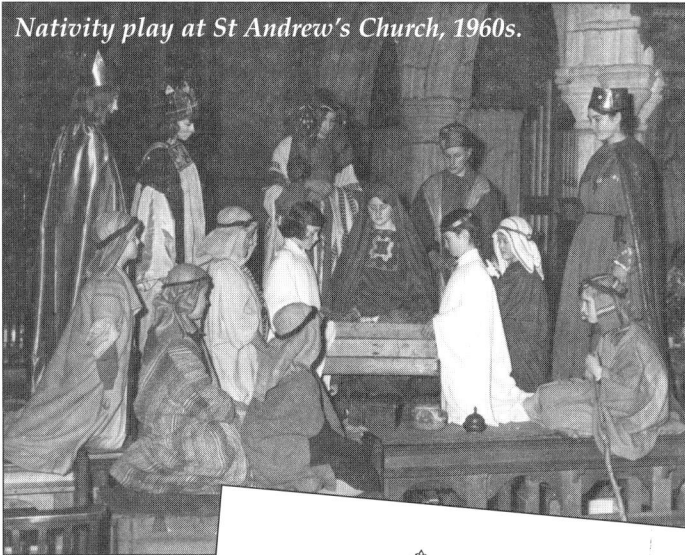

Nativity play at St Andrew's Church, 1960s.

Below: *Funeral card – Ann Arscott of Lower Trecott, 1895.*

Main picture, below: *Bell-ringers, July 1997. Left to right: Bill Folland, Karen Squire, Raymond Squire, Chris Clayton, Chips Rivett, Linda Pope, Frank Bye, Gwyn Williams.*

Bottom left: *Revd Mark Butchers, St Andrew's Church, 1997.*

Bottom right: *St Andrew's Church, 2001.*

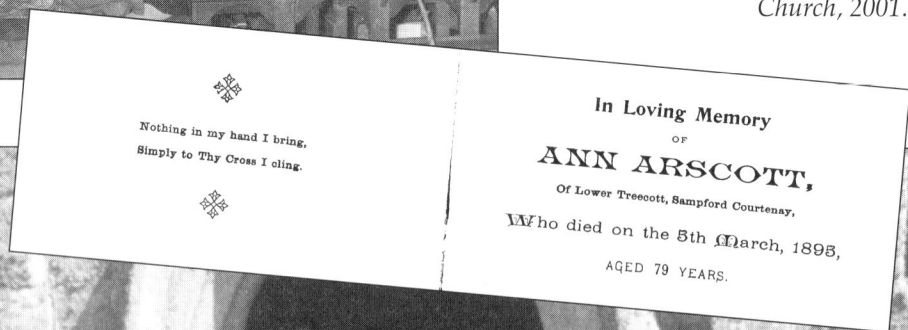

Nothing in my hand I bring, Simply to Thy Cross I cling.

In Loving Memory OF **ANN ARSCOTT,** Of Lower Treecott, Sampford Courtenay, Who died on the 5th March, 1895, AGED 79 YEARS.

Arthur Squance was instituted in 1947. He had worked in mining and shipbuilding parishes in the North, so it was a great change for him and Mrs Squance to come to rural Devon. He had done great work in the Durham diocese, of which cathedral he had been made a canon. In South Shields during the war, he had run a pig club in the garden and in Sampford Courtenay he kept pigs, geese and bees. The Squances at first lived in the old rectory, but the house in later years proved too much for them; unlike the previous rector they had no domestic help. They were, therefore, pleased to move into the new rectory in 1959. Several people remember Canon Squance visiting each of his parishioners every Easter and Christmas. He retired from Sampford Courtenay in 1960 and died at Hatch End in 1963.

The next rector, David Bickerton, when living in Hertfordshire, came to Devon on holiday, read Professor Hoskins' description of Sampford Courtenay and decided to become a country parson. Revd Bickerton was instituted in 1961 and lived throughout his incumbency at the new rectory. He was a bachelor and his housekeeper for 25 years, until 1979, was Grace Coles. In his later years, Audrey Reddaway looked after him. He played an active role in the parish and was a keen local historian. He was a parish councillor from 1971 until 1985 (chairman during the later years), chairman of the Village Hall Management Committee for 15 years and chairman of the Britain in Bloom Committee. In the 1960s he set up a youth club in the village. He had a fine singing voice and was a member of the choir of St David's Church in Exeter. As well as being rector of Sampford Courtenay and Honeychurch, from 1977 he was also priest-in-charge of Exbourne and Jacobstowe. By 1985, at the age of 75, he was finding the four parishes too much to cope with and he retired to Okehampton. On his retirement, he said:

I have been a country parson for many years and things for us now are very different. It is very sad that there is no longer a priest in each village. It is a part of village life that is lost to the younger generation.

For a while David Bickerton took occasional services at St James' Chapel in Okehampton. He then moved to North Tawton, where he died in 1994, aged 84. He was laid to rest in his beloved Sampford Courtenay. Betty Wilkins, in the parish magazine, paid him a fitting tribute:

David was rector of Sampford Courtenay for nearly a quarter of a century and in that time he came to know and love everyone and everything in Sampford Courtenay... and Honeychurch too... Their concerns were his concerns. Every lane, every farm and cottage was familiar to him and he had an interesting tale to tell about each... It is not surprising that years after

his retirement, in fact till the end of his days, to most Sampford Courtenay folk he has remained rector.

In April 1986, Arthur Parsons, a retired clergyman, temporarily took over the four parishes of Sampford Courtenay, Honeychurch, Exbourne and Jacobstowe. He was the last incumbent to occupy the rectory. He resigned in October 1987 and his place was filled in June 1988 by Anthony Gibson, who was the first rector to take on the four parishes of Sampford Courtenay, Honeychurch, North Tawton and Bondleigh, residing in North Tawton. Exbourne and Jacobstowe became part of a united benefice with Hatherleigh and Meeth. Revd Gibson resigned in February 1993 to take office as rector of St Peter's Church, Tiverton. Mark Butchers was appointed in September 1993. He was involved in the establishment of the Prayer Book Rebellion display in the church and organising the celebrations held in 1999 to commemorate the 450th anniversary of the event. In that year he was appointed as chaplain to Keble College, Oxford, and left Sampford Courtenay. The rector in 2003, Brian Ardill, instituted in November 2000, comes from Northern Ireland and was for many years a university lecturer in mathematics.

Church House

Theirs is yon house that holds the parish poor,
Whose walls of mud scarce bear the broken door;
There, where the putrid vapours, flagging, play,
And the dull wheel hums doleful through the day;
There children dwell who know no parents' care;
Parents, who know no children's love, dwell there.
Heartbroken matrons on their joyless bed,
Forsaken wives, and mothers never wed;
Dejected widows with unheeded tears,
And crippled age with more than childhood fears.
From 'The Village' by George Crabbe, 1783.

Church House, or the church rooms as it is now called, has played many roles apart from that of the parish poorhouse. It was built in around 1500, although was considerably altered in the late-nineteenth century. The upper room at the south end of the building was used for the Manor Courts, held at first by the Courtenays and then by King's College. The original oak table, benches and chairman's seat, which are all mortised to the floor, survive.

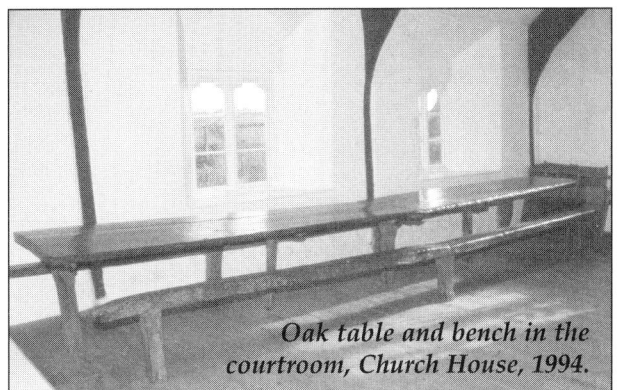

Oak table and bench in the courtroom, Church House, 1994.

Left: Village square – old Methodist chapel Sunday school with outside staircase, c.1915. In the mid-distance Little Albury Cottage can be seen to the right of the Sunday school and Pound Cottage to the left of the far end of the church rooms' wall. Both cottages have now gone.

The sayde pishoners of Sampford Courtenay intendinge and keeping Church Ale for the benefit of the said Church and givinge thereof convenient warninge by the space of one moneth unto the said Stephen and Gartrude... shall and may for that purpose quietly and peaceably enter into, use, occupie and enioye the said butterye and other room aforesaide during all suche tyme as they shall so keep their said Church Ale.

The plan of the building, with two storeys and an external flight of stone steps to the upper floor, is common in Devon. The church house generally evolved from the lord of the manor's brew house. In it was held the parish feast or 'church ale', the profits of which went to the church. Ales were held after church services on holy days; the churchwardens were responsible for brewing the ale and baking the cakes, for which the parishioners made a small payment.

Church House in Sampford Courtenay is largely constructed of granite rubble and was originally thatched, but probably acquired a slate roof at the end of the nineteenth century. The building was owned by the lords of the manor but, by the early-seventeenth century, the copyhold was held by three prominent landowners in the parish. In February 1615 the copyhold 'of all that tenem't of landes with appurtenances called the Pishe House otherwise the Church House' was granted to:

Wyllyam Tyckell the younger, John Ellys and Nicholas Legge during the lyves of them to the only use benefitt and behoofe of the pishoners of Sampford Courtenay and to none other use intente nor purpose.

An indenture drawn up in October 1615 recorded the subletting of part of the building to 'Stephen Heathman, taylor and Gartrude his wiffe'. The parish officers, with the consent of the parishioners, on payment 'of the some of fower pounds', and at an annual rent of 'sixteen pence of good and lawfull money', let to the Heathmans:

All that one lower roome called the butterye and so muche ffrom the sayde buttery in and of the said house downewardes as contayneth seaventeene ffoote in lengthe, to be severed and enclosed from the residue of the said house.

There were various conditions attached to the lease, which included satisfactory maintenance of the property, the building of a chimney and a requirement relating to church ales:

It would appear that the Heathman family ran the tailoring business for many more years. Roger Heathman the elder followed Stephen and Gertrude and in 1668 a further lease granted to another Roger Heathman 'all those five under rooms now severed and inclosed in the south end of the pish house.' The terms of the lease were the same as in the earlier agreement, including that regarding the holding of church ales. Roger, and then William, Heathman were recorded as making clothes for the poor between 1676 and 1698. William Heathman died in 1700 and it is likely the business then ceased.

Parish records indicate the existence of a parish loom or looms between 1767 and 1830; it is not known where these were operated, but they were possibly in Church House. Legal and maintenance expenses relating to the property were charged to the poor rates in the seventeenth century and probably thereafter, until the middle of the nineteenth century, to the church rates. As the nominated 'lives' on the copyhold died, new names were added, on payment of a 'fine' to the lords of the manor. The first reference to the possible use of part of the building as a poorhouse was in 1697: 'Pd. for caring of Humpery Harvey goods from home to Sampford Towne Church House, 2s.0d.' Humphrey Harvey, 'in his sickness', was receiving poor relief at this time.

A bond in 1739 confirmed that Church House was being used as a poorhouse from that time at least:

We Simon Newcombe and George Lacey... did... take of the Lords of the Mannor of Sampford Courtenay to and for the sole use, benifitt and behoof of the poor of the said Parish a reversionary copy of Court Roll of and in the Church House.

After this date, numerous entries in the books of the overseers of the poor, refer to the poorhouse, for example: '1781 John Lethbridge to drawing William Ellis to the Poor House 2s.6d.'

The upper room, as well as being used for the Manor Courts, was also a schoolroom, possibly from 1720, but certainly from 1786 until 1837. Following the formation of the Okehampton Union in 1836, most of the poor would have transferred to the Union workhouse and the school moved downstairs. The school moved to new premises in 1880. In 1840/1 Church House Cottage was occupied by poor families at a nominal rent. The occupants were Tristram Vanstone and his wife at 3d. per week, Mary Piper and her daughter at 2d. per week each and Elizabeth Westaway at 2d. per week.

A Vestry (a meeting of the parish officers) in March 1840 was held to decide what was best to be done with 'that building commonly known by the name of the Poor House.' Nothing appeared to be resolved as in 1856 the problem was resurrected, 'the overseers having received a notice of presentment for the delapidation of the same.' The parish did not feel disposed to expend any money in repairing the premises, 'so that the Lords of the Manor will be allowed to take possession of the property if they think proper.' King's College at this stage must have assumed responsibility for the building. *Billing's Directory* of 1857 listed part of Church House as being occupied by poor families rent free, presumably the cottage, which later in the century became the schoolmaster's house. During the later part of the nineteenth century one of the large rooms was used as a Sunday school. A letter from the bursar of King's College to Revd Little in 1895 indicated that the college kept the premises in structural repair, but Grant added:

As the only return we get is 5s. a year from the School Board and the very occasional use of the Court Room... It is open to question whether we can afford to go further than this. The parishioners should show some interest in having the rooms made cheerful and habitable for clubs and school purposes.

Little in his reply referred to the building as the 'reading-room', indicating that this had been established at some stage after 1880. The reading-room, which was a social club, is described in Chapter Ten.

During the twentieth century, Church House was used for a variety of purposes. For a while the building continued to be used as a court house, a Sunday school and the reading-room. It was also used for Parish Council meetings, but these subsequently moved to the Village Hall. When King's College sold the manor in the 1920s, it donated Church House to Sampford Courtenay Church. The cottage ceased to be occupied by the head teacher and in recent years has been let, whenever possible, to parishioners who are in some way connected with the church. The two large rooms provide a venue for various social gatherings.

The Chapels

Apart from the ancient Chapel of St Mary, established at Sticklepath in 1140 and later served from Sampford Courtenay, there is evidence of another chapel of ease in the hamlet of Sampford Chapple. Field names here suggest its former existence: Outside Chapel Field, Inside Chapel Field and Chapel Meadow. Bishop Grandison's registers on 6 June 1329 recorded the institution of John Swayne de Somerton as chaplain, on the presentation of Hugh Courtenay. On 13 November 1371, Bishop Brantyngham's registers refer to the 'Chapel of St Leonard in Sampford Parish'. This seems to be the chapel from which the hamlet is named, but it had lost any independent status by 1549, although the date of its vanishing is unknown.

Celebration at the Village Hall to mark the reopening of the Methodist chapel following the roof refurbishment, 1958.
Left to right, standing: *Winnie Wooldridge, Renee Piper, Amy Seaward, Audrey Reddaway, Shirley Reddaway, Phyllis Piper, Emily Cockram, Daisy Westlake, Betty Robertson, Barbara Johnson, Emily Arscott, Clarice Shead;* seated: *Mary Cleverdon, Mrs Sherwood, Becky Horn, Sarah Sherwood, Beatrice Reddaway, Valerie and Rose Hawking, Lena Sanders.*

Laying memorial stones at the new Methodist chapel Sunday school, 1933.

The birth and growth of Methodism during the eighteenth and nineteenth centuries split the community into two sections, political as well as religious, for the chapel absorbed almost everyone who held Liberal or Socialist views. The Methodist Society was established by John Wesley in 1740 and separated from the Church of England in 1791. Under the ministry of an evangelist named William O'Bryan, in 1815 the Society of Bryanites or Bible Christians was established at Shebbear in North Devon; the society joined the United Methodist Church in 1907. In 1932 most of the Methodist groups were united as the Methodist Church we know today. The supreme authority of the Methodist Church is the Conference, which comprises equal numbers of both ministers and laymen.

Richard Pyke, who was born in Sampford Courtenay and spent his early years in the parish (see Chapter Eleven), was president of the Methodist Conference in 1939. In his book *The Golden Chain* he described the birth of the Bible Christians:

Above: *Certificate presented to John E. Hawkins on completion of over 50 years as a Methodist preacher, 1930.*

Opposite: *Church of England Temperance Society pledge signed by Richard Hill, 1894.*

The working men were often little better than serfs. Their complete lack of education and the meagre pittance which they received for their labour both contributed to the abject hopelessness in which most of them passed their lives. When wheat was at famine prices, a shilling a day was regarded as a reasonable wage for these sons of toil... The Bible Christian Church was born out of this.

John Wesley did not find the morals or the manners of the Devon people all that he might have desired. Too often the clergyman of the village was noted chiefly for his zest in hunting or his bonhomie in the public house. On one occasion when Wesley was speaking at North Tawton his opponents brought up the huntsman with his pack to drown his voice but 'the dogs behaved better than the people. The language was as base, foul and porterly as ever was heard in Billingsgate.' Wesley had a poor opinion, too, of the people of Okehampton; Sticklepath was more hospitable and appeared to have been the one bright spot for him in the county. A Wesleyan chapel was erected in

Sticklepath in 1816, but it is not clear when Nonconformism first came to Sampford Courtenay village. Pyke recorded that William Mason from Winkleigh Mission was the first Bible Christian who ever visited Sampford Courtenay, the result being the formation of a society in the village. No date was given but it must have been in the mid-nineteenth century as Pyke's father Samuel, born in 1834, was a convert in adult life.

The Sampford Courtenay Bible Christians initially met in the upstairs room of the small building, now a single-storey garage, adjacent to the Alberries cottages in the square. An outside staircase gave access to the upper floor. In 1876 Robert Hawkins senr of Beerhill, who had purchased the cottages from King's College, gave a small plot of land nearby for the construction of a chapel. The cornerstone was laid on 3 April 1876 and the chapel opened on 8 March 1877. At the opening celebration 160 visitors and friends sat down to tea and at the evening meeting the chapel was so crowded that many could not get in. The chapel contains but one memorial, in memory of Robert Hawkins' grandson, killed during the First World War:

In loving memory of Edwin John, son of J.E. & H. Hawkins of Solland in this Parish, who died of wounds in France, October 24th 1918, aged 20 years. Interred at Escaudoevres.

The heart may shiver at the thought,
Of sacred ties so rudely riven,
But lo! Eternal peace is bought,
Earth's sorrows swell the songs of heaven.

There was never a resident minister at the chapel, although two of Robert Hawkins' sons, Robert junr and John, were local lay preachers, both for over 50 years. John Hawkins farmed Solland and, during the early part of the twentieth century, Methodist circuit rallies were held there. The circuit comprised 12 local Methodist churches. To Richard Pyke, Robert Hawkins junr was his guide and friend:

I have always thought of him as the last of the Puritans. He was tall, broad-shouldered and bearded, with a benignant eye and gentle voice... His balanced virtues, his unquestioned probity, his saving common sense, gave a completeness to his character which commanded the esteem of all who knew him.

When the new chapel was opened, the old meeting-room was used as a Sunday school. Becky Horn remembered, as a child in the 1890s, attending the Sunday school and going, in her best clothes, with her sisters to Beerhill where she was lifted into a wagon and taken off to tea in Winkleigh. In later years there were chapel outings to the seaside. In the early-twentieth century, John Hawkins' daughter Irene and her sisters were Sunday-school teachers and also played the organ in the chapel. A new Sunday school was opened in November 1933. An article in the *Western Morning News* earlier that year deprecated the plans for the new building:

Threat to picturesque village – we learn of plans for a new Sunday school to be built of red brick with an asbestos roof... this projected introduction of a note of

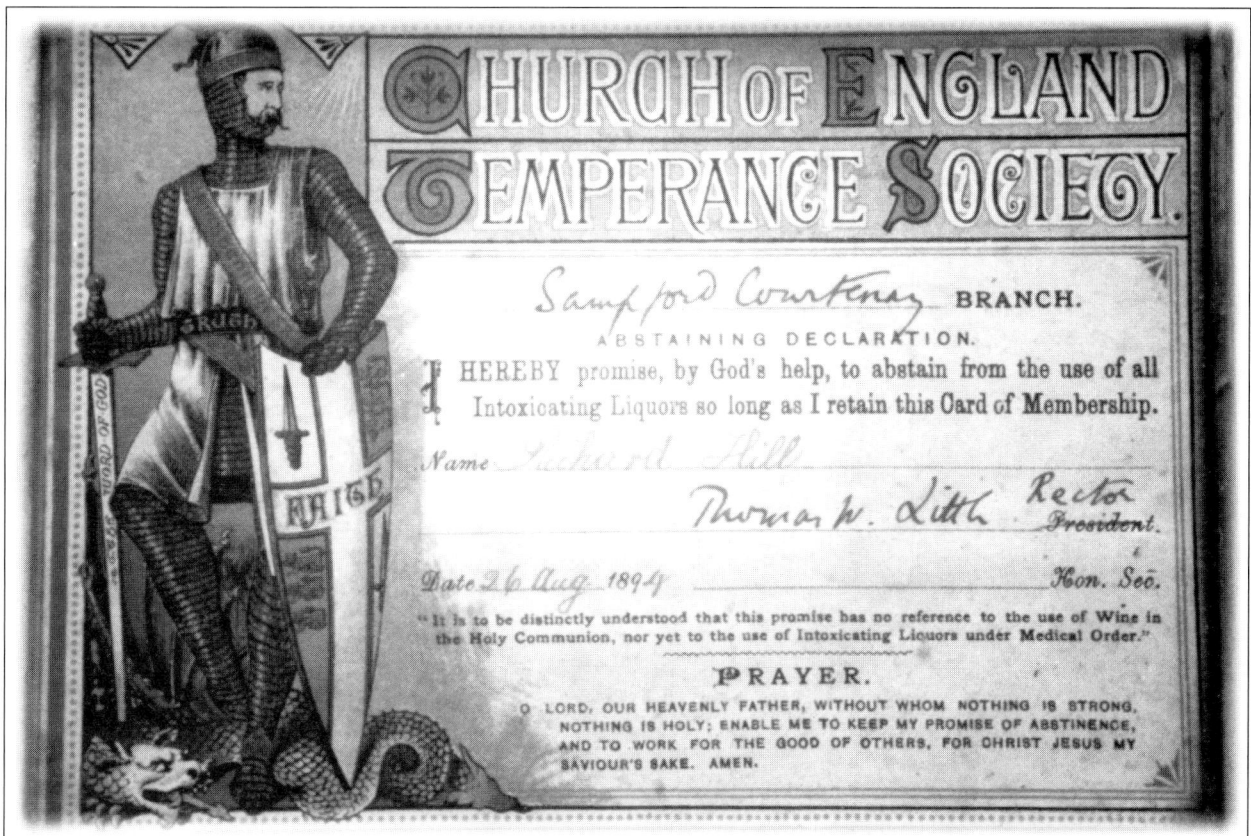

modernity appears particularly incongruous. From an artistic point of view red brick buildings with their ghastly asbestos roofs have nothing to commend them, unless it is cheapness. They are quite out of place in... old-fashioned villages.

The building went ahead, but incorporated 'stone-effect' rendering and an asbestos slate roof which blends in fairly well with the surroundings. It is no longer used as a Sunday school.

In about 1900 Bible Christian services were also held in the waiting-room of Sampford Courtenay railway station. A congregation of about 20 people assembled each Sunday afternoon at 3p.m. William Brock, who farmed Restland, drove his daughter Katie by pony and trap to the station, where she played the harmonium. The Brocks left Restland in 1910 but the services continued. According to Mavis Sleeman, on one occasion in 1912 when the appointed preacher failed to appear, William Reed, who lived at Hatherton, volunteered to conduct the service, which began for him 70 years of preaching. At that time he was an Anglican, but

Katie Brock of Restland Farm, c.1900.

he had gone to the service with a young friend who was a Bible Christian. He became a Bible Christian, although his friend subsequently became an Anglican. Les Beer remembers a Methodist Sunday school being held in the station waiting-room in the 1930s; this stopped at some point during the Second World War.

The Temperance Movement

There were frequent references in the village school records to attendance by the children at Temperance teas, Band of Hope teas and bazaars and White Ribbon Army teas and processions. The Temperance movement appeared to be active in both church and chapel at the end of the nineteenth and beginning of the twentieth centuries.

Many people signed the pledge to abstain from all intoxicating liquor.

A member of the Church of England Temperance Society in Sampford Courtenay worthy of mention is Richard Hill, who signed the pledge in 1894. This must have caused problems with his father Samuel, who was landlord of the New Inn.

∞ Church Weddings ∞

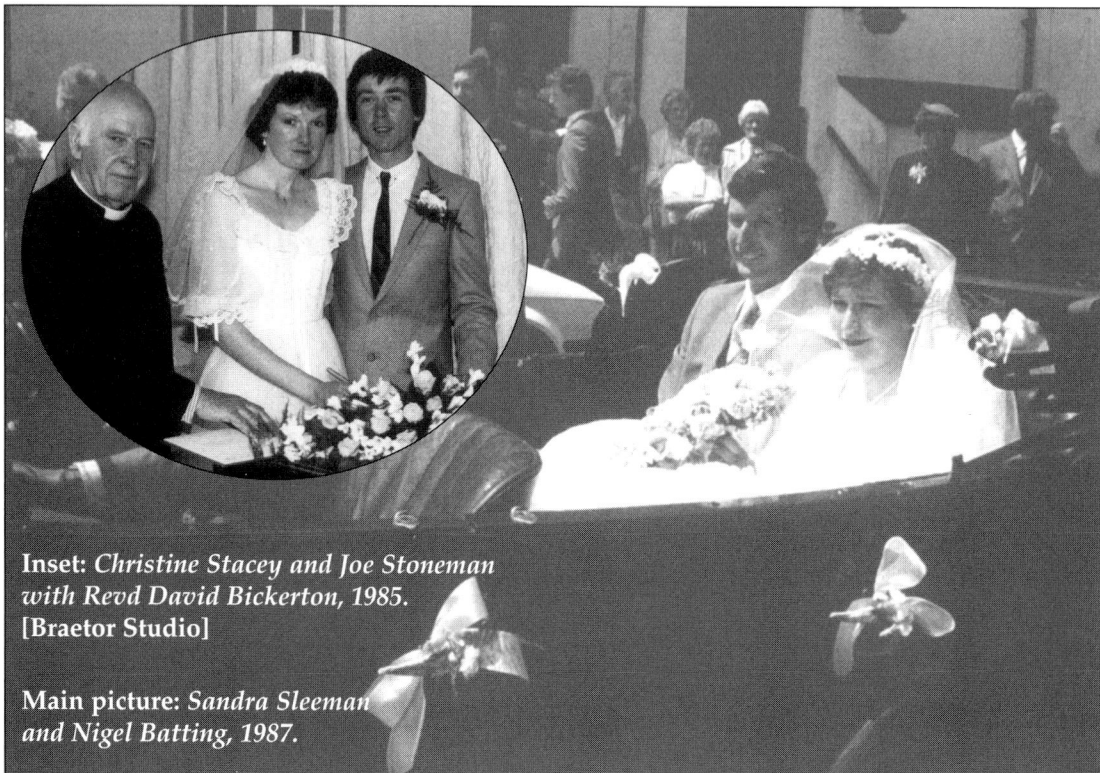

Inset: *Christine Stacey and Joe Stoneman with Revd David Bickerton, 1985.* [Braetor Studio]

Main picture: *Sandra Sleeman and Nigel Batting, 1987.*

∽ *Church Weddings* ∽

Above: *Monica Scoble and Dennis Turner, 1951/2.*

Right: *Audrey Reddaway and Phil Reddaway, 1950.*
(The couple are distantly related – they have a
common great-great-grandfather.)

Below: *Margaret Squance and Robert Murray, 1950.*

Chapel Weddings

Above: *Ivy Reddaway and Bert Coates, 1944.*

Left: *Rosemary Beer and Antony Wilk, 1976.*
[Braetor Studio]

Below: *Rose Hawking and Derek Peard, 1972.*

Chapter Three

HONEYCHURCH

*Honeychurch has one of the simplest and most appealing interiors
of all English country churches. It lives up to its delightful name in
a way that so rarely happens, and just to see it on a fine morning
puts one in a good humour for the rest of the day.*
From *Devon* by W.G. Hoskins, 1954.

Farms, Cottages and Families

Honeychurch is remarkable in that it has changed very little in almost 1,000 years. The name probably derives from a personal name – 'Huna'. It is likely that Huna's church was founded in the tenth century by the owner of the small estate of 607 acres which was carved out of the large parish of Sampford Courtenay. Huna endowed his church with the tithes of this land. 'Honechercha' at Domesday 1086 is described in Chapter One; the five holdings (the lord's demesne farm and the four villein farms) survive, together with a small farm created at some later date out of the glebe lands. Walter's demesne farm is Middleton (formerly Middle Town) which lies immediately west of the church. The four villein farms are Westacott, Slade, Bude and East Town. The population of the parish in 1086 would have been about 30.

By 1242, apart from Westacott and Rowtry (held by Richard Cadyo), 'Hunichurche' was held by William de Legh, Walter de Mumlaunde (Munyland) and Adam and Margery (Margaret) de Hunichurche. The Honeychurch family took their name from the manor and there is no evidence that they were ever resident in the parish. According to Pole, who was writing in the early-seventeenth century, in 1295 the manor was held by Ralph de Honichurch and in 1345 by Elias and Adam de Honychurch.

In the early-eighteenth century the manor was sold by the Honeychurch family to the Glynns. In 1797 it was purchased from Edmund John Glynn by the Honourable Newton Fellowes. The Fellowes family (also called Wallop) resided at Eggesford and owned property in North Tawton. According to Revd Fulford Williams in the *Transactions of the Devonshire Association*, the manor passed by purchase to Sir Roper Lethbridge (of the Manor House, Exbourne) in 1900. In 1913 Edith Prideaux (see below)

recorded Sir Roper as being lord of the manor as well as patron of the Honeychurch living. However, *Devon Notes and Queries 1903* and *Kelly's Directories* until the 1930s listed the Earls of Portsmouth (Fellowes/Wallop family) as lords of the manor. It is not known which assertion is correct.

The 1545 Subsidy Roll of those paying tax in Honeychurch included William and Richard Canne, Henry Drue and Henry, Simon and William Wekes. Coincidentally, the Weeks family (no known relation) farm in Honeychurch in 2003. The 1641 Protestation Returns, which listed all adult males, included Oliver and Richard Cann, William Brook, Christopher and Richard Newcomb and Daniel Wekes.

A terrier of the glebe lands compiled in 1631 listed those paying church rates as follows:

William Weeks, gen	*xiid.*
Symon Underhill for Westintoun	*xiid.*
Christopher Newcomb for Slade	*xiid.*
Richard Cann for Westacott	*xiid.*
William Brooke for Bowoode	*viiid.*
John Westaway for Wilcocks	*iiiid.*
Symon Baker for pte of Chattasen	*id.*
Honychurch Mill	*id.*

This is puzzling as it seems that either Middleton or East Town, presumably Middleton, was described as 'Westintoun'. Bude is a contraction of 'Bowoode'. By the 1781 Land Tax Assessments the farms had more or less acquired their modern names – the Parsonage, Middle Town, Westacott, Slade, Bood, and Easton Town. Tax was also paid on Chadavins Park, Willcocks Tenement and the Mills. Chadavins Park was a small parcel of land in the parish belonging to Chattafin Farm, Exbourne. Willcocks Tenement was a smallholding which, until the end of the nineteenth century, possessed a dwelling-house adjacent to East Town farmhouse. The *Exeter Flying Post* in 1851

Left: *Remains of the old malt-house, Honeychurch, 2001.*

Right: *Victorian letter-box, Honeychurch, 2002.*

advertised the property for sale by auction at the New Inn in Sampford Courtenay. At the time it consisted of 'a comfortable farmhouse and requisite farm buildings and about nine acres of arable, meadow, orchard and pasture land', and was owned by Richard Raymont and occupied by Robert Folland. In 1881 it was occupied by a farm labourer and his family, by 1891 it was uninhabited and by 1901 no longer mentioned, the land presumably having been absorbed into East Town. An existing farm building could have formed part of the old farmstead. It is possible that Honeychurch Mill was still working in the early-nineteenth century, with Thomas Stoneman as the miller. By 1814 Mark Sloman of East Town had acquired the property, when it may well have ceased operation. It had certainly done so by 1838 when the building was a farm-worker's cottage. The last occupants of Mill Cottage, listed in the 1881 census, were John Dayment (or Dimond), a farm labourer, and Mary Cockram, his housekeeper. John Dayment died in 1886 aged 72 and the cottage probably became derelict soon after. It is possible to identify the site of the mill at the bottom of Mill Lane close to the Hole Brook.

In 1841, in addition to those mentioned above, there were three other properties in Honeychurch. There was an uninhabited cottage near Middleton, which by the time of the 1889 Ordnance Survey map had disappeared. There was a cottage at Slade, which was occupied by a farm labourer and his family until the 1880s, but by 1891 it was uninhabited and at the time of writing is a farm building. In recent years a different outbuilding at Slade has been converted into a dwelling-house. A second property at Middleton, situated opposite Slade, was the last of the Honeychurch cottages to be occupied. Thomas Stoneman operated a malt-house here in around 1810, but its origins were possibly earlier. By 1822 John Raymont was the maltster, followed by Richard Raymont in 1841, although they lived at Willcocks Tenement. By 1851 Richard Raymont and his brother were farming Bowmead (Beaumead) Farm in Sampford Courtenay, and *Billing's Directory*

of 1857 recorded George Slo(w)man as the maltster. Sloman was still running the malt-house in 1861 but by 1866 it appeared to have ceased operation. However, the malt-house cottage was occupied by farm labourers until the early part of the twentieth century. The 1901 census recorded the Ching family living there, but it is thought that a family called Pinn were the last inhabitants, remaining there possibly until the 1920s. In the 1940s the galvanised roof fell off and the building subsequently deteriorated, although parts of the walls remain.

Of the ancient Domesday farms, Slade boasts the oldest farmhouse, described by Pevsner as a late-medieval house of high quality. The Grade II* listing identifies the building as mid-fifteenth century. The farmhouses at Bude, Westacott, Slade and East Town were all rebuilt in the eighteenth or nineteenth centuries. Various members of the Sloman family farmed Middleton and East Town throughout the nineteenth century. It is likely that they were responsible for rebuilding the two properties; much grander houses have replaced what were probably modest cob farmsteads. Part of the older house at Middleton remains.

By 1893 the acreage of Honeychurch parish had mysteriously increased from 607 acres (1838 Tithe Apportionment) to 679 acres, and by 1902 to 787 acres. The transfer in 1884 of Venn Farm (comprising 83 acres) from Bondleigh to Honeychurch, does not account for either increase. At Venn in 1851 there were two farm-workers' cottages; by 1881 these were unoccupied. The old walls of the cottages existed during living memory but have now disappeared. Following the Local Government Act of 1894 the parish of Honeychurch was united with Sampford Courtenay for civil purposes. At some stage in the mid-twentieth century, Rowtry Farm was also transferred from Bondleigh to Honeychurch. Rowtry was farmed by the Seawards from 1850 until 1878, but by 1883 it was unoccupied. Just before the turn of the century, Rowtry Villas were built close to the old farmhouse, probably by the Sloman family, as two farm-workers' cottages for East Town. By the 1920s the two cottages had amalgamated to form Hillside Villa (now Hillside). The old seventeenth-century farmhouse at Rowtry has survived but is now used as a farm building.

Various families farmed in Honeychurch for several generations. The Weekes or Wykes family go back to at least 1524, but probably earlier. However, the family had disappeared from the parish by the late-seventeenth century. It is possible that they were related to the Weekes of North Wyke in South Tawton. In 1681 the Newcombes (who were at Slade in 1631) were still at Slade, and at 'Westtontonne' and 'Boode'. By the 1760s they no longer appear in Honeychurch records although there were Newcombes in Sampford Courtenay until the twentieth century. Various members of the Brook family (also first mentioned in 1631) farmed both Slade and Bude in the eighteenth and nineteenth centuries. The last member of the family recorded in the parish was Thomas Brook, who was at Slade until the early 1930s. Westacott was owned and farmed by the Dunnings during most of the eighteenth century, followed by the Fishers, Vanstones and Hills in the nineteenth and early-twentieth centuries. By 1816 John Sloman was at Middleton. Maud the widow of Thomas Sloman, who had moved from The Barton in Sampford Courtenay, was the last member of the family to live at the farm. She died in 1950. East Town was farmed by the Stonemans in the late-eighteenth century and the Slomans (Mark, Richard, Simon and Thomas) from 1807 until 1919. The property has reduced to a smallholding in recent years with the majority of the land now forming part of Hillside. At the time of writing the five Honeychurch holdings are farmed by families long established in the parish; three are third generation.

The population of Honeychurch reached a peak of 66 souls in 1801; by 1901 this number had reduced to 44 and at the time of writing there are 26 inhabitants.

The Parsonage

It is not known when the first parsonage was built in the parish. Rectors of Honeychurch are recorded from 1261 but they were not always resident. A parsonage house certainly existed in 1631. In 1670 a presentment was issued by the rural dean to Revd Hernaman, the rector, that 'the parsonage house of Honeychurch is in decay and stands on posts.' The rector answered the charge as follows:

To the said presentment Christopher Hernaman, Clerk Rector of Honeychurch, maketh answer that there is one post fixed in the outside of the wall of the said parsonage house which hath been so placed there for the space of 30 years or thereabout and that the house is not in any danger of falling but is in good and sufficient repair in all parts thereof.

The building referred to is almost certainly the present Glebe Farm. A glebe terrier compiled in 1679, during Simon Rattenbury's incumbency, described the parsonage as comprising two under rooms, two chambers and an adjacent barn and shippen. A 1727 terrier, when George Baron was the rector, gave a more detailed description:

One dwelling house in length about nineteen foot, the walls of it are of earth and covered with reed and contains one under room called the Hall. The floor of it is made with stone. It is neither wainscoted nor ceiled. Another little room on the right hand of the entrance called the milkhouse, the walls of earth and covered with reed. The floor of earth. One uper room called the Hall chamber and covered over with reed.

The outhouses are two, viz. one barn adjoining to the east end of the dwelling house in length about twenty four foot, the walls of earth and covered with reed, and one stall house, usually called the shippin, adjoyning to the west end of the dwelling house, twelve foot in length, the walls of earth and covered with reed.

The terrier also gave details of the glebe lands and the 'surplice fees' which were 'two pence for offerings for everyone above the years of sixteen, one shilling for marrying and six pence for churching.' All tithes were 'due in kind with heath penalty and garden penalty.' The clerk was paid ten shillings a year out of the church rates but there was 'no settled fee for any sexon that we know of, neither have we any such one within our parish.'

A terrier in 1745 recorded the addition of a kitchen and two cellars to the parsonage, and a total of three chambers, all of which were 'plaistered with white lime mortar and floored with boards of elm.'

The 1781 Land Tax Assessment identifies that certainly by then, but probably before, the glebe lands and parsonage were being let by the rector. Revd Robert Taylor presumably held the Honeychurch living in plurality with another and resided elsewhere. It appears likely that the old parsonage, from this time onwards, was not occupied by the Honeychurch rectors. A new rectory was built in 1895/6 but was only occupied by one incumbent – William Bentley, who was rector from 1894 to 1905. Both parsonage houses were sold by the Church Commissioners in 1915; the relative problems are covered below.

The Rectors until 1874

Honeychurch had many difficulties with its rectors. The parish was so small and the annual stipend so modest it was unlikely that any minister would wish to hold the living as his sole source of income. The annual sum in lieu of tithes payable to the rector in 1838 was only £48, compared to £650 payable to the rector of Sampford Courtenay in 1842. Inevitably there were complaints about absentee ministers.

In 1680 the inhabitants of Honeychurch petitioned the Bishop of Exeter that, although they had previously complained that the rector Symon Rattenbury was 'not supplying his place as he ought to do' and the bishop had visited him to charge him to do so, the minister was performing his duty 'but once a month for a long time and that commonly in the afternoon.' It is not known if Rattenbury was suitably admonished by the bishop and reformed his ways, but he continued as rector until his death in 1704.

In 1723 the churchwardens and parishioners of Honeychurch were obliged to complain to the bishop again:

> About eleven years since, Mr George Baron, Clerk Rector, was presented and inducted in to the rectory and pish church of Honeychurch aforesaid, and for five years last past hath served also at Thorverton and Netherexe about 20 miles distant and hath preached but one Sunday since at Honeychurch, so that the sacraments are not kept, children are not catechized nor His Majesty's proclamations are not read nor observed. The chancle nor parsonage are not kept in good repair so that the service of God and dutys of religion are neglected and parishioners forced to wander abrode every Lord's day. Therefore we humbly beseech your Lordship that we may have prayers every Lord's day.

This petition contained two interesting comments. Firstly, the residents of Honeychurch were reliant on their rector to read the King's proclamations; presumably many could not read. Secondly, as was then common practice, the rector was responsible for the maintenance of the chancel of the church, whilst the parishioners looked after the nave. Again, how the problem was resolved was not recorded. George Baron continued in office until his death in 1756. Possibly his absence was covered by the appointment of a curate or the use of neighbouring clergy, which was to happen frequently in later years. It is doubtful that the bishop, Lancelot Blackburne, took any action. He was himself away from the diocese for long periods and under him there were fewer candidates for ordination than at any other period; of the few he did institute to livings some were required to suit his convenience by appearing at London or Bath for the ceremony. By the middle of the eighteenth century, nearly half the incumbents of Devon parishes were non-resident. This increasing laxity of the established Church was to lead to the growth of Nonconformity.

Unfortunately for Honeychurch matters worsened. In December 1816 Charles Sandby was appointed rector and he discharged his duties even less satisfactorily. Examination of the parish registers during his incumbency (1816–31) reveals his officiating on only one occasion – in 1817, soon after his induction. Thereafter Sandby seemed to disappear. In January 1831 Francis Bassett, Sandby's curate, who lived at Broadwood Kelly, wrote to the bishop that 'the incumbent of this parish has not made his appearance here for some years, nor do I know in what part he resides'. It appeared that the tithes were collected by Thomas Brook of Slade who, after paying the curate, remitted the balance to John Alliston of London. Alliston at this time was the owner of the advowson (the right to appoint a priest to an ecclesiastical benefice). Alliston revealed that Sandby was in receipt of regular payments (credited to a bank account) in connection with the Honeychurch living, from Queen Anne's Bounty Fund (for the benefit of the poorer clergy). However, neither Alliston nor the Bounty Office knew Sandby's whereabouts, although the Bounty Office agreed to withhold their next payment. Whether Sandby was ever traced through his bankers is not known, but it seems that he never again put in an appearance at Honeychurch and Thomas Upjohn, the curate of Jacobstowe, took on the living.

Further inspection of the registers suggests a non-resident rector for many more years. During the incumbencies of Thomas Upjohn and his successor Samuel Hands Field, a variety of different curates and other ministers officiated at church ceremonies. In 1848 Dr Hodgson Brailsford, who was rector of Exbourne, also became rector of Honeychurch. In 1868 a communication to the diocesan registrar revealed that all was not going well with Brailsford: 'The duties are unsatisfactorily performed by him in his two parishes of Exbourne and Honeychurch that the parishioners are up in arms against him.' Brailsford was instructed to appoint a curate. Although his total income from the two livings was £600, he claimed he could not afford 'the infliction of a curate's stipend'. By 1870 Brailsford had still failed to comply with the instruction and was neglecting to provide the required number of services. Moreover, those he did provide were 'performed in a hurried and unsatisfactory manner'. How the problem was resolved is not known; the registers show no evidence of the appointment of a regular curate. Brailsford continued in office until his death in 1874.

The Rectors from 1875 and the Annexation of Honeychurch by Sampford Courtenay

At this point the patronage of the Honeychurch living should be mentioned. Beatrix Cresswell listed many different patrons throughout the centuries, including the Honeychurch, Strechleghe, Hillersdon and Dunning families. *Hennessy's Directory* recorded John Alliston of Cornhill, London, holding the advowson from 1832 until 1875, but this was incorrect. He certainly held it in 1831 and it would seem likely that he probably acquired it before this.

A conveyance (held in the Exeter diocesan records) transferred the advowson from him to Revd Hodgson Brailsford in 1852. On Hodgson Brailsford's death in 1874, the advowson passed to the executor of his estate, his brother Revd Edward Brailsford, who by all accounts was 'not a very honourable man to deal with'. Correspondence to him from the bishop's office, asking that dilapidations to church property at Exbourne and Honeychurch be made good out of the estate, was answered by 'a very insolent letter'. The beneficiary of Hodgson Brailsford's estate was his son Arthur who, as the apparent new holder of the advowson, declared himself willing to grant the living of Honeychurch to Revd Edward Theed, the rector of Sampford Courtenay, provided that Theed resigned the living to him as soon as he became qualified to hold it. Arthur Brailsford, presumably, was in the process of taking holy orders. Accordingly, Theed was offered the living as a *'locum tenens'*. Surprisingly, Theed accepted the offer and applied to the bishop for permission to hold the two benefices. At the time, the total net income from Sampford Courtenay was £625 and that from Honeychurch a modest £89. Theed was granted permission and held the living until his death in 1893, employing the services of a curate. What happened to Arthur Brailsford was not recorded.

When Theed took over responsibility for Honeychurch, the official annexation of the living by Sampford Courtenay and the possible transfer of Sticklepath to Belstone was broached to King's College, the patrons of Sampford Courtenay. In 1878 Theed wrote to the college saying that, under the late Dr Brailsford's will, the advowson of Honeychurch was ordered to be sold for the benefit of his widow and daughter and he advised the provost to take the opportunity to purchase it. He suggested that the farm cottage and buildings on the glebe should be pulled down in preference to the expense of rebuilding them. The college duly offered to purchase the advowson, at a price of £300, permanently uniting the two parishes. Edward Brailsford, the trustee, declined the offer, asking for £1,300. Although he later reduced his request to £850 and then to £400, the matter remained unresolved. In the meantime, Theed organised the necessary repairs to the glebe property; possibly because his cook was to marry the tenant William Croote! In 1886 Mrs Brailsford died and, although her solicitors offered to take £300 for the advowson, King's College for some reason did not take up the offer. The advowson passed to William Kelland and in 1890 from Kelland to Revd Frederick Bussell at a purchase price of £220.

Following Theed's death, in 1893 and again in 1894 Bussell approached King's College to resurrect the desirability of officially uniting Honeychurch with Sampford Courtenay. His original intention had been to hold the living of Honeychurch with six months' residence at his house in Exbourne (The Manor House). He had secured sanction from the bishop

and promise of permission from the archbishop for a licence of non-residence but then was prevented from taking the living by the statutes of Brasenose College, Oxford, of which he was a fellow. He had no wish to remain patron if he could not take the living himself. He thought the rector of Sampford Courtenay 'the right and proper person to take charge' and offered to sell the advowson for £360. Unfortunately, the new rector of Sampford Courtenay, Thomas Little, professed himself 'in no way inclined to jump at the plan'; responsibility for both Sampford Courtenay and Sticklepath was quite enough, and he did not want a second church on his hands needing restoration (see below). The college therefore did nothing and the advowson passed at some stage after this to Sir Roper Lethbridge, the subsequent owner of The Manor House, Exbourne. In October 1893 Thomas Stanley was appointed rector of Honeychurch, followed by William Bentley in September 1894. Revd Bentley was also rector of Brushford, of which Bussell was patron.

In 1901 Charles Grant, the college bursar, drew up a plan for the ideal ecclesiastical arrangement of Sampford Courtenay, Honeychurch and Belstone, which he dispatched to the Bishop of Exeter. He suggested making two parishes out of the three, one consisting of Honeychurch and the greater part of Sampford Courtenay, and the other of Belstone with the southern portion of Sampford Courtenay including Sticklepath. At about the same date Sir Roper Lethbridge wrote to the college explaining that he was 'compelled by personal and family reasons to sell the advowson at once.' The college professed themselves unwilling to repeat their previous offer of £300, the market value of advowsons having fallen. There were now two other negative factors at Honeychurch – the 'very bad state of repair of the church' and the encumbrance of a new rectory (built in 1895) 'which was worse than useless to the rector of Sampford Courtenay'. The college did not want responsibility for either but suggested Lethbridge approach them again when the living fell vacant. In 1905 'the whole question of Honeychurch turned up again unexpectedly'. Little wrote to Grant:

You will know that Revd Bentley, rector of Honeychurch, has been preferred to a living in the Peterborough Diocese. How, no-one knows or guesses, but that is the fact.

Rumour had it that Bentley, who was by then 72, drank and his family lived in straitened circumstances. Apparently, the tenant of Glebe Farm, John Reed, was obliged as a condition of his tenancy to take Bentley by pony and trap to and from his other living at Brushford. With the Honeychuch living thus falling vacant, Lethbridge again broached the possibility of the amalgamation of the two parishes. Lethbridge offered to take the new rectory, which had cost about £800 to build, as the equivalent of the advowson. By then the living had reduced in value, the commuted tithe being £35 and the rent from the glebe only £25 a year. Grant did not consider this a good idea; he thought any money derived from the sale of the rectory should be invested for the benefit of the living. Little was worried that if he accepted Honeychurch he would be pressed to do something about the dilapidations of its church, and he had 'had quite enough to do in that way at Sampford Courtenay.' However, by January 1906 Little had announced his impending move to a new preferment. Bentley had duly departed in May 1905 but the next official institution of a rector in Honeychurch was not until September 1910. The church was first served on a temporary basis from Monkokehampton by Revd Alfred Marshall, then from Exbourne by Revd Oldham. In 1906 there was a development in the suggested annexation of Sticklepath to Belstone. Both Little and Grant thought this a good idea in principle as dispensing with Sticklepath could be combined with the acquisition of Honeychurch, but agreement on the details of the proposal could not be reached with Lucas, the patron of Belstone (see Chapter Two).

It appeared that Marshall of Monkokehampton had declined the Honeychurch living because of the cost of putting right dilapidations at the new rectory (said to amount to over £90). The circumstances under which the rectory was built were strange to say the least. There appeared to be no faculty for it, which probably caused the next rector of Honeychurch, Arthur St Leger Westall, in 1911 to enquire of the bishop's office if it was a 'legal parsonage'. His enquiry revealed more detail about the property. Apparently in 1894 Queen Anne's Bounty had held the sum of £800 belonging to Honeychurch, arising from benefactions and grants in 1817 and 1894, towards which Bussell had contributed £75. In 1894 on Bussell's discovering he was unable to hold the living, and his cousin at Exbourne, Revd Oldham, refusing it, two small livings – Honeychurch and Brushford – were put together. A new house was built for the incumbent, the old parsonage being considered unsuitable. Bussell submitted plans for the new parsonage, which cost £770 plus £30 for new roads. The plans were approved by the bishop and the Governors of Queen Anne's Bounty and the house was built between July 1895 and July 1896. According to Bussell, he had contributed £200, raised at interest, to the building costs. It was rather a grand house and Bentley, the only incumbent to live there, presumably could not afford to run it and it fell into disrepair. By October 1906 William Surtees had been appointed rector at Sampford Courtenay. Lethbridge soon

offered him Honeychurch, the only stipulation being one Sunday service and a celebration of Holy Communion at least once a month. Surtees declined; with responsibility for Sticklepath as well as Sampford Courtenay, he was unable to take on any more services on Sundays – 'the time not the will was lacking'. He too did not want the financial liability of the dilapidations at both the church and the rectory. By this time Revd Oldham of Exbourne was taking Sunday afternoon services at Honeychurch.

In 1907 the possible annexation of Sticklepath to Belstone had still not been resolved, although the bishop was urging that something be done about the Sticklepath/Honeychurch question, which he called 'this tiresome matter'. He suggested to Lethbridge that he take only part of the proceeds of any sale of the Honeychurch rectory in exchange for the advowson, the rest being added to the endowment of the benefice.

There was fear that the Crown might intervene 'owing to lapse', the living having now been vacant for over two years. By the end of 1907 the rectory was being let to a Mrs Smales and her daughter, who did some poultry farming. Surtees and Rawlence, the college land agent, drove over to Honeychurch to have a look at the building and 'when they were speering about', Mrs Smales observed them from an upper window and concluded they were burglars making up their minds where to gain an entrance during the night. The two ladies did not sleep all night but kept 'watch and ward most carefully'. Mrs Sloman of Middleton put them right the next morning as to the identity of the 'burglars'.

By early 1908, no further progress had been made with the negotiations. Sticklepath and South Zeal were being worked together by an assistant curate and Surtees had agreed to undertake Honeychurch with an agreement from the bishop that he would not be responsible for the dilapidations. This informal arrangement continued until September 1910 when Arthur St Leger Westall, who had been instituted as rector of Exbourne in February that year, was appointed rector of Honeychurch. Why he was appointed at this stage was not recorded. In April 1911 Surtees, who was then rural dean, commented in the visitation book that both the church and rectory house were in such a bad state of repair as to need immediate attention. During the last few months of Westall's incumbency (1912 or 1913), Queen Anne's Bounty advanced the sum of £50 to carry out repairs to the rectory, although in March 1914 the rural dean commented that it was money thrown away as the repairs had not been properly carried out. In June 1913 Alan Morris was instituted at Exbourne and in November of that year at Honeychurch. Revd Morris' daughter Irene at the time of writing lives in Sampford

Revd Alan Morris, Rector of Honeychurch 1913–25.

Courtenay and, at 96, is the oldest inhabitant of the parish. She remembers her father, throughout his incumbency at Honeychurch, cycling from Exbourne to conduct the weekly services.

By the end of 1914 Lethbridge, the patron, and the diocese decided to sell all the glebe property. In November Frederick Bussell, by then rector of Brushford, appeared on the scene again and offered £350 for the rectory. The following month he offered £535 for the rectory, the old parsonage and 25 acres of glebe land, but by the end of the month he had backed out: 'I find myself quite unable to complete my promise, private reasons alone, both personal and connected with raising the money needed are to blame.' It transpired, from an article in *The Times*, that Bussell had lost a recent court case concerning tithes and had had to foot the bill for legal costs. In August 1915 the property was put up for auction. The rectory was described as 'an elegant and well-built country residence in splendid order and repair' and the glebe farmhouse and outbuildings 'all in first class repair'. Presumably considerable work had been carried out to bring them to this state of perfection! Thomas and Ella Anstey from Iddesleigh acquired the two houses and 63 acres for £1,160. After the outstanding mortgage with Queen Anne's Bounty was settled, the balance was invested by the Ecclesiastical Commissioners, producing about £50 a year for the benefice.

During Alan Morris's incumbency all appeared to run smoothly and, as far as can be discovered, the annexation with Sampford Courtenay remained in abeyance for several years. Revd Henry Burnaby continued to be responsible for Sticklepath, possibly with the assistance of a curate. According to the diocesan records, in June 1922 King's College finally agreed to buy the advowson of Honeychurch – no price was recorded, and the purchase was finalised on 24 May 1923. What is strange is that the college bought from Frederick Bussell, although *Kelly's Directory* in 1923 recorded Honeychurch still in the gift of Lady Lethbridge. Somehow Bussell must have managed to get involved at the end. In 1927 the union of Sampford Courtenay and Honeychurch was finally effected by the Ecclesiastical Commissioners, as was an alteration of the boundaries of the parishes of Sampford Courtenay and Belstone in respect of Sticklepath. Alan Morris had died in December 1925; Honeychurch was subsequently served by Revd Edward White, who was appointed rector of Exbourne in November 1926. He continued to serve until Revd Hyson, the rector of Jacobstowe, resigned in October 1930 and White became the first incumbent of the united benefice of Exbourne and Jacobstowe. It was at this date that Revd Burnaby took responsibility for Honeychurch and relinquished Sticklepath to Belstone. The details of the sale of the Sticklepath advowson have not been discovered. From 1930 the rectors of Honeychurch have been those of Sampford Courtenay and at the time of writing Honeychurch is part of the united benefice with Sampford Courtenay, North Tawton and Bondleigh.

The Church

Huna's tenth-century church was replaced completely in about the middle of the twelfth century by the small stone building in existence today. The original Norman nave and chancel remain; some Norman work is still in evidence,

Above: *Font and cover, St Mary's Church, April 1983.*

Inset: *Ringing the bells at St Mary's Church, 1991. Left to right: Chris Clayton, Verity Heffer, Raymond Squire.*

St Mary's Church, 1991.

∾ St Mary's Church ∾

Exterior, c.1913.

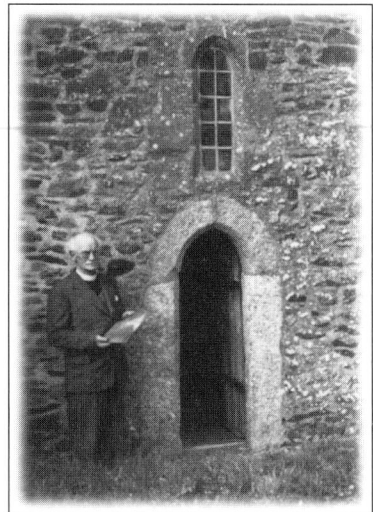

Top right: *Canon Arthur Squance at the priest's door, 1950s (reopened when the church was restored in 1914).*

Interior, c.1913.

Churchyard gate, 1991.

Bottom right: *Interior looking west, 1997.*

Interior looking east, 1991.

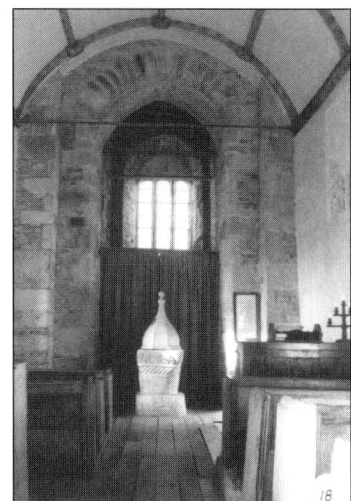

such as the south window of the chancel with its deep splay, a small round-headed opening in the north wall of the nave and two corbel heads now situated on either side of the south door. These were described by the architect Alfred Powell in 1914 as 'creations of ungainly shape but full of wolfish life.' The granite font, a sculptured tub font of unusual design, is also twelfth century. The dedication of the church was first recorded in 1466 when an entry in the episcopal register of John Bothe, the Bishop of Exeter, referred to 'St Mary of Honeychurch'.

The buttressed tower was added in the late-fifteenth century, probably replacing an earlier Norman structure, and is in neat Perpendicular style, in contrast to the coursed rubble of the rest of the building. On the north side of the tower is a shallow newel staircase which continues up only as far as was absolutely necessary to reach the belfry, there having been no money to spare at the time of construction. Of the three bells, the second and tenor are contemporary with the tower and the South Tawton churchwardens' accounts for 1569 appear to determine the origin and date of the treble:

> *Item – iiis iiiid payed for wynyng of the sayd belles & to iii mens labor to go with them to Honichyrche & for haye for the oxen wch caryed them.*
>
> *Item – iis vid payed for ther meate & drynke wch carryed the bells to Honychyrche.*
>
> *Item – payed to John Blakedon to se the bells weyed at Honychyrche & to iii men to go wt hym thether. And £iiii payed to the belfounder at Northwyke.*
>
> *And iis xd for John Blakedon & ii men to way the bells at Honeychyrche.*
>
> *And xiid payed to ii dayes labor & charges at Honychyrche when the bells were yn castyng.*
>
> *And iid payed for carryng of a yowke to Honychyrche payed to Thomas Byrdeall at Exeter for his seconde payement.*

Thomas Byrdall, who was at that time running the Exeter foundry, was evidently casting in Honeychurch in 1569, so it hardly seems possible that the treble was not made by him. The inscription on the treble bell is jumbled and each source examined records it slightly differently. The inscription on the second bell: *'lebs [for Plebs] ois [omnis] plaudit ut me tam sepius audit'* was a stock inscription of the Exeter foundry: 'The people all rejoice the more often they hear me.' The tenor bell inscription: *'Est michi collatum ihe istud nomen amatum'* was another common one: 'To me is given Jesus that beloved name.'

In the fifteenth century the chancel arch was rebuilt and several windows altered or added in place of the small Norman windows. The church was reseated at the same time, or perhaps given seats for the first time, and these medieval benches remain substantially untouched to this day. Most are of plain oak but some have roughly carved ends. The plain box pews on the

south side of the nave are eighteenth century. The church was also given a wagon-roof at the end of the fifteenth century, which, being adorned with much carving is rather handsome for so small and plain a church. The work is fairly crude but undoubtedly, at the time it was done, funds must have been available from some pious and generous patron. The porch was added last of all on the south side during the late-fifteenth or early-sixteenth century. The pulpit is Elizabethan or early-seventeenth century and the altar rails an example of simple country carpentry of seventeenth- or eighteenth-century date. The font cover is seventeenth century. On the north wall are the remains of a large painting of the royal arms of Elizabeth I, with part of an inscription decipherable: 'Elizabeth Regina... God save the Church, our Queen and Nation.' The east window of the chancel was designed and built in 1958 (see below). A number of medieval cooking pots are displayed in the chancel; these were discovered in 1914 when the priest's door in the south wall was reopened after a period of about 200 years. It is possible that they were used to fill up the doorway, with other material gathered from a rubbish dump close by. There is but one modest monument within the church to the Dunning family of Westacott. A small portion of what was possibly the old cross is situated in the churchyard.

The church is delightfully unspoilt; it remains just as described by W.G. Hoskins in 1954:

> *Honeychurch is one of the simplest and most unsophisticated country interiors in the whole of England... We push open the heavy door, and with it the centuries roll back: this withdrawn Norman church on the site of one even older, small and aisleless, only a plain nave and chancel: there was never any need to enlarge the church at Honeychurch. There at the back under the curtained tower arch, is the mutilated font of Bishop Bartholomew's time, crowned unevenly by a worn, slightly comic, cover of Jacobean date; here are the leaning wormy benches of rustic carpentry – some 15th-century carpenter from Sampford Courtenay no doubt made them – the pulpit from which the doctrines of the Elizabethan Church were the first to be heard, the curtains, the plastered and bossed roof, the plain granite chancel arch. It is all so worn and uneven, not a straight line anywhere, soaked with so many centuries of the Latin Mass spoken to a small gathering of Devonshire farmers and labourers and their house-holds. In the light from the clear glass of the windows, we almost hear again the mumbled Litanies and Collects on 18th-century Sunday mornings, the murmur of the Lord's Prayer and Psalms spoken in broad Devonshire voices, the immemorial words of the English Sunday they knew by heart.*

St Mary's, Honeychurch, owes its preservation from any kind of Victorian 'restoration' to the fact that it was always a small parish without a squire and, as

Hoskins commented, 'There is occasionally something to be said for not having too much money.' One puzzling matter is the incorrect dedication of the church, from the end of the nineteenth to the middle of the twentieth century, to St James the Less. All nineteenth-century trade directories, including *Kelly's*, gave the proper dedication to St Mary. According to Beatrix Cresswell, the dedication to St James, augmented to 'the Less' at a later date, was given without authority in ecclesiastical sources in 1782. The Ordnance Survey map of 1889 gave the dedication of St Mary but the revised edition of 1904 gave it as St James. In 1958 Hoskins confirmed that the dedication to St Mary was the proper one, given in John Bothe's register of 1466 and Oliver's *Monasticon* and Bacon's *Liber Regis* of 1786, the two latter being very accurate sources. From 1958 Canon Squance reintroduced the correct dedication.

The want of money in the parish, augmented by the proliferation of absentee rectors, was to cause many problems for the church and the small community caring for it. These were documented in the rural dean's visitation book. In 1826 Archdeacon Froude required the churchwarden 'to renew the seats in a uniform manner'. This was the same archdeacon who compelled the rector of Sampford Courtenay to tear out the old pews at St Andrew's Church. Renewal of the seating and other remedial work were to be completed over a three-year period. Although the rural dean issued several subsequent reminders, little was done, presumably because of lack of funds, and luckily the old pews survived. Frequently the dean referred to the necessity of keeping the ivy, which was growing both outside and inside the church, under control. The roof and the tower continually seemed to require attention and, at each visitation during the 1830s and '40s, there were numerous recommendations for repairs to be carried out. The churchwardens and parishioners did their best; some work was done and, in the 1850s and '60s, the fabric appeared in a fair condition. However, the following three decades saw much deterioration:

1872 *Nothing seemingly has been done to the church which is getting into lamentable state of decay. Slating on south side of roof in very bad repair letting wet in on the floor underneath and down the south wall. The ivy inside is not removed. Slates are wanting in the roof of tower. Light can be seen through... The wet is coming in all down the north side of tower... The gate of churchyard has no hinges or lock.*

1874 *Everything connected with this church disgraceful and a bitter reproach to any Christian land – it is to the credit of the parish that they have reslated the roof – serious complaint is made which I shall at once forward to the Bishop of the neglect and carelessness of the Rector for the spiritual welfare of his people* [Revd Brailsford].

1890 *The roof of chancel and nave is sound and the Queen's Arms are well preserved. Beyond this no word of commendation can be said.*

1896 *It is very sad to see this very interesting old church in its present condition. The church yard gate is a wreck – a portion of bank adjoining has fallen down. The masonry in front of the porch is defective, also the roof of the nave in several places. The tower seems to take wet everywhere. The ivy along the south front is doing much damage. The building is in no better condition. The floors have fallen in and the seats are following after – nothing as becometh the House of God. The fabric is so small that a comparatively small sum would make all things comely.*

The archdeacon strongly recommended a complete restoration and that the advice of an experienced architect be sought. During 1897 and 1898 some improvements were carried out, including the construction of a new east window. However, in 1898 the dean commented:

A costly and imposing church gate has been erected as a memorial of the 60th year of the Queen's reign. It speaks much for the zeal and liberality of these [sic] *who erected it, but I should doubt if it is very ecclesiastical in its character or in keeping with the place and surroundings.*

In 1901/2 an appeal was launched by the Bishop of Crediton for a complete restoration. Architect George Fellowes-Prynne, who had been responsible for the restoration of the church at Sampford Courtenay in 1899, had drawn up recommendations for St Mary's, Honeychurch. The outward pressure of the roof had caused the chancel arch to crack and part. The chancel wall was also cracked, and the south wall of the nave and the porch walls were dilapidated. The tower floors and roof were in a rotten condition and the west door off its hinges. The flooring in the nave was in a very bad state. Fellowes-Prynne recommended complete re-flooring, the foundation of a dry drain externally to keep the damp from the walls and foundations and the introduction of buttresses on the north and south sides to stay any further damage from the outward thrust on the walls. He also suggested renewal of the east window (the recent wooden replacement), rebuilding of the porch and major repairs to the roofs. He estimated the total cost would be about £800. By 1903 the buttresses had been built but the porch had not received attention. In 1905 the rural dean recorded the porch having been rebuilt but the interior of the church still 'in a deplorable state of decay and dirt'. A newspaper report in December 1907 announced the possible closure of the church, owing to the dilapidated state of its interior and the paucity of funds to put it in suitable repair, although a contemporary account in another newspaper denounced this rumour as erroneous.

In 1911 William Surtees, the rector of Sampford Courtenay and rural dean, recommended that the complete restoration of the church should be taken in hand. He referred to many evidences of dilapidation including further movement in the chancel arch in spite of Fellowes-Prynne's buttresses. In 1913 Edith Prideaux made an extensive report on the church to the Exeter Architectural Society. In it she dispelled the myth, claimed by the Bishop of Crediton and others, that the whole building, including the tower and chancel arch, was twelfth century. Apparently, when she had examined the carved bench ends, a youthful Honeychurch parishioner had asked 'whether it was true that the carving was so very ancient that it had been done with a flint axe before iron tools were known.' She had had to 'disappoint his antiquarian hopes'. Miss Prideaux also drew attention to the ivy which was 'doubtless very picturesque' but as she said 'if we want picturesque ruins by all means let us grow ivy; but if we want sound and serviceable buildings it must be ruthlessly eradicated.' Her report urged the need for immediate restoration of the church. In 1914 the Bishop of Crediton once again launched an appeal for funds and the architect Alfred Powell was invited to advise on the steps necessary to preserve the building. Alan Morris was by then rector of Honeychurch and played an important role in the project.

Bill Weeks of Hillside with his first baler, 1957.

Extensive repairs to cracks in the tower were needed. The bell cage and floor below the bells were to be strengthened and made sound. The south wall of the nave was to be underpinned if necessary and the buttresses on the north and south walls rebuilt on deep foundations with their bases projecting further from the walls. Powell advised complete re-laying of the nave floor, re-slating the roof with local rather than Welsh slate, new oak wall plates on both north and south walls and the insertion of a tie-beam halfway along the nave to keep the rafters from spreading. Other recommendations included the retention of the wooden east window introduced in 1897. He thought it an example of the careful work of some local craftsman and, as such, an integral part of the history of the old building. He stressed the importance of not attempting to introduce any kind of new ornamental work in the church which would jar upon its original and unique medieval character. He estimated the total cost of the work at about £300.

Presumably the necessary money was raised as work commenced in the spring of 1914 and all the recommendations appeared to be carried out. Unfortunately, the lengthening of the south buttress necessitated the moving of a gravestone and the family representative objected, declaring: 'Why not pull the wall down and build it up afresh', and later: 'The cost of the whole work is far too great; one can put up a new house for £300.' At this time it was revealed that there had been no churchwarden at Honeychurch for 20 years. However, it seemed that Miss Hockaday, who lived at Middleton, acted as warden and she was later appointed officially. In October 1914 the Bishop of Crediton officiated at the reopening of the church.

In 1917 the bishop and rural dean visited the church and recorded it as 'in exceedingly good order'. During the ensuing years the old building was carefully looked after by the churchwardens, who included Richard Weeks from 1936–40, followed by his widow Clara from 1940–55 and his son Bill from 1965–96. In 1947 the dean reported: 'All in very good order and the church shows that care and attention has been expended on it.' In 1956 Canon Squance arranged for Bertram Shore to inspect and report on the condition of the church. Shore recommended the construction of a new bell frame and the introduction of a more suitable granite window in the east wall of the chancel. In 1958 the two schemes were implemented at a cost of £770 and the new bell frame and window dedicated by the Bishop of Exeter in October. Dr Satow of Westacott carved a candelabra, which still hangs in the chancel, out of the old bell frame. Although in the early 1960s electric power lines were erected through Honeychurch, electricity has never been connected to the church. However, oil-lamps and candles on winter afternoons seem much more in keeping with the ancient character of the building.

Under the supervision of the churchwardens, being at the time of writing Jose Reddaway and Lorna Weeks, the small church has remained in good order, although encountering from time to time the problems inevitable with old buildings. Compliments regularly adorn the rural dean's book:

1986 A very faithful group of people work hard and well to keep their church.
1990 The church is beautiful and rightly regarded as a treasure.
1994 It is always a great joy to visit St Mary's, it is truly a gem set in beautiful countryside.

During 2001 a complete restoration of the tower was carried out at a cost of £46,000, made possible by many generous donations. In 2003 funds are needed to preserve the rare Elizabethan wall painting on the north wall. Work has started on the project and a larger portion of the painting has been uncovered.

Sunday services at St Mary's reduced from weekly to fortnightly in the 1970s and to monthly in the 1980s, due to the increasing commitments of the rector. Nevertheless there are always many visitors to this charming little church.

Honeychurch Well

There is an old well, situated at Rowtry Cross, which was used for many years by the villagers. This was filled in when mains water arrived in the parish. It has recently been restored to commemorate the new millennium, the work being carried out by local residents.

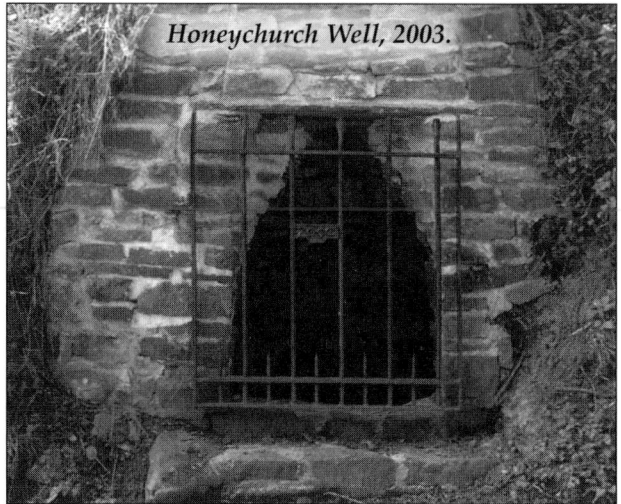

Honeychurch Well, 2003.

∞ Church Weddings ∞

Left: *Wedding of Teresa Squire and Derek Caplan, with Revd Anthony Gibson* (left) *and Revd David Bickerton* (right), *July 1991.*

Bottom left: *Wedding of Valerie Squire and David Letheren, October 1983.*

Below: *Wedding of Sylvia Squire and Robert Redman, March 1984.*

Chapter Four

HARD TIMES

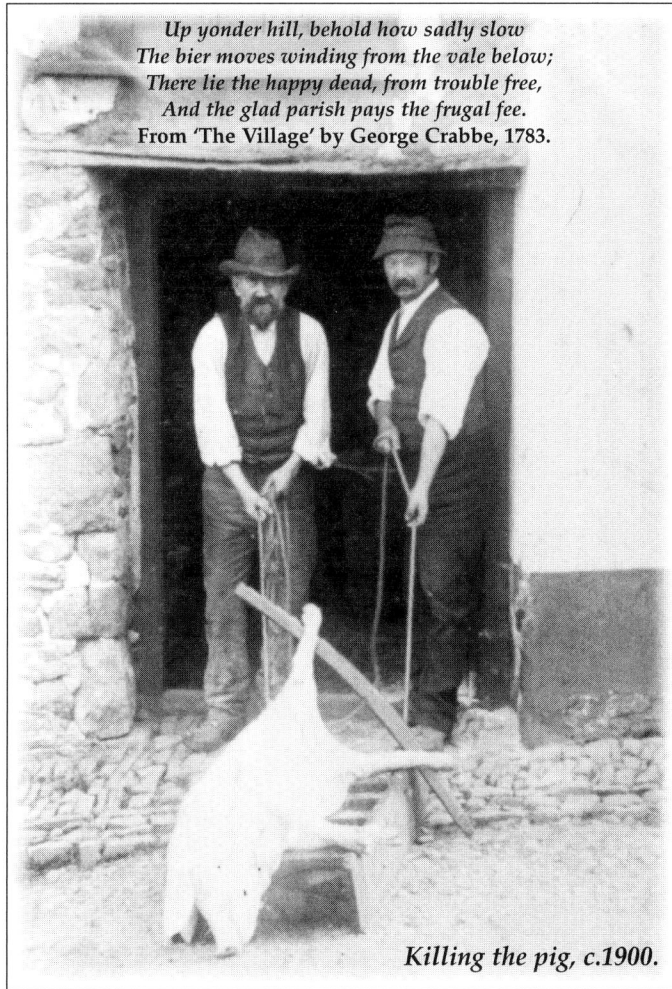

Up yonder hill, behold how sadly slow
The bier moves winding from the vale below;
There lie the happy dead, from trouble free,
And the glad parish pays the frugal fee.
From 'The Village' by George Crabbe, 1783.

Killing the pig, c.1900.

The Agricultural Labourer

The number of farm labourers in Devon in the early-sixteenth century was about a third of the whole rural population, rather more than in many English counties. A statute of 1563 required maximum rates of wages paid to labourers in husbandry to be fixed from time to time. It was a punishable offence to offer, or to take, more wages than the official maxima. In the Devon assessment of 1594 the Justices fixed the maxima at 7d. a day without meat and drink from 1 November to 2 February and 8d. a day for the remainder of the year. Where meat and drink were provided, the rates were 3d. or 4d. a day for the same two periods. At harvest

time, the labourer might take 1s. a day, or 6d. with meat and drink. Young workers and women were paid less than this. Over the following two centuries wages rose from 8d. a day to 1s. or 1s.2d. for the greater part of the year, but the cost of living had more or less trebled. Those who lived in were better off with food, drink and, possibly, clothes provided; it was the increase in the cost of these items that hit the day labourer and his family. By the beginning of the nineteenth century, Charles Vancouver and others described the labouring class of Devon as poverty-stricken and degraded.

By the middle of the century wages were still only between 7s. and 9s. a week with three or four pints of cider daily. However, task work, such as weeding, supplemented the basic wage and the labourer often had an allotment on which he could grow potatoes and other vegetables. Many labourers also kept a pig, which was estimated to be worth 6d. a week to the family. A good employer might also allow the gathering of sticks for fuel and provide some corn (for bread) or milk and butter. The labourer dug his garden by moonlight, in the early morning or on Sundays. Children as young as seven or eight were soon sent off to work in the fields as the few shillings they earned contributed an important part of the family budget. Meals were very basic – barley bread and potatoes, with some wheat broth seasoned with a small piece of bacon and herbs. The bacon was fat and all the stews were greasy. Tea accompanied each meal, but tea-leaves were reused many times over with blackberry leaves added to eke them out further. The labourer's cottage was small, damp and badly ventilated, with bare floors (of beaten earth in the earlier years). According to Richard Pyke in his autobiography *Men and Memories*:

> *A carpet would have been laughed out of court as silly and pretentious... Windows were small and were never opened... The night air was regarded as enemy number one. To open a bedroom window was considered to be flying in the face of providence. This may have had something to do with the prevalence of consumption. There were nearly always two or three persons in the last stage of that fatal disease. The bell that tolled, when they were laid to rest, used to harrow my heart.*

By the time the cost of the bare necessities of life had been met, there was little left. If money could be spared, the labourer could join the village benefit society, but in 1808, out of a total population in Sampford Courtenay of around 1,000, only 52 men and 24 women belonged to the two friendly societies then in existence. Thus, in times of need – unemployment, sickness or old age – most labouring families had to fall back on the parish for charity.

The Poor Laws

In the early part of the sixteenth century, apart from the monasteries who did much to support the impotent poor, the rector was regarded as the person whose responsibility it was to organise the relief of those in need. Statutes required him to urge the wealthier members of his parish to contribute liberally. Following the Poor Law Act of 1563, responsibility passed to the parish. The law required that two suitable persons should be appointed 'gatherers and collectors of the charitable alms of all the residue of people inhabiting in the parish.' In 1572 the office of overseer of the poor was created – an elected parish official who supervised collection and distribution of charitable funds. From 1597 parishes could levy a poor rate on all occupiers of lands and other property, paupers were to be provided with work and supplies of materials were to be kept for this purpose. Sampford Courtenay records indicate that the poor were set to work spinning and weaving for the local woollen-cloth industry and occasionally on the maintenance of the local roads.

The Poor Law Act of 1601 established a system which was to remain virtually unchanged for the next 200 years. Parish poor relief was organised by the two churchwardens, together with two or more substantial landowners who acted as overseers of the poor. There were four overseers in Sampford Courtenay parish; two covered the northern part, including the village, and the other two the southern part, which included Sticklepath. The Vestry clerk kept the accounts, for which he was paid in later years. In Honeychurch there was only one overseer and he appeared to keep the books himself. The post of overseer was performed on a rotation basis and was unpaid; those farmers who held more than one property had to take a turn for each. The duties must certainly have taken up much of their valuable time and must in many cases have been undertaken with some reluctance. Very often the rector, or a woman landowner, would appoint a deputy to cover his or her turn. The records of the overseers of the poor in Sampford Courtenay and Honeychurch, which cover a period stretching from the 1670s to the 1830s, identify some overseers and clerks who were obviously more capable (and more literate) than others.

The Law of Settlement Act of 1662 enabled overseers to remove from their parishes any stranger who was unable to convince them of his or her ability to obtain work within 40 days or who did not rent property worth £10 a year. However, workers could obtain temporary employment outside the parish (e.g. at harvest time) by means of special certificates issued by the overseers of their home parish which guaranteed to take them back. The Settlement Act of 1697 enabled strangers to settle in a new parish, provided that their home parish agreed to take them back should they ever have need of poor relief. By the same Act, every pauper and his wife and children were required to:

> *Wear upon the shoulder of the right sleeve of the uppermost garment... in an open and visible manner... a large roman P together with the first letter of the name of the parish... in red or blue cloth.*

Any pauper refusing to wear such a badge was to lose his relief or be whipped. Sampford Courtenay in 1697 recorded the issue of 'pauper badges':

> *Pd Will Hethman for setting up the bages one the poore folks sleeves 2s.10d.*
> *Pd for shag and thred for make the bages 10d.*
> *Pd Will Row for whiping of Mary Easterbrooke 1s.0d.*

Probably Mary Easterbrook refused to wear her badge; she was certainly on poor relief at this time. By the late-eighteenth century, the poor were excused the imposition of wearing the badge 'upon proof of very decent and orderly behaviour'.

The overseers of the poor books recorded the poor rates collected from the owners of property in the parish and itemised how the funds were disbursed each year. Certain individuals were on regular weekly and, later, monthly pay, which varied from 6d. to 1s.6d. per week in 1683 to an average of about 7s. per month in 1830. The recipients appeared to be the elderly, the sick, the widowed and unmarried mothers. The impotent poor were often resident in the poorhouse but others were receiving 'out-relief' to tide them over a difficult period of illness or unemployment. The desperate plight of many is illustrated by a letter written in 1773 by a well-wisher to John Dart of Underdown, one of Sampford Courtenay's churchwardens:

The necessity of Hannah Inch has obliged me to trouble you again in order to beg that you will be so good as to send her something for her and her children for they are in a most deplorable condition. Her husband is still in the hospital and it is very doubtful whether he will ever be cured; she likewise begs that you will support her as it is impossible she can maintain herself and her two children upon what she can earn. I should not take the liberty of writing to you if I was not very well satisfied of her great industry to provide for her family, the poor creature herself is at present in a very bad state of health.

Entries in the poor books often indicated general poverty:

1812 *Paid to 38 poor people on a/c of the high price of corn £4.15s.0d.*
1831 *Paid to labourers who were refused employ in the severe weather £1.19s.10d.*

Clothing and Bedding

The purchase of clothes and shoes for the poor formed a large part of parish expenditure and give an indication of the sort of dress worn at the time:

1676 *Pd. for a coats cloth for Sisly Crispin and for makeinge 8s.0d.*
Pd for a paire of bodies for Allice Gaurde 1s.5d.
Pd for two aperrons for Allice Gaurde 1s.10d.
1683 *Pd ffor a pare of showes for Richard Small 3s.6d.*
Pd for a coat and wascoatt for Henery Tayler 10s.6d.
1686 *Pd for cloath to make Rich. Rowe a shirt and drawers and a paire of drawers for Simon Rowe 7s.1d.*
Pd for a coate and wascoat for Grace Nortrop 9s.0d.

1687 *Pd for a hat for Geo. Coombe 1s.4d.*
1695 *Pd for a paire of breeches for Geo. Babb 5s.0d.*
1758 *For 6 yds of serge to make Eliz. Gatton a gown at 1s.2d. a yd 7s.0d.*
For whale bone 4½d.
For a handkerchief 7½d.
1764 *For whitels for Margaret Narraway's child 1s.4d.*
1769 *A lethern stay for Paiks maid 3s.8d.*
1781 *Elizabeth Langmead junr: to three mobs 1s.6d.*
1810 *John Veal and John Easterbrook a shirt each 11s.10d.*
James Bond's boy a frock and coat 3s.9d.
1831 *To a smock frock for Richd Jackman 5s.10d.*

Beds and bedding were provided, possibly for use in the recipients' own cottages but more likely for the poorhouse:

1767 *3 yds of barrons for a beadsheet for Anstace Veal 2s.4½d.*
A nech of reed to put under Margt Ellies bedtie 2½d.
1768 *For a coverled for Margaret Ellies 4s.0d.*
1786 *John Ffrost: to a rugg and filling his bedtye 5s.0d.*
1830 *To bedding provided for the inmates of the poor house during the late severe weather £2.12s.5d.*

Clothes, shoes and bedding were often repaired:

1683 *Pd for cleets, lether & neailles to mend Rich. Small 2 pare of showes 1s.6d.*
1769 *For 1 yrd of lasting to mend Ellies coat 1s.4d.*
1812 *To repairing Ann Moors bedding 4s.6d.*
1822 *Wm Dunn callico for repair his shirts 6d.*
1823 *To cuting & nailing poor peoples shoes at Sticklepath 2s.9d.*
To webbing & sarge for repairing Anth'ny Hawkens' clothes 3s.1d.

Illness and Death

The parish paid for medical treatment, such as it was, for those in regular receipt of poor relief and probably for many who were in work. The cost of a visit from the doctor would have been prohibitive for the average farm labourer:

1758 *For 3 purges one for John Frost & 2 for Elinor Bennett 9d.*
1759 *For a hors for Hanah Hewood to doctor 6d. [Honeychurch].*
Pd for bleeding Hanah in the foot 1s.0d. [Honeychurch].
1764 *For a pot of ointment for old Yeo 1s.6d.*
1769 *For curing Mary Frost of the itch 2s.0d. [The itch was a skin disease which was treated with sulphur ointment.]*
1783 *Doctor Legg: for reducing a fractured leg & medecines for Ann Peckett £2.6s.0d.*
1784 *Joan Jackman: towards curing Wm Newcombe*

family of scald heads 12s.0d. [This was a skin disease of the scalp.]
1830 Mr Budd for leeches etc. £1.6s.0d.

According to Vancouver, writing in 1808:

Scrophula, sore or bad legs, are very common in the district to both sexes of the peasant order at an advanced time of life, upon the heads and other parts of young persons of the same order and before they attain the age of puberty. Among those who live above the condition of the common labourer, this disease is not so generally noticed.

An unusual entry in the poor accounts for 1784 recorded the payment of 3s., 'For striking Grace Battishal for the Kings Evil'. Scrofula was also known as the 'King's Evil' because of the custom of treating it with the divine power of the royal touch. The parish gave a certificate to the afflicted person who presented himself before the King, by whom he was touched with a gold medal. It is unlikely that anyone living in Devon could have taken advantage of this. Striking here may refer to some form of topical treatment. Grace Battishall or Battishill appeared in local records on several occasions. She was probably the same person who featured in the *Exeter Flying Post* in 1775:

Missing – This is to give notice that, whereas my wife Grace Battishill is elop'd from me and gone the country with another man who is married and hath a wife and child now living in the parish of South Tawton. She is a set grown woman, of middle stature, and hath got a child with her, named William, who is about seven years of age. This is to caution the public that whoever credits her, I shall not pay them. The man that is gone with her, shews much of the smallpox. The mark of William Battishill.

By 1779 Grace Battishall was on poor relief and in 1783 she gave birth to another child, but by 1785 she had died, the parish paying the burial expenses. In 1778 her son William was apprenticed to Joseph Dennaford of Frankland.

In the eighteenth century smallpox was widespread and the poor were inoculated against the disease at the expense of the parish:

1822 To innoculating 26 poor children by Dr Legg £3.5s.0d.
To ditto 33 ditto by Dr Budd £4.2s.6d.

In 1742/3 the Devon and Exeter Hospital opened for the treatment of the poor. The parish, upon payment of a subscription, was allowed to send a restricted number of in-patients and out-patients to the

Left: *Wood's Cottages, c.1900 – note the unsurfaced road.*

Right: *Rectory Hill, c.1910 – note the cottages on the left, which have now disappeared.*

hospital. In 1812 Sampford Courtenay was paying five guineas a year. The local Justices could order that in-patients should be supplied with proper clothes to keep them warm and clean when admitted to hospital:

> 1768 For close for Eliz. Yeo when she was carried to hospital 7s.1¼d.
> 1786 Sarah Rapson: to clothing fit to go into the hospital 19s.9d.

However, excluded as in-patients were those:

> ... supposed incurable, suspected of being consumptive, to have the smallpox, itch or any infectious disease, women big with child, persons disordered in their senses or children under seven.

The cost of burying the poor was met by the parish and often included those not on regular relief but whose families could not afford the unexpected outlay:

> 1783 Thos. Kepple in need & expenses burying his child 12s.6d.
> 1786 To a coffin for Eliz'th Rapson 8s.0d.
> To 5 yds of burying crape at 8½d. pr yd 3s.7d.
> To ½ lb sope & ½ lb candles 10d.
> To wood 6d.
> To making her grave 2s.0d.
> To laying forth 2s.6d.
> 1786 Two coffins for Westaways child and Harris child 8s.0d.

Among the most interesting of the burial entries are those relating to burials in woollen fabric under the Acts of 1666 and 1678. These provided that: 'No corpse of any person... shall be buried in any shirt, shift, sheet or shroud... other than what is made of sheep's wool only.' Heavy penalties were imposed on parishes neglecting to comply with this ruling. Special books or printed forms were often kept for making the relative affidavit. Within eight days of the funeral, an oath had to be taken affirming that the law had been complied with. The Act was repealed in 1814.

Settlement and Removal

Under the earlier Poor Law Acts it had become almost impossible for the poor to move at all – the parish was virtually their prison – but the 1697 Act allowed them to reside in a new parish, provided that their parish of birth or legal settlement agreed to receive them back if they fell upon hard times. A settlement certificate enabled the bearer to move from one parish to another. The settlement examination was the written evidence of a formal enquiry into an individual's past to identify the parish responsible for providing his or her relief. The removal order specified that the person named was

to be deported from one parish to another, the receiving parish being responsible for supporting that person. Endless time and vast amounts of money were spent on contested settlement cases. From 1776 to 1815 the annual expense of litigation across the country grew from £35,000 to £287,000. Constables spent much of their time transporting paupers. Half the business of every Quarter Sessions consisted of appeals on orders of removal, at an expense which often would have covered the cost of the pauper's maintenance many times over. Sampford Courtenay and Honeychurch were no exceptions and there were numerous instances of settlement disputes. In 1778 in Honeychurch:

> Paid Mr Thomas Luxmoore about parish trial £9.3s.9d.
> Paid for an order to carry him [the pauper] to Coleridge 6s.0d.
> Paid for bringing the paupers to Exon £1.1s.0d.
> Paid for counsel advice befor the trial £1.1s.0d
> Paid for coppy of his register an three warrants 2s.6d.
> Paid for carrying the paupers to Coleridge 3s.6d.
> Paid for a jorney an expences to attend at the sessions 10s.0d.

The total cost of the case, including some other expenses, was £12.18s.3d., representing a large proportion of Honeychurch's total disbursements (£32.8s.11d.) for that year.

Sampford Courtenay's litigation costs included:

> 1814 To a journey to South Molton and a copy of an order of removal of Thos. Furneaux & family from North Tawton to the parish of Sampford Courtenay 8s.6d.
> To the expences attending an appeal to the Quarter Sessions against the said order of removal £36.1s.10½d. [It would seem that Sampford Courtenay lost the case as Thomas Furneaux subsequently received relief.]
> 1820 Expences of an appeal against the removal of Ann King from South Tawton to Sampford Courtenay £22.8s.8d.

Bastardy

> Next at our altar stood a luckless pair,
> Brought by strong passions and a warrant there;
> By long rent cloak, hung loosely, strove the bride,
> From every eye, what all perceived, to hide.
> While the boy-bridegroom, shuffling in his pace,
> Now hid awhile and then exposed his face.
> From 'The Village' by George Crabbe, 1783.

In the sixteenth and seventeenth centuries the birth of an illegitimate child in a country parish seems to have been an unusual event, but such occurrences became more common in the early-eighteenth century and even more common from 1750 onwards.

In many cases the parish officers used their considerable powers almost to compel the marriage of any woman found pregnant – the 'knobstick weddings', so called because of the staves of office carried by the churchwardens of the time. A bastard child took its settlement in the parish of its birth so, when the likely father came from a different parish, it was in the interests of the woman's parish to arrange a hasty wedding to ensure the child's settlement in the father's parish and the subsequent deportation of the family. An interesting case is described in the Honeychurch poor book of 1719:

> Pd. Richard Ffrost for keeping Eliz. Bartlett seaven weeks 6s.0d.
>
> Pd. for a warrant and mittimus [warrant for committal to prison] ag't Will'm Soper 4s.6d.
>
> Pd. Richard Ffrost 3 dayes labour at Exon about the marriage of Wm Soper and Eliz. Bartlett 4s.0d.
>
> Expence at the wedding 12s.0d.
>
> Paid for lichence to marry them £1.0s.0d.
>
> Paid Wm Soper in money £1.10s.0d.
>
> Pd. Mr Swetin to marry Soper and Bartlet 9s.0d.
>
> Pd. for a deliberate to fetch Soper out of the bridwell to be maried 14s.6d.
>
> Paid for 4 summons ag't Jacobstow, Sampford and Exbourn about Sopers settlement 2s.0d.
>
> Pd. for an ord'r on Jacobstow 4s.6d.

Of Mr and Mrs Soper we hear no more; John Dunning, the overseer at the time, for a modest sum of money, had apparently dispensed with the problem of Elizabeth Bartlett.

A subsequent entry in the poor book, which is undated but appears to have been added many years later, rather intriguingly reads:

> In the year one thousand seven hundred an nineteen
> A comical account their may be seen
> About a couple who learnt to dance Jack on the Green.

The rhyme is unsigned but in another hand is added 'Thomas Stonman maltster Honeychurch wrote the above rhyme'. Jack in the Green was a folk figure from pagan times linked to the green men prominent in church-roof bosses. In a fertility ritual performed on May Day, Jack, a man dressed in a frame of greenery, was led in procession around the village. Jack feigned death and then came to life to comfort and dance with his disconsolate May Queen. Perhaps the suggestion here was that the Sopers had duped Honeychurch parish into giving them money. There is evidence of several other knobstick weddings in the Sampford Courtenay poor books, for example: '1790 Expences to taking up & marrying John Short & Jane Westaway £3.15s.2d.'

Other methods of dealing with the problem of a bastard child were either to make the father liable by bond for the maintenance of his child himself or to allow him to discharge his responsibility by payment of a lump sum or regular contributions to the mother through the parish officers. In 1783 Mary Cann made oath before the Justices that the father of her bastard child was John Phillips of Belstone 'he having had carnal knowledge of her body'. John Phillips was apprehended by the constable of Belstone, taken before the Justices and ordered to pay Mary Cann 8d. per week towards the maintenance of her child. In 1784 Mary was brought to the poorhouse and received 1s. per month from the parish. An early-seventeenth-century Act had ordered that 'lewd women who have bastards' should be committed to a house of correction. Another young woman who found herself in unfortunate circumstances was Elizabeth Discombe. Elizabeth had been apprenticed as a young child to one of the Sampford Courtenay farmers and Sampford Courtenay was therefore her parish of legal settlement. She must have left the parish and returned in 1788 following a settlement examination by the Justices. By 1789 she was receiving poor relief and had had a child: 'Eliz'th Dishcombe to her laying in and midwife 13s.8d.' The following year the father of the child was apprehended: 'Expences taking up and carrying Henry Parish to justice 17s.8d.' In August 1790 he was 'adjudged to be the reputed father of the bastard child' and was ordered to pay to the churchwardens and overseers of Sampford Courtenay the sum of 10d. per week, 'for the keeping of the child for and during so long time as the said child shall be chargeable to the parish.' Elizabeth Discombe was ordered to 'pay... the sum of 5d. weekly in case she shall not nurse and take care of the said child herself.' What happened to her over the next couple of years is not known but in March 1792 a removal order was issued in Exeter in respect of 'Elizabeth Discombe single woman and Ann her bastard child aged about 3 years.' They had been apprehended in the parish of St John in Exeter 'as rogues and vagabonds, to wit, wandering abroad, lodging in the open air, and not giving a good account of themselves.' Upon examination of Elizabeth Discombe, it had been established that Sampford Courtenay was the place of her last legal settlement. A removal order was issued instructing the Exeter constables to convey the 'vagabonds' to the next parish on the way to Sampford Courtenay. Thereafter, they were to be delivered to the constables of each parish through which they passed until they reached Sampford Courtenay where they were to be 'provided for according to law'. Elizabeth once again found herself 'on the parish' at Sampford Courtenay.

There were numerous other similar cases. The settlement examinations make interesting reading as they demonstrate the low wages domestic servants were receiving at this time – about £3 or £4 per year at the beginning of the nineteenth century. In the majority of bastardy cases the unfortunate man named as the putative father, if he was unable to find securities, had to spend a few months in gaol, waiting to appear at the Quarter Sessions. Presumably the greatest number of bastard births have no record except in the parish register of baptisms, and maintenance of the child was settled out of court.

Apprentices

Apprentices were of two kinds – those by voluntary consent and 'parish' apprentices, who were poor children bound by the parish authorities. Both sorts of apprenticeship gave legal settlement in a parish. The system of apprenticing poor children was much more common in Devon than in any other county. Records exist of 'parish' apprentices bound by indenture in Sampford Courtenay from 1740 until 1842. The children varied in age from seven to 12 years, occasionally 13 or 14; by 1818 the youngest age had risen to nine years. Examination of the register reveals that many were bastards, orphans or one of their parents had died. The trade was usually husbandry for boys and housewifery for girls and the term of apprenticeship was until 21 years of age for boys and 21 years or marriage for girls. Occasionally the records identify a different trade. John Avery was bound 'to Nathanial Hole of Belstone, taylor, to be instructed and taught the art or mystery of a taylor.' Mary Westlake was bound to John Frewins to learn serge weaving.

Occupiers of land worth £10 per annum or more were compelled to receive regularly, in turn, a parish apprentice; if they refused a fine had to be paid. In 1821 the Sampford Courtenay rector, William Beauchamp, paid £10 to the overseers in lieu of taking an apprentice due to him for the glebe. In certain cases masters could apply for discharge of their responsibilities towards their apprentice. In 1802 Henry Cottle, 'dark in one eye', was apprenticed to William Brook of Beer. It was agreed in Vestry that he should be freed from his master if he should get blind in the other eye. In 1807 Ann Eastabrook, aged eight, was bound to William Arscott of Trecott. In 1817 Arscott applied:

... for the discharge of the said Ann Eastabrook for divers misdemeanors which she hath committed against him particularly by being with child which child is likely to be born a bastard.

The expense of the support of Ann and her child subsequently fell on the parish, although the latter was able to secure an order for payment against the father.

An Act in the mid-eighteenth century permitted the cancellation of indentures of those apprentices 'whose masters use them ill'. An Act in 1793 authorised the punishment of masters for ill-treatment of their apprentices. In 1794 a complaint was made before the Justices by William Palmer, apprentice to John Brook of Sampford Courtenay:

That he the said John Brook hath misused and iltreated him the said apprentice, by which cruel and barbarous iltreatment the said apprentice is become a criple – and whereas the said John Brook hath appeared before us, in pursuance of our summons for that purpose, but hath not cleared himself of and from the said accusation and complaint, but on the contrary, the said William Palmer hath made ful proof of the truth thereof before us upon oath.

Palmer was discharged from his apprenticeship, but there is no evidence of any punishment given to Brook. Apprentices occasionally 'eloped' from their masters and, indeed, notice was posted in the local press, including the *Exeter Flying Post* in September 1765:

Sticklepath, Sampford Courtenay. Whereas on Friday the 6th of September William Hutchins, an apprentice, did elope from his master, George Underhill, miller... Notice is hereby given that whoever shall harbour or employ him after this publick notice, shall be prosecuted to the utmost severity of the law. If any person can give notice of him, so as his said master may have him again, he shall be handsomely rewarded. He is about 5 feet 6 inches high, ruddy complexion, brown flaxen hair, and wore a light-colour'd cloth coat and breeches, and was bred to husbandry.

The parish paid the fee for the apprenticeship indenture and met the cost of clothing each apprentice:

1740   Pd for 5 pare indentures   £1.0s.0d. [Honeychurch].
*   Pd for clothing the five printeses   £2.10s.0d. [Honeychurch].*

By the mid-1830s the apprenticeship scheme was falling out of favour. In Sampford Courtenay the last apprentice was bound under the 'old system' in 1836 and, over the following years until 1842, just a handful of 'volunteers' were apprenticed in the parish.

Other Charges to the Poor Rate

Discharged soldiers and sailors were exempted from the penalties attached to vagrancy and numerous such men and other travellers passed through the parish, sometimes going no further:

1752 Paid for a coffen for an old travaler dyeing in this parish 7s.0d. [Honeychurch].
1787 Relieved distressed seamen with a pass 2s.0d.
1800   Pd to tow seafaring men from Sumeset to Cornwall 3s.6d. [Honeychurch].
1834 To board & lodging, medical attendance, funural expence etc. of a traveling vagrant who died from the smallpox at Sticklepath £3.11s.2d.

There were numerous intriguing and often amusing charges to the parish purse:

1683   Pd Robert Crispen & Will Ffors to draw out Roger Symes & his goods when the house was ffallen downe   2s.0d.

1688   Pd John Underhill for himself and his horse and their entertainment   12s.6d.

1689   Pd William Knapman to goe to the bath £2.10s.0d.

Pd for carying of William Knapman to the bath   6s.6d.

Pd William Knapman to goe to a dockter   6s.6d.

1689   Pd to a briefe for boor captivs in slavery £2.10s.0d.   [Briefs were royal mandates for collections towards some deserving cause, often for the redemption of captives (especially those of the Barbary pirates).   However, in some instances, much less than half the money raised was ever received by the supposed beneficiary.]

1762   For a special warrant for searching Eliz. Western's house in finding of the money tool   2s.0d.

1766   Wm Bailey 1 shoe new & the other mended 2s.6d.

1790   To two men watching by Will'm Bird   5s.0d.

To meat & drink & drawing him to the belfry   3s.0d.   [Perhaps this was the parish lock-up.]

1824   Expence of keeping two men 7 dys & nights with Mary Brookland she being insane   19s.0d.

1830   To singing the lunatic list   3s.0d.

Over the years the poor books include many an interesting spelling and turn of phrase:

1678   Pd ffor for the cureinge of Richard Row son legg that was brocked   2s.6d.

1689   Pd John Wonnacott for acofeing [a coffin] for Elizabeth Smyth   8s.6d.

1689   The some of our dusbusments is £78.10s.0d.

1761   The 22 day Sept. pd for alle & caks crowneation day   10s.6d.   [Honeychurch].

1763   Pd William Huxtable for a jorney to Bytheford about the millety   2s.6d.   [Honeychurch].

1763   Dis Bustid All is £7.7s.2½d.   [Honeychurch].

1799   Paid Christ'r Stoneman for the instrouckings for the land tax   2s.0d.   [Honeychurch].

Increased Costs and the Poor Law Amendment Act, 1834

Money paid out of the poor rates was in the form of outdoor and indoor relief.   From about the mid-eighteenth century Church House was used as a poorhouse, but whether it was ever used as a workhouse is not clear.   There were numerous references to maintenance of the parish looms and of teaching poor people to weave, but where this work took place is not known.   Over the period covered by the overseers of the poor records, in both Sampford

Green Cottage, 1933 – note the old pigsty on the right. **Left to right: Mrs and Mr Yeo, Lewis Lampey, Emma and Charles Reddaway.**

Courtenay and Honeychurch, the cost to the ratepayers escalated dramatically.   In Sampford Courtenay the total disbursements for 1680 were £58, by 1760 this sum had risen to £153, by 1790 to £323 and by 1810 to £658.   In Honeychurch costs during the initial years were negligible at only a few shillings, but by 1780 had risen to £23 and by 1817/8 to £36.   These increases were typical of the whole country; the cost of supporting the poor nationally had risen from £1.9 million in 1785 to £4.1 million in 1803, and by 1817 to £7.9 million.   This was due to several factors.   The period from 1793 to 1815 was one of almost continuous war and of much political and social unrest; there was an agricultural depression and an increase in unemployment.   Wages had not increased in line with the cost of living. Moreover, in 1795 the Speenhamland system was introduced in the Berkshire village of Speenhamland and was soon adopted widely in Southern England. The scheme set out a scale of poor relief based upon the size of the family and the price of bread.   The amount of relief given was calculated on the price of a gallon loaf of bread and the number of dependants a man had.   This encouraged employers to reduce wages in the knowledge that the parish would make up the difference and resulted in a significant increase in claims for relief.   Another contributory factor was the significant increase in litigation costs. Figures indicate that between 1800 and 1836 about ten per cent of the populations of Sampford Courtenay and of Honeychurch were receiving some form of poor relief, but the figure is almost certainly much higher than this as many of the recipients would also have been claiming for dependants.

The problems of the rapidly increasing expenditure on the poor led to the passing of the Poor Law Amendment Act of 1834.   This greatly reduced the payment of outdoor relief and encouraged conditions in workhouses to be made as unpleasant as possible so that they would be considered places of last resort. Parishes were grouped into unions managed by Poor

Law guardians who were elected locally. Outdoor relief was not immediately prohibited as there were insufficient workhouses. Sampford Courtenay and Honeychurch became part of the Okehampton Union. One of the last entries in the Sampford Courtenay poor book in July 1836 read: 'To refreshment for the poor when examined by the guardians at Okehampton 11s.6d.'

The Okehampton Union contained 28 parishes and there was much rebellion against the new laws. Large assemblages of men, using threatening language, gathered to intimidate the guardians and a company of infantry from Plymouth had to be stationed at Okehampton. Relief was taken to each of the parishes by relieving officers and loaves of bread were delivered by a contractor. In nearby South Tawton relief was withheld in consequence of riotous proceedings in which the bread contractor's carts and bread were destroyed. However, in Sampford Courtenay there was no resurrection of 'rebellion spirit' and the new procedures appeared to be accepted meekly. Poor rates continued to be levied on the parish until well into the twentieth century. In 1919 the Ministry of Health was made responsible for the Poor Law and in 1946 the modern system of social security was established.

Parish Charities

Funds for the support of the poor were regularly donated by local benefactors. Losses of such funds occurred frequently. One source of loss was the English law of Mortmain. Another was the custom of handing the money to local tradesmen upon whose bankruptcy or death the money was lost. Some losses of charity funds were the result of mere carelessness. Sampford Courtenay and Honeychurch in their administration of charity funds appeared to exhibit all of these problems.

In 1673 the total of the 'Parish Stock Money' at Sampford Courtenay was £53.17s.6d. and comprised the following charitable donations:

Willm Harpure Rector there £7.0s.0d. [Rector in 1549]
Willm Beare of Littcott £1.0s.0d.
Henry Elles of Combe £1.0s.0d.
John Rapson of Weberhill 15s.0d.
John Elles of Barton £1.15s.10d.
Thomas Slowman 10s.0d.
Ralph Williamson £2.0s.0d.
John Wotton 5s.4d.
Phillipp Sloman £3.6s.8d.
Thomas Elles of Trickott 10s.0d.
William Tickell of Exon 10s.0d.
More added by the pish 4s.8d.
Sum is £18.17s.6d.

Additionally, John Sloman of Throwleigh, Lawrence Underhill and Sir John Acland had each contributed £10 and Widow Shilston of Okehampton £5. Sir John Acland's money was to be used for the apprenticing of poor children and Lawrence Underhill's to be lent to tradesmen without interest. The rest of the money was held by a variety of different landowners in the parish at interest. Each Easter this interest was distributed amongst the poor, but was paid haphazardly; some years as much as five years' interest was accumulated by a particular holder of funds before distribution. Also, in 1617 John Sloman had granted a dwelling-house and herb garden to the parish, the rent of which was to be annually bestowed upon the poor. The cottage, Beacon House, was situated at Beacon Cross and was let at 3s. and then 5s. per year. The cottage fell down in around 1700 but the land continued to provide an income. Donations were occasionally made by other benefactors and immediately given out to the poor.

From the original total of stock money held (£53.17s.6d.) by 1727 most of Sir John Acland's £10 had been lost. Lawrence Underhill's £10 disappeared from the records soon after, as did the odd 17s.6d., leaving £33. The £33 was held in equal amounts by the two churchwardens, who distributed the relative interest each year until 1785. In that year it was agreed at a Vestry to credit the £33 to the overseers of the poor accounts and to pay the annual interest of £1.12s.0d. thereafter out of the poor rates.

In 1822 inquiries into the administration of local charities were held in every parish by the Charity Commissioners. The report in 1824 recorded the loss of both Sir John Acland's and Lawrence Underhill's money and pointed out that the parish's actions in respect of the remaining £33 of Stock Money 'was unauthorized and incorrect'. The report also gave details of more recent charitable gifts for the benefit of the poor. John Langmead in 1795 had left 10s. a year to be paid out of the moiety of Langmead's tenement in Sticklepath; this subsequently was made void under the Mortmain Act. John Tickell in 1801 had given £100 to be invested in three per cent Consols with the dividends to be distributed amongst the poor at Christmas each year.

Another inquiry was held by the Charity Commissioners in 1912. The payment of the interest on the Stock Money had not been paid in living memory. John Langmead's charity was no longer in force. The Beacon garden (Sloman's charity) was still being let, to Sidney Bolt, but at 2s.6d. per year. Tickell's charity was still in existence but the £100 stock had been substituted in 1849 by a deposit of £87 in the Devon & Exeter Savings Bank; this in 1912 had risen to £90.0s.4d. The income from Sloman's and Tickell's charities was distributed each year.

Honeychurch in the early years also had a fund of 'stock money' held for the benefit of the poor, but this in 1683 amounted to only 40s. The money was held by two families in the parish, and the interest distributed to the poor. In 1757 the £2 held reduced to £1, with no explanation given, and it is not known what happened to the other £1. In 1889 William Kelland paid the sum of £8.7s.6d. to the Official Trustees of Charitable Funds for investment in three per cent Annuities, the dividends to be applied each alternate year for the benefit of deserving persons. The 1912 inquiry declared that there had been no distribution of the income since 1904.

In 2003 the Sampford Courtenay Poor Fund, operated by Revd Ardill and two other trustees, encompasses the three remaining charitable gifts for the two parishes – those of John Sloman, John Tickell and William Kelland. The capital sum is now invested by the Charity Commissioners and the income paid to a local bank. No distributions have been made from the fund in living memory.

Friendly Societies

As mentioned above, in 1808 there were two friendly societies in Sampford Courtenay. These must have been in existence for several years before this date – entries in the overseers of the poor book in 1769 and 1770 mention purchase of warrants 'for stewards of the club', possibly one for each of the two organisations.

Becky Horn and her mother Rebecca Cooper both belonged to the Female Society and Becky kept a copy of the articles of agreement formulated in 1788. These were drawn up at the house of John Harvey, presumably Harvey's in Town. He was possibly connected with the woollen-cloth industry and many of the women members may have been outworkers for North Tawton Mill. At entrance each member had to pay 1s. to the stock and spend 3d., and 8d. per month afterwards, 6d. of which was to be put to the stock and 2d. spent in the society room immediately. Members each had to pay 6d. for a sheet of the printed articles, although it is doubtful if many of them could read. Any member, having been a payer for one year, not being able to 'follow her employment, provided the same did not arise from her own carelessness or folly, or from the gout or venereal disease', was able to claim benefit. Any proven fraud caused exclusion of the member. Pay was 6s. per week if confined to bed and 3s. per week 'walking-pay'. When £3 had been received, £3 more at 3s. per week was paid, followed by a further £3 at 2s. per week. No member was to receive

more than £9 in any one sickness. If a member continued in employment while under pay, she forfeited double the sum received. There was also a form of pension benefit; long-serving members reaching the age of 60 and then incapable of labour could receive 2s. per week for life. The fund also covered the cost of the funeral of a member, being £1.5s.0d. Each surviving member had to contribute 1s., the total being given to the deceased's next of kin. Every member within a four-mile radius had 'to attend and follow the corpse, according to the seniority of their entrance, and behave in a becoming manner.' Any member not attending the funeral was fined 1s.

Various penalties were imposed for misdemeanours:

If any member curse, swear, profane the Lord's name, promote gaming or debauched discourse, abuse the steward's table, or make any disturbance during meeting hours, she shall forfeit 2d. for each offence on conviction.

Rebecca's Cottage – note the old bread oven and kettle on chimney crook.

Above: *Harvey's in Town and Higher Town, c.1910 – note the outbuilding to the left of Higher Town where the fire-engine was housed.*

Below: *Female Society – Articles of Agreement, 1788.*

WE, Inhabitants of SAMPFORD-COURTENAY and Places adjacent, &c. agreed upon the following ARTICLES :

I. THAT this Society shall consist of any Number of Members, not exceeding One Hundred ; and that it shall ever be held and kept within the Town of Sampford-Courtenay, as long as Four Members shall resolve to continue the same; and if any Member directly or indirectly propose its Dissolution, she shall forfeit Five Shillings.

II. That Three Stewards shall be chosen at every third monthly Meeting, to receive and disburse the Money, and visit the Sick. And if any Member so chosen shall refuse to execute the Office, or procure a proper Member to do it for her, she shall forfeit One Shilling. And a Clerk shall be appointed to keep a just Account of the Receipts, Payments, &c. who shall be paid Six Pence per Month, and have a reasonable Recompence for extraordinary Duty ; and if detected in any Fraud, he shall forfeit Two Shillings and Six Pence, or be discharged.

III. That no Person shall be admitted who has a natural Infirmity, or exceeds the Age of Forty Years : And if it be proved that any such Disorder or Superannuation was concealed at her Admission, she shall be immediately excluded.

IV. That a Box be kept at the Meeting-House, in which the Accompt-Books, Cash, and other Property of the Society shall be deposited.: And that the Master or Mistress of the House shall give good Security to one of the Stewards or the Clerk, for the Safety and due Return thereof. That no Money shall be lent, or expended, (except as directed by these Articles) without the Approbation of the major Part of the Members; and if the

Above: *Old cob woodsheds or pigsties between Fir Cottage and Bank Cottage, seen in 2001.*

Right: *Old cob building, formerly a cottage, opposite The Barton, in 2001.*

Striking another member or divulging the transactions of the society to a non-member could result in exclusion. Any member convicted of felony was to be excluded and any member having an illegitimate child was to forfeit 10s.6d. to the stock or be excluded.

The Female Society continued until closure in 1911. Under the Lloyd George National Health Insurance Scheme of 1912, only organisations with 10,000 members were approved. The men's equivalent society, however, converted into Court 'Courtenay' of the Ancient Order of Foresters. The Foresters had been formed in 1834 out of an earlier society, the Royal Foresters, which probably dated from about 1745. The conversion in Sampford Courtenay brought with it £661 in funds, suggesting a flourishing pre-existing society. Court 'Courtenay' met in the old schoolroom; the secretary was William Parsons and the first treasurer William Brealey. From 1914 until closure, in around 1940, the treasurer was Richard Brealey. The solemn initiation ceremony, always carried out during the nineteenth century, but less frequently in the twentieth, contained the following exhortation to the new member:

In your domestic relationships, we look to find you, if a husband, affectionate and trustful; if a father, regardful of the moral and material well-being of your children and dependants; as a son, dutiful and exemplary; and as a friend, steadfast and true.

In 1914 Court 'Courtenay' had 75 voluntary members and 63 state members, of whom 33 also belonged to the voluntary sector. The number of voluntary members had fallen to 11 by 1940, suggesting most members could not afford the contributions to the extra benefits voluntary membership brought. However, the state section remained buoyant. The First World War caused a dip to 55, then numbers grew to 82 in 1931–32, then gradually declined again to 55 by 1940. The Foresters had an annual dinner and 'club walk' in the village (see Chapter Ten).

Chapter Five

FARMS AND FARMING

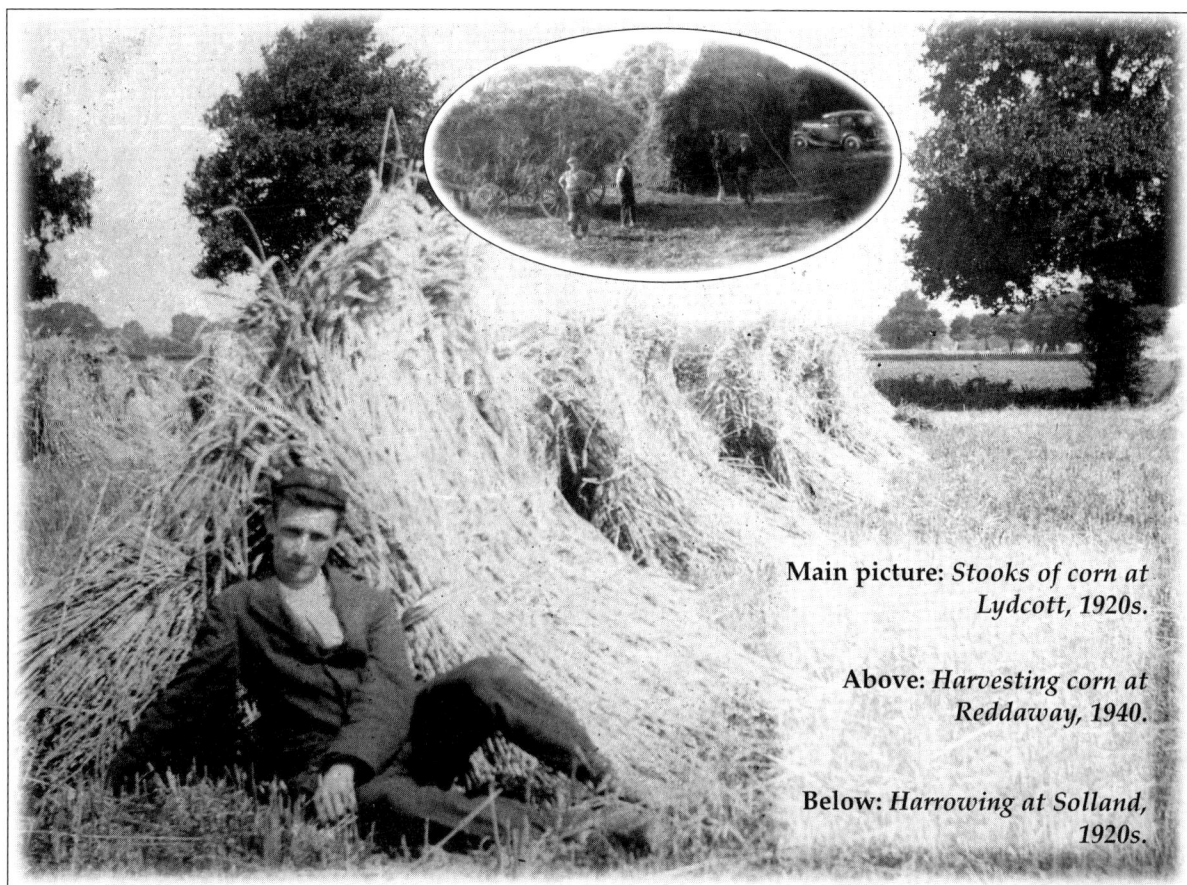

Main picture: *Stooks of corn at Lydcott, 1920s.*

Above: *Harvesting corn at Reddaway, 1940.*

Below: *Harrowing at Solland, 1920s.*

The Farms

The history of the Sampford Courtenay farms could fill a book of its own, but in these pages there is only room for the briefest detail of each property. King's College, Cambridge, acquired the manor in 1570; its survey carried out at the time is held in the College Archive Library. Although it is written in medieval script and in Latin, most of the entries could be deciphered. There were 23 free tenants:

Richard Wood at Whitbroke [Withybrook].
John Weekes at Bewlands.
John Slowman at Fulforde [Fullaford].
Willmus Westwaie at Honycott [Honeycott].
Andreas Upcote at Lake in Belsome.
Symon Froncke at ?.
Phineas Snell at Paies [Paize].
Willmus Tycyll at Cleston [Cliston].

Johes Redway at Redwey [Reddaway].
Ricus Oxenham at Dyvercoute [Davencourt].
Thomas Bannot at Bowmeade [Beaumead].
Laurencius Herman at Harforde [Halford].
Thomas Holman at Underdowne.
Henricus Weyley at Wely [Willey].
Georgius Brokeden at Restlonde [Restland].
Johes Alforde at Coscombe [Corscombe].
? Gypforde at Lydcote [Lydcott].
Jacobus Snell at ? in Belsonne.
Johes Bowden at ?.
Willmus Anste at Sticklepath.
Johes ? at Lake.

It was not possible to decipher two others. The 'tenants of indenture' held 73 properties, most of which had been annotated by the college with the more modern names:

Richard Alford at Trehill.
Alicia Mayne at Langmead and Taylors Downs, South Town.
Johes Knapman at Higher Tricott.
Robertus Ellys at Nine Cotts.
Alicia Ellis at North Barton.
Johes Ellys at East & West Barton.
? 'In Cliston'.
William Ellys at Middle Tricott.
? at Southay.
Willmus ? at Higher Langbear.
Johnna Ellis at Combe and Chapell Land.
Agnet Upcote at Westhill.
Agnet Walsh at West Hatherdon.
Richard Quicke at Higher Solland.
Johes Broke at The Lake.
Johes Raddon at East Hatherdon.
Philippus ?: Fourth part of Samford Wood.
Johes Rapson at Webber Hill.
Willmus Ascote: Fourth part of Samford Wood.
Johes Dun: Fourth part of Samford Wood.
Joem Johes at Appledore.
Ricus Slowman at Rowdon Mills.
Johnna Ellys at Yondhill.
Johanna Chastey at Aller.
Johanna Broke at Falcadon.
Willimus Underhill at Frankland and Middle Solland.
Willimus Segar at Brook, Lower Incott, Strayer Moor and Saltacre.
Ricus Cerose at Fullaford.

Andreas Rapson at Fentown.
Thomas ? at Lower Langbear.
Alicia Chastey 'In Southtowne'.
Robertus Haywood at West Underdown.
Robertus Newcombe at Balle.
Chistiana Aller 'In Cliston'.
Willimus Ellis at West Tricott.
Willimus Come at Radcomb.
Robertus Ablebridge at Lower Solland.
Symon Wicke at North Berehill.
Willimus Lege at South Berehill.
Willimus Legge at West Rowden.
Robertus Parrys at East Rowden.
Symon Northcombe at Middle Rowden.
Johes Newcome 'In Cliston'.
Willimus Ascote at ?.
Willimus Rapsome at Higher Incott.
Matteus ? 'In Cliston'.
? at Lower Underdown.
Philippus Thorne at Middle Underdown.
Thomas Ellys at Lower Tricott.
Willimus Ascote at Wood or Atwoode.
Thomas Ellis at ?.

Six properties were listed 'In Samford Town' and two 'In Town'; these presumably were village tenements. Seven cottages were also included. Two names were indecipherable. Thus in 1570 the manor comprised about 90 holdings. In 1809 King's College arranged for a full survey of the tenanted farms to be carried

Left: Charity Hawkins (later Sanders) of Beerhill, c.1890.

Below: The Barton, c.1940.

Left: Eleanor Hawkins of Beerhill, c.1890.

out by Messrs Webb, Webb & Atwood. This survey, which was updated in 1821, gives an interesting picture of the copyhold farms and cottages. Examination of subsequent records, including the 1842 Tithe Apportionment, the census returns and the King's College sale catalogues, provides evidence of the survival of many of the ancient families through several generations and the gradual consolidation of the farms into larger units.

Higher Quarterwood or Bowmead Wood in 1809 became Higher **Agistment** by 1842. The 1851 census returns recorded two cottages at Higher Justment. By 1871 Higher Ajistment was uninhabited but by 1873 Justment was occupied by John Newcombe. Between 1842 and 1888 (probably in the 1870s) a new farmhouse was built on a site north of the old property. From 1901 the farm was variously described as Justmant or Agistment and in 1921 was sold by King's College to the tenant Henry Hawkins.

Aller in 1809 was occupied by William Brook(e) but the buildings were in a ruinous state. In 1837 Isaac Brook was the tenant; in 1891 the farmhouse was uninhabited and in 1901 occupied by a farm labourer. When King's College sold the combined farms of Trehill and Aller in 1921, the house at Aller had disappeared. Some farm buildings remain.

Appledore in 1809 was farmed by the Slomans. In 1837 it was run by Susanna Snell, followed by other members of the Snell family until the 1880s. By 1891 the house was uninhabited and in 1921, when King's College sold the property, Appledore and Coldacott were farmed by Albert Frost of Westhill. The farmhouse had by then disappeared, although a new house was built in the 1930s. Two cottages on Appledore Hill (one at a slate quarry) had gone by 1881.

Arscott's in Town (Middletown) was originally a village tenement. The land was farmed with other holdings from 1809 onwards, firstly by the Heathman family and then the Snells. The Snell family were in occupation until the 1930s; King's College probably sold to them by private treaty.

Ball was farmed by John Quick in 1809 and George Quick in 1842. The Quick family disappeared from the parish in around 1860. In 1891 William Horn, the Parish Clerk, was the tenant and in 1923 the farm was sold by King's College to the subsequent tenant Robert Reddaway. At the time of writing most of the land is farmed with North Corscombe.

The Barton (derived from bere-ton meaning barley town) was originally the lord's demesne farm. By 1809 the farmhouse at North Barton had disappeared and John Brook(e) was the occupier at East (South) Barton. By 1842 Philip Brook held the properties. South Barton farmhouse was partially rebuilt in the second half of the 1800s. The Brooks were followed by Thomas Sloman and then the Langs; King's College sold the farm to Thomas Lang. In recent years most of the land has been absorbed into Langmead and Beerhill and a barn has been converted (Weirford House).

Beaumead (Bowmead), a freehold property, by 1842 was farmed with Coombe by the Raymont family. The farmhouse was occupied by farm labourers from 1871 to 1891, the land probably being absorbed by Wood or Agistment. The house then became empty and is currently used as farm buildings by Agistment. Little Bowmead was uninhabited by 1881.

Beer was owned by Sir Ipsley Tuckfield in 1842. The Reddaway family farmed there for many years at the end of the nineteenth and into the twentieth century.

South **Beerhill** was in a dilapidated state in 1846. By 1855 William Hawkins was farming both North and South Beerhill. The house at South Beerhill was probably then abandoned; part of it remains but is used as a farm building. The college sold Beerhill to William and Charity Sanders (née Hawkins).

Brook was near Stock Bridge. In 1809 William Tickle held the copyhold and James Cockram was the tenant. The Cockrams were in occupation until the 1870s but by 1881 the land was farmed by the Southcombes of Wood and a young family lived at Brook Cottage. By 1891 the cottage was uninhabited and when King's College sold Brook as part of Wood in 1921 the cottage was being used as cattle pens. In 1943 the cottage was still 'suitable for renovation as a dwelling' but now just part of a wall remains.

Bude was bought by the Lethbridge family in 1918 and is now in Sticklepath parish.

Chapel (Chapple) Lands was north-east of Wood; Thomas Heathman was the tenant in 1809 and 1842. From 1851 the cottage was occupied by farm labourers, but had disappeared by 1901. The land was sold by King's College as part of Wood Farm.

Chapple Agistment, owned by King's College, comprised 59 acres south-west of Ratcombe; no homestead was recorded at the property.

Chapple Moor was held jointly by several tenants in 1842, but was sold by the college as part of The Barton. It was purchased by the Forestry Commission in 1969/70.

In 1842 Great (or Lower) **Cliston** was still owned by the Tickle family, who held the freehold in 1570 (and probably earlier). Richard Page (probably two generations) was the tenant from 1837 until the early 1880s, followed by the Sanders family. The other properties at Cliston were owned by King's College. Down's Cliston and Aller's Cliston were so called from family

Great Cliston during the 1920s.

Above: *Halford Manor, 2002.*

Left: *The Cleverdons of Higher Cliston, 1925.*
Left to right, standing at rear: *Walter and Leslie;*
front: *Mary with baby Mary, Kenneth and Henry.*

names; there were Downs and Allers in the parish in the sixteenth century and Margaret Aller still owned the copyhold of Aller's Cliston at the end of the eighteenth century. By 1837 both were farmed by William Coombe and by 1851 the house at Down's Cliston was uninhabited. The Coombe family continued at Cliston until 1910. When King's College sold Down's and Aller's Cliston in 1925 only farm buildings had survived at Down's Cliston. The land now forms part of Great Cliston. The Newcombes farmed Middle Cliston in 1809 (the family had been tenants of a holding 'In Cliston' in 1570) but from the 1850s the Dayments were in residence. Confusingly, from around 1882 Aller's Cliston became known as Middle Cliston and Middle Cliston as Higher Cliston. Miss Elizabeth Dayment ran Higher Cliston from 1896 until the 1920s. In 1927 the property was sold by King's College to Henry Cleverdon, the grandfather of the occupant at the time of writing. In 1809 East Cliston was a separate holding; by 1851 the farmhouse had become two cottages and the land amalgamated into Middle (subsequently Higher) Cliston. The cottages were unoccupied by 1871 but have been restored as one dwelling-house in recent years. There is a barn conversion at Middle (Aller's) Cliston.

Coldacott was variously called Quarterwood, Appledoor Wood and Coldecotte. In 1809 Thomas Ellis was the tenant. The Ellis family were prominent in the parish in the 1500s. By 1837 Coldacott was farmed with Appledore by the Snells. The cottage at Coldacott was still in existence in 1901 but only farm buildings had survived when King's College sold the property as part of Westhill in 1921. There are now two modern bungalows near the site of the old farmhouse.

Coombe was a separate holding in 1809; by the 1820s William Bolt was the occupier. In 1842 John Raymont was farming both Coombe and Beaumead and the house at Coombe was occupied by a farm labourer. By 1861 the house was uninhabited. Coombe formed part of Wood when sold by King's College to Samuel Southcombe. The cottage at that time was being used as cattle pens. The former site of the property is now in the middle of Berrydown Plantation, but only fragments of masonry remain.

Coombehead and **Higher Coombehead** are now in Sticklepath parish.

There were eight properties in **Corscombe** hamlet in 1842. By 1881 the land was farmed by Richard Raymont, John and William Westaway and William Reddaway. By 1891 only five properties were listed. At the time of writing these five – Higher, Lower and Middle Corscombe together with Corscombe Down and a cottage (previously South Corscombe) – survive. A cottage at Middle Corscombe, used as a farm building for some years, has now been restored, but two cottages, one adjacent to Lower Corscombe and one on the right-angle bend to the north of the hamlet, have disappeared. There is now a modern bungalow at North Corscombe.

Cross was farmed separately in 1842 but between 1851 and 1901 was occupied by farm labourers. The cottage has survived, although most of the land is now farmed with Reddaway.

Davencourt (also Daveycourt) was farmed as a separate holding until the late-nineteenth century, for many years by William Reddaway. The house was then occupied by farm labourers and fell into a bad state of repair until it was restored in recent years.

Dornaford was a sub-manor. The farmhouses at Higher Dornaford and Dornaford Park and a cottage were all uninhabited by 1871 and have now gone. A new property at Dornaford Park is outside the parish boundary. Lower Dornaford farmhouse remains (renamed Higher Dornaford on the 1888 Ordnance Survey map) and there is a twentieth-century property called Dornaford House on a new site. Dornaford was farmed by the Snell family from the late-nineteenth century until the mid-1900s.

Falcadon was a separate holding in 1809 and in 1851, but by 1881 the house was being used as a farm-labourer's cottage. The property was purchased from King's College by Philip Tilden of Rowden. Although the schedule identified a cottage, the catalogue did not give details of the building. In recent years a modern bungalow has been built on the site.

Frankland remained virtually unchanged from 1570 until 1991. The Dennafords were the tenants in the eighteenth century and the Dayments in the nineteenth and the farm was bought from the college by Stanley Pike. The land is now divided.

North **Fullaford** was owned by King's College but South Fullaford was a freehold property. By 1837 the two holdings had amalgamated and were farmed by the Slomans until the 1890s, followed by the Bolts. The house at North Fullaford and a second house at South Fullaford had disappeared by 1851. The college sold the land and farm buildings at North Fullaford to Sydney Bolt.

The **Glebe** lands, which totalled 85 acres in 1842, are now divided.

Halford was a sub-manor in the thirteenth century, and was owned during the 1700s and 1800s by the Snell family. Halford Cottage, which was opposite the house, disappeared in living memory although another cottage at Halford remains. The house at Little Halford, once Halford Mill, had gone by 1881. There were also two cottages on Halford Moor, just north of the footpath to Trehill. By 1891 these were uninhabited and have now disappeared.

Hammett's Hill with 17 acres was one of the village tenements in 1809. The cottages (Hammett's Hill Cottage, Virginia Cottage and Rebecca's Cottage) were sold by King's College in 1929.

Harvey's in Town in 1809 had 73 acres and four dwellings and Mary Harvey held the copyhold. King's College sold the cottages in 1929 but the land had already been absorbed into other holdings.

In 1809 West and East **Hatherton** were separate holdings. Mary Tickle held the copyhold of East Hatherton. By 1837 William Tucker was farming both and in 1851 one of the houses was occupied by a farm labourer. By 1861 only one house was listed. Hatherton was sold by King's College to Thomas Southcombe.

Hayrish in the nineteenth century was called Irish. There were two dwellings – Irish Farm with 96 acres, occupied in 1881 by William Davey, and Little Irish. The latter was uninhabited by 1901 and has now disappeared. In recent years the old farmhouse and a cottage on a different site have been restored and the property, with land from Davencourt and Langabeer, is now a sporting estate.

Higher Town with 105 acres was occupied by John Reed in 1809 but by 1842 had been divided into separate holdings. John Ward, the King's College carpenter and sub-agent, lived in the farmhouse at the end of the nineteenth and beginning of the twentieth centuries.

Lower and Higher **Hole** (small tenements with cottages) in 1842 were situated just east of Trehill, north and south of the footpath from Halford. One of these was uninhabited by 1851 and the other was not mentioned after this date. By 1857 the land belonging to Hole was farmed with Aller.

Honeycott was farmed by George Quick, with Ball and Restland, in 1842 and by Bernard Legg of Lydcott in 1857. There were two cottages, the current property and another south-west of it; both were occupied by farm labourers during the late 1800s. The latter property had disappeared by the beginning of the twentieth century.

King's College did not record a house at Higher **Incott** in 1809, although the 1842 Tithe Apportionment did, when Higher and Lower Incott plus **Ventown** (or Fentown) were farmed by Mark Lock. In 1851 Mark Lock

---

The catalogue text (Lot 1):

Lot 1
(Coloured Pink on Plan).

PLEASANTLY SITUATE AND EASILY ACCESSIBLE

MIXED HOLDING

known as

"Frankland Farm"

embracing a total area of about

77 a. 0 r. 18 p.

VACANT POSSESSION can be had on the 10th day of October, 1925, subject to an Agreement with the Vendors to the date of Completion.

THE FARMHOUSE

situated just off the Sampford Courtenay—Honeychurch Road, contains:—
ON THE GROUND FLOOR :—Entrance Lobby; Dining Room, about 16 ft. x 14 ft.; Drawing Room, about 15 ft. 6 in. x 14 ft. 9 in.; Large Kitchen; Dairy; Leanto Pump-house with well of good water.
ON THE FIRST FLOOR :—Landing; 1 medium-sized Bedroom and 2 large Bedrooms; and approached by separate staircase :—Men's Bedroom and Apple Store.

THE FARM BUILDINGS

which are substantial and commodious, comprise:—Store with Loft over, adjoining Farmhouse; Barn; Poultry House; Piggeries; 3-bay Open Linhay; Loose Box; Leanto Calves' House; 2-bay Open Linhay; 3-stall Stable; 6-ties Shippen and Roothouse, with Loft over; Calves' House in 3 divisions; Large Barn, floored throughout; Leanto Poultry House; Detached 4-bay Cart Linhay.

SCHEDULE

No. on Plan	Description	A.	R.	P.
	Sampford Courtenay Parish.			
1832	Arable			
1833	Rough Pasture	9	1	14
1849	Arable	6	3	23
1850	"	5	1	13
1855	"	6	0	32
1861	" (Pasture by Tenant)	5	1	34
1862	Orchard	3	3	5
2097	Pasture	1	2	21
2099	Farmhouse, Buildings, Garden, Yards, etc.	1	3	29
2100	Pasture		3	14
2101	Orchard	1	3	19
2102	Arable		1	12
2117	"			
2118	" (Pasture by Tenant)	3	0	11
2119	"	3	0	35
2120	" and Row (Pasture by Tenant)	4	3	16
2121	" (Pasture by Tenant)	8	0	3
2122	Old Quarry		1	9
2123	Arable and Row		2	11
		2	3	34
	A.	77	0	18

Outgoings:—
Commuted Tithe Rent Charge ... £ s. d.
Land Tax (apportioned) ... 9 9 5 ... 1 16 0
The Timber on this Lot has been valued at £60 (sixty pounds).

King's College sale catalogues. Above: Frankland Farm, 1925; below: Hammett's Hill Cottages and Rose Cottage, 1929.

The catalogue text (Lots 12 and 13):

LOT 12
(coloured Green on Plan).

Another Picturesque Block of Four Devon Cottages

known as

" Hammett's Hill "

together with their Gardens and Sheds, comprising an area of about

0 a. 2 r. 19 p.

2 COTTAGES, No. 1726c on Plan (in the occupation of Mr. W. Knott and Mr. H. Sanders), each contains :—Living Room, Back Kitchen, 3 Bedrooms, Pantry, Coal House and E.C.
2 COTTAGES, No. 1726d on Plan:—
1—(in the occupation of Mr. W. Piper), contains:—Living Room, Kitchen, Scullery, 3 Bedrooms, and E.C.
2—(void), contains:—Living Room, Kitchen, 3 Bedrooms, and E.C.
There is a Pump House and Well shared by these two Cottages.
The Court, containing 4 Piggeries and 4 Linhays, is shared in common.

SCHEDULE.

No. on Plan.	Description.	A.	R.	P.
	In Sampford Courtenay Parish.			
1681b	Garden		1	10
1726c	Two Cottages, Gardens and Sheds			34
1726d	Two Cottages and Sheds			15
	A.		2	19

This Lot is let on Quarterly Tenancies.
Outgoings:—Commuted Tithe Rent Charge, 5d.
As to Tenant's Fixtures, see Notes and General Remarks.
N.B.—A Right of Way is reserved through the covered way in No. 1726c of this Lot, as at present enjoyed by the tenants and adjoining owners.

LOT 13
(Coloured Yellow on Plan)

Freehold Reversion to

The Attractive Cottage and Garden

Numbered 1684c on Plan. It occupies an excellent corner site in Sampford Courtenay, and comprises an area of about

0 a. 0 r. 19 p.

The Accommodation is as follows:—Parlour, Kitchen, Back Kitchen, Pantry, 2 Bedrooms, Wood House.
As to Tenant's Fixtures, see Notes and General Remarks.
This Lot is sold subject to a former Copyhold Interest determinable on Lives, and there is a Quit Rent Payable to the Vendors of fourpence per annum. The present Lives are 67 and 68 years of age respectively.

Langmead, c.1920.

Above: *The Bolts of Sampford Courtenay, c.1916/17.*
Left to right, standing: *Sydney and sister Ellen from Fullaford, Tom from London, William and his housekeeper (Mrs Dunn) from Underdown, Charles from Langmead;* seated: *Grandma Emma from Fullaford with young Mary (Charles' daughter).*

probably lived at Lower Incott and the other house was uninhabited. A farm labourer lived at Ventown. By 1861 only one house was recorded at Incott and when King's College sold Incott and Ventown in 1925 the cottage at Ventown had disappeared. A bungalow was built at Ventown in the 1980s.

The Lake (also Trelake or Daylake) was occupied by John Sloman in 1809. The college survey recorded the buildings as being in a very bad state. A new house was built in 1818, but in 1881 and 1891 was uninhabited and in 1901 no longer mentioned. The land was sold as part of West (Higher) Rowden by the college but the only building to survive was a large cattle shed. Most of the land now forms part of Withybrook.

In 1809 Higher and Lower **Langabeer** were farmed as separate holdings; John Newcombe was the tenant at Higher Langabeer. In 1842 William Jackman was the tenant at Lower Langabeer and Thomas Dawe at Higher Langabeer. By 1871 William Newcombe was living at Lower Langabeer and by 1891 was farming both holdings. However, by 1921 when King's College sold the Langabeers, the Newcombes were still the tenants but the house at Lower Langabeer had disappeared and they were living at Higher Langabeer.

Most of the land is now farmed with Willey.

In 1809 and 1842 the Legg family were the tenants of **Langmead** and South Beerhill and in 1851 John Legg was living at the former. (The Legg(e) family were at South Beerhill in 1570.) By 1856 William Bolt was the tenant at Langmead and the Bolt family remained there until the late 1920s, Charles Bolt buying from King's College in 1925.

Longfield (now Nos.1 and 2 Shores' Cottages) was a small tenement of three acres in 1809, which was sold by the college in 1929.

Lydcott, one of the thirteenth-century sub-manors, was farmed by the Legg family from the 1830s until the 1880s. Lydcott Cottage was unoccupied in 1901.

Moils Moor in 1809 was a village tenement with 55 acres occupied by William Heathman. The house, which possibly burned down in the mid-1800s, may have been on the site of the present Post Office.

Ninecotts, a village tenement with 11 acres, included the New Inn and the cottages (now gone) opposite Rose Cottage. In 1809 Simon Sloman held the copyhold and in 1842 John Snell was the tenant.

Cattle at Lydcott Farm, 1945.

The Reddaways of Reddaway Farm, 1930. **Left to right, back row:** *Maurice, John (J.I.), William junr and Mary;* **front row:** *Herbert, William senr, Emily Jane and Hetty.*

North Town (also Stuckeys) in 1809 comprised two dwellings and 16 acres. It was sold with four acres by King's College in 1929, by which time one of the cottages was being used as a farm building.

Oxenpark, a tenement of 22 acres, in 1842 was owned by Theodore Tickle, who also owned Great Cliston. A homestead was recorded at the property but it is likely it was already uninhabited.

Paize in 1842 was owned by Lord Clinton and farmed with Great Cliston by Richard Page. For much of the twentieth century it was occupied by the Sanders family. Some of the land is still farmed by a descendant of the Sanders family. There is a recent barn conversion.

Pitt, which was south-west of Lydcott, was farmed separately in 1842 but by William Snell of Appledore in the 1850s. The house was then occupied by farm labourers but was uninhabited by 1891 and probably disappeared soon after.

Ratcombe was farmed by William Lang of Withybrook in 1837. From 1851 until 1891 two farm labourers and their families lived there but by 1901 just one family. In 1921 the college sold the property to the tenant, Thomas Lang of The Barton. The cottage had been re-roofed and repaired and was last occupied by two old ladies in the mid-1920s. No signs of the cottage now remain, although parts of the outbuildings have survived. The land is now part of Restland.

Reddaway was a sub-manor held by Galfrid de Radeweye in 1242. The Reddaway family, who have lived in and around Sampford Courtenay parish for the last 750 years, are all descended from Galfrid. Members of the family have farmed Reddaway on and off over the centuries. Thomas Reddaway was in residence in 1851. He and his four brothers all died childless and the farm passed to his sister's son William Reddaway Knapman. Robert William Reddaway, the son of William Reddaway of Beer Farm, at first farmed Ball but in 1924 took over Reddaway Farm as a tenant of the Knapmans. Robert's son, John Isaac, or 'J.I.' as he was known, subsequently bought the property, which is now run by his son, another Robert.

Restland in 1842 was owned by George Quick, who also owned Honeycott but who was farming and living at Ball. A farm labourer was living at Restland farmhouse. Restland was occupied by John Brock in the late-nineteenth and early-twentieth centuries. The family left the farm in around 1910 and the house eventually fell down. Restland Cottage, built at the end of the nineteenth century, is now the farmhouse.

In the 1809 King's College survey three properties were listed at **Rowden** – West, Middle and East. West (subsequently Higher) Rowden was farmed by John Sloman in 1809, Thomas Sloman in 1842 and George Sloman in the 1860s and '70s. East Rowden was farmed by Simon Newcombe in 1809, by Edmund Dennaford in 1842 (when it was described as Lower Rowden) and from the mid-nineteenth century until

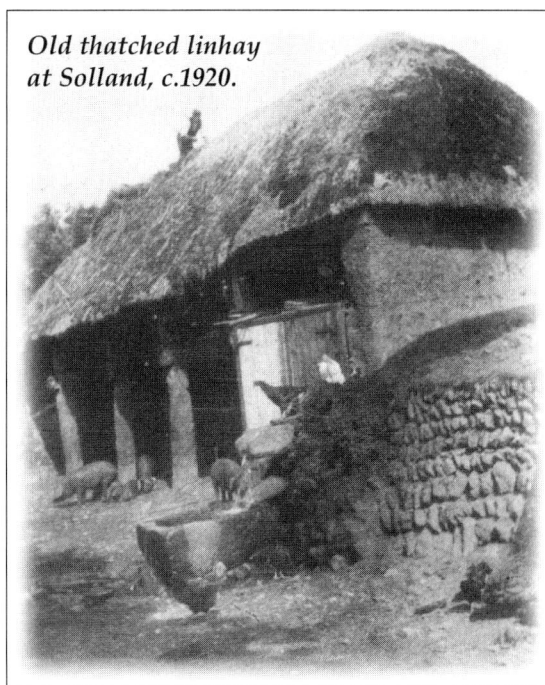

Old thatched linhay at Solland, c.1920.

1920 by the Slomans. The 1809 survey recorded John Newcombe as the tenant at Middle Rowden, but he was possibly living at Higher Langabeer. No house was recorded at Middle Rowden but this was probably a mistake as the 1842 Tithe Apportionment map clearly shows a house on the property, situated between West and Lower Rowden. In 1881 two houses were recorded at Middle Rowden, presumably the old house and a new building (now called the White House) to the north of it. These were occupied by two members of the Davey family who were farming Higher and Middle Rowden. The old house has now gone. The Rowdens were acquired by the architect Philip Tilden in the 1920s (see Chapter Eleven). Lower Rowden is now called Rowden Manor. Another property known as East Rowden (or Little Rowden), which was not owned by the college, was situated at Peckets Ford. Over the years it was variously farmed, occupied by farm labourers or uninhabited.

Upper, Middle and Lower **Solland** were farmed by William Kelland in 1809. The college survey recorded:

The tenant wishes to take down the barn, linney and house at Lower Solland. They seem to be unnecessary, there being two other homesteads on this site and the house and other buildings at Middle Solland have lately been much repaired and improved.

No sign of Lower Solland now remains and the old farmhouse at Upper or Higher Solland was replaced at the end of the nineteenth century by two farmworkers' cottages. The Kellands were resident at Solland until 1894. John E. Hawkins then acquired the tenancy and subsequently bought the property from King's College. The family remained the owners until 1995 when John E. Hawkins' grandson, another John, sold the farm.

Solland Farm, 1920s.

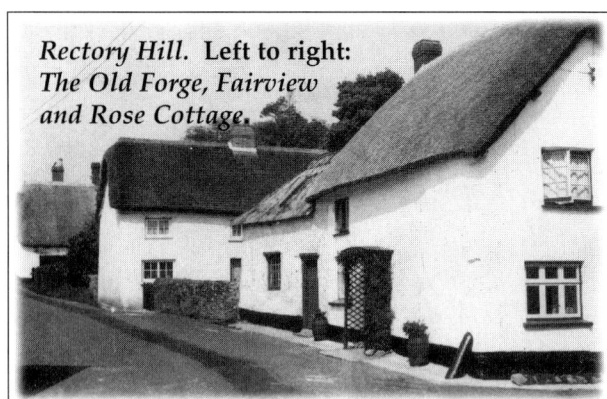

Rectory Hill. Left to right: The Old Forge, Fairview and Rose Cottage.

Lower Trecott, c.1910.

In 1809 John Snell was the tenant at **Southey** (Southay). In 1842 another John Snell was the tenant but he was also the landlord at the New Inn and a farm labourer lived at Southey. The house was still occupied in 1881 but by 1891 it was empty. Part of the old building was still in existence until the 1970s when the owners pulled it down and built the present house.

In 1809 James Snell owned the copyhold of **South Town**; by 1837 William Sanders was the tenant. George Sanders senr and junr farmed South Town from around 1850 until 1909, followed by John Harris. Fred Taylor bought the farm from King's College in 1928. There is an adjacent barn conversion.

Taylor's Downs in 1809 was a village tenement of 23 acres belonging to Rose Cottage on Rectory Hill. John Legg owned the copyhold.

In 1809 there were four farms at **Trecott** – Middle, West, Higher and Lower Trecott. Middle and West Trecott had already amalgamated; Wilmot Arscott owned the copyhold and William Coombe was the occupier. The survey recorded: 'West and Middle Trecott are so mingled that there would be much trouble in separating them.' The farmhouse at Middle Trecott was being used as a farm-workers' cottage. West and Middle Trecott were subsequently farmed by the Hern family, followed by William Arscott by the late 1870s. The Arscott family continued there until the 1920s when Richard Hill bought the farm from King's College. In 1809 Higher Trecott was farmed by John Brooke and Lower Trecott by another William Arscott (no apparent relation to the one at West Trecott). By 1842 William Arscott's son, another William, was farming both properties. William was living at Lower Trecott and Higher Trecott became a farm-workers' cottage. When the college sold Lower Trecott in 1929 the house at Higher Trecott was being used as a farm building. The land holding had reduced; presumably some had been absorbed by West Trecott. Lower Trecott was purchased by the Jones family, the children of the sister of a third William Arscott. The house at Higher Trecott has since been restored and an adjacent barn has also been converted into a dwelling.

Trehill in 1809 possessed a farmhouse and two cottages. In 1842 it was farmed separately but by around 1880 had amalgamated with Aller. By 1901 John Page was farming Trehill and Aller; King's College sold the combined properties to the Page family in 1921. Although the cottages appeared to have fallen out of use by 1851, they have since been reinstated and there is also a barn conversion. The land has been absorbed into other holdings.

In 1809 King's College recorded West, Lower and Middle **Underdown** all being farmed as separate holdings. By 1842 William Sanders was farming West Underdown with South Town. Thomas Heathman of Middle Underdown was also farming Little Underdown which may have been carved out of Paize. By 1891 the same family were farming Paize and Little Underdown, and they probably re-amalgamated. By then Middle Underdown farmhouse was uninhabited. By 1901 William Holmes was living at Lower Underdown; West and Middle Underdown were not listed. King's College sold Lower and Middle Underdown to the tenant William Southcombe in 1923 when the houses at West, Middle and Little Underdown had either fallen down or were being used as farm buildings. At the time of writing Dunn's Dairy operates from the farm.

Webber Hill in 1809 had two houses, one of which was 'newly built'. At Webber Hill Wood (later called Blackstubbs) there was another recently built house. Both holdings were farmed by John Drew, followed by William Bolt by 1837. In 1871 and 1881 Blackstubbs was uninhabited, although occupied again by a farm

LOT 10
(coloured Brown on Plan).

The Noted Block of Four Old-time Thatched
Cottages and Gardens

formerly known as

"Wood's Cottages"

No. 1725c on Plan, situate in the Village of Sampford Courtenay, and
comprising an area of about

0a.   2r.   30 p.

3 COTTAGES (in occupation of Mrs. M. Seward, Mrs. J. Pike and Mr. S. Cole)
each containing:—Living Room, Back Kitchen, 2 Bedrooms and E.C.

COTTAGE (in occupation of Mrs. Wm. Goodwin), contains:—Living Room, Back
Kitchen, 1 Bedroom and E.C.

Together with this Lot there are:—7 Pigstyes, 3 Linhays; 2 Wood Sheds and
Fowls House.

The Cottage in the occupation of Mrs. M. Seward is let on a monthly tenancy. The
remainder are let on quarterly tenancies.

Outgoings:—
Commuted Tithe Rent Charge, 3s. 4d.

As to Tenant's Fixtures, see Notes and General Remarks.

LOT 11
(coloured Pink on Plan).

The Accommodation Pasture Lands

Situate in the Village of Sampford Courtenay.

SCHEDULE.

No. on Plan.	Description. In Sampford Courtenay Parish.			A.	Area R.	P.
1680	Pasture	...	...	1	3	31
1681a	ditto	...	...		2	10
1726e	Lane ...	...	...			8
1729a	Shrubbery	...	...			10
				A.	2 2	19

This Lot is let to the Rev. H. Beaumont Burnaby on a yearly Ladyday tenancy.

Outgoings:—
Commuted Tithe Rent Charge, 17s. 11d.

As to Tenant's Fixtures, see Notes and General Remarks.

N.B.—With this Lot is sold a Right of Way through the covered way in
No. 1726d of Lot 12, as at present enjoyed by the tenant and other adjoining owners.

Above: *King's College sale catalogue, 1929 –
Wood's Cottages.*

Below: *May and Nellie Jones at
Lower Trecott, c.1920.*

In commemoration of the Queen's Jubilee.

THE PROVOST AND FELLOWS OF KING'S COLLEGE

REQUEST THE PLEASURE

company

AT DINNER IN THE COLLEGE HALL

on Wednesday, July 13, 1887, at 6.30 P.M.

KING'S COLLEGE,
CAMBRIDGE.

Above: *Dinner invitation from King's College
to William Arscott of Lower Trecott, 1887.*

William Arscott of Lower Trecott, c.1920.

**The Horn family at
Webber Hill, 1920s.**

labourer in 1891 and 1901. By the mid-1850s William Bolt had moved to Langmead and a John Drew was once more listed as the tenant. By the 1870s John Newcombe was possibly farming Webber Hill from Agistment. By 1881 he had moved to Webber Hill, leaving his son, another John, running Agistment. By 1906 William Horn was the tenant at Webber Hill and he bought the property from King's College in 1921. The cottage at Blackstubbs was then uninhabited and has since disappeared. Webber Hill was divided into three properties in the late-twentieth century, but most of the land has been absorbed into other holdings.

Westhill was farmed separately in 1809 but run by Stephen Southcombe of Wood in 1842. By the 1890s Westhill had been amalgamated with Appledore and Coldacott and was farmed by the Frost family. Westhill, together with Appledore and Coldacott, was sold by King's College to Albert Frost in 1921. The land is now farmed from Appledore. There is a recent barn conversion.

Westwood (Lower Justment/Agistment), which is south-west of Wood Farm, was farmed separately with about 45 acres in 1809, 1842 and 1851. The house was occupied by a farm labourer in 1871 but then disappeared. The land was probably absorbed into Agistment.

There were four properties at **Willey** in 1842, all owned by Thomas Lethbridge, who lived at East Willey. By the 1850s Willey comprised two holdings and by 1891 had consolidated into one farm, with a house and two cottages. The present buildings are nineteenth century in origin.

Withybrook was owned by the Lang family from 1829 until 1898, then let to several tenants until John Sleeman bought it in 1946. His son Arthur took over in 1952 and rebuilt the farmhouse. The farm is now run by Arthur's son, David, with land from other holdings. There is an adjacent cottage which was built in the mid-nineteenth century.

Wood Farm was a separate holding in 1809 and was run by Stephen Southcombe with Westhill in 1842. The Southcombe family continued at Wood and by 1921 had also acquired Brook, Chapple Lands and Coombe – 322 acres in total. They bought from the college and remained in residence until the 1950s. The land is now farmed from Agistment.

Wood's was a village tenement with 56 acres and six dwelling-houses (including Forge Cottage) in 1809 and Thomas Heathman was the tenant. Four cottages at Woods (now two) and Forge Cottage were sold by the college in 1929.

Yondhill was farmed by the Hill family throughout the nineteenth century. The property was sold by King's College to the tenant, William Ash, who married Elizabeth Hill.

Youldon was farmed separately until the 1860s. In 1881 and 1891 the house, which was situated south of Youldon Bridge, was recorded as uninhabited and presumably disappeared soon after, the land being absorbed into other holdings. There are now two modern properties at Youldon on different sites.

Thus the consolidation of the holdings over the course of the nineteenth and early-twentieth centuries can be identified, leading to many of the farmhouses falling empty. Some houses were occupied by farm labourers for a while but the gradual introduction of labour-saving machinery reduced the number of men required and these too fell empty.

Farming in the Nineteenth Century

The land's as wet as wet can be:
How bothered my poor pate is!
There's Brisk and Boxer cruel galled,
And Tidy Mare is gripy; ...
And all the sheep have got the scab;
And wool's a-going down;
And I've to draw my produce in,
Vull vorteen miles to town...
Us can't get on if times don't mend;
'Tis raly quite alarming:
I only wish my lease was out,
I'm zure I'd give up farming.
From 'Farming in Devonshire' – *Sighs, Smiles and Sketches*
by J.G. Maxwell, 1860.

Little is known of farming in Sampford Courtenay before the nineteenth century. The 1809 survey gives details of field usage and annual yields plus some general remarks about the lands within the parish:

The northward part, ... lying west, north and east of and round the village, consists of red rich useful land; the southward part of inferior land and extensive tracts of poor moory heath land. The moors were plowed many years ago and some few pieces are now occasionally plowed; but so many successive crops of corn are taken, and then the land is laid down in such bad condition that it remains good for very little for many years to come. Much stock is kept on some of these moors in summer, consisting of young bullocks, colts and Dartmoor sheep. The lands in general, especially those south of the village, might be much improved by draining.

The chief crops in the parish in the nineteenth century were wheat, barley, oats and roots.

Manor Courts

King's College held an annual court in the upper room of Church House, which two of the fellows of the college attended. One of these was sometimes the provost. Revd Fulford Williams described one such visit in 1826 when the provost drove up through the village 'in a coach and four, between two lines of bowing tenants, each man given a new smock and each women a new bonnet and gown for the great occasion'. The steward, as the lords' representative, presided over other meetings. To help him he had a

The Pound with the Methodist chapel and Sunday school in background, 2001.

jury of local landowners who presented matters to be dealt with at the court, which included the conveyance of land to new tenants and the appointment of manorial officers. The proceedings of the court were inscribed in the rolls; these were written in Latin until the mid-eighteenth century. However, a court roll book, covering the period 1763 to 1830, has survived and this is in English. From this we can identify the various officers. For example, in 1794 Thomas Heathman was tythingman, William Reed was reeve (both responsible for law and order) and John Avery was pound keeper (the pound was for stray animals).

Freeholders held their land by socage tenure and they had certain obligations to the lords of the manor. They paid a relief when succeeding to their property and an annual rent. They had to attend Manor Courts, but less frequently than unfree tenants. By the beginning of the sixteenth century the majority of unfree tenants had become copyholders, holding their lands by copy of court roll. The copyholders had to attend meetings of the court and had to use the lords' mill. Copyhold was normally held for three lives and then reverted to the lords when it was either re-granted or kept 'in hand'. The copyholder usually put forward his own name, together with those of his wife and heir, or alternatively two of his children. Entry fines had to be paid and these were adjusted to reflect the true value of the land. All tenants were eligible for election as jurors. Those who failed to attend the courts were fined. The most irritating of all feudal dues were 'heriots' which compelled the surrender of the best beast on a tenant's death. One can imagine that the best beast was kept well out of sight when the steward called. Some examples of the above practices were:

1764 We present Simon Newcombe's death on Cliston and a heriott due to the Lords... and Christopher Newcombe to be the next life.

1764 We present all tenants that have made default this day and amerce [fine] them one shilling each.

1794 At this court came William Arscott of Sampford Courtenay yeoman and took of the Lords a certain tenement called Lower Trecott for the lives of William Arscott his son aged 21 years and Dorothy Arscott his daughter aged 15 years... to have and to hold the said tenement unto the said William Arscott for the lives of William Arscott

and Dorothy Arscott his son and daughter. William Arscott hath given a fine in hand paid of £280.

1774 We present the death of Honour Frost a life on the Manor Mills and the Mills to be in the Lords' hand.

1797 We present the death of John Legg late a life on Langmead, South Beerhill and Higher Incott and 3 heriots due for same.

1814 We present that on the death of John Newcombe late a life on Middle Rowden an heriot of the best beast has been seized for the use of the Lords which has since been commuted to a pecuniary heriot and accepted and paid to the Lords being the sum of £7. [This became common practice.]

Other presentments for various misdemeanours included:

1792 We present Richard Dinnaford for making an encroachment on a cottage within the said Manor he having no right so to do and cutting down timber without leave either from the Lords or the steward.

1802 We present Mary Earle, formerly Drake, for a chimney belonging to a cott house being ruinous and dangerous to His Majesty's subjects.

1820 We present Richard Reed for a nuisance in building pig sties in the church path.

1822 We present Joseph Arscott for having carried away or suffered to be carried away large stones several feet in length being part of the dwelling house belonging to West Trecott and having used them in making a vault in Sampford Courtenay Church for the Westlake family and also for topping one oak and 14 elm trees without leave.

Many copyhold properties were 'underlet' (sublet) on short-term leases. Any copyholder wishing to 'demise a copyhold' had to apply to the lords for a licence to do so and the term was not to exceed 14 years. The owner of the copyhold was granted a dispensation of non-residence on the condition that he ensured that the buildings were kept in good order and the land well managed and cultivated. A fine had to be paid at £10 per cent on the annual rent of the premises. In 1814 licences were granted to 13 copyholders, including John Newcombe for Middle Cliston, John Russell for Frankland, William Tickle for North Barton and Robert Hawkes for North Beerhill. In 1844 19 copyholders were presented at the Manor Court for underletting without licence. Unusually King's College continued copyhold tenure until well into the nineteenth century, although nationally most copyhold had been replaced by leasehold well before this time. At some stage, certainly by the 1830s, they were granting 14-year leases and by the time they sold the manor in the 1920s, the farms were held on annual and the shops and cottages on quarterly or monthly tenancies. Just one property (Rose Cottage) was still copyhold.

Tithes

Tithes were a continuing source for grievance. A tithe was a tax of a tenth part of the annual produce of land or labour, formerly levied to support the Church and the clergy. Farmers were liable for the payment of great tithes, which represented the fruits of the earth – corn, hay, wood, fruit etc., and small tithes, which were payable on animal products such as lambs, colts, calves, wool, milk, eggs and honey. Tithes were payable to the rector of the parish. Tithe owners were entitled to claim payment of tithe in kind and to enter farms to exact their claims. Payment in kind was a cause of endless disputes between farmers and tithe owners and having to make a contribution to the Anglican Church was an obvious irritation to the Nonconformists. Also tithes fell most heavily upon land enjoying agricultural improvement, the tithe owners, as 'sleeping partners', enjoying the benefits of higher yields. In 1727 the Sampford Courtenay rector, William Donne, recorded:

Great tythes of all sorts of corn and clover are uncontest'd in kind but the parishioners have pretended prescriptions as to smal tythes, viz. meadows, calfs, colts, milcking, lambs and I durst not call upon them to bring in the aforesaid, for that it would raise a war betwixt us. They w'd not sign my claims nor I theirs.

John Heath, the rector in 1745, recorded the same problem. However, the duty was converted, by the Tithes Commutation Act of 1836, into a money payment known as the tithe rent charge. Tithe rent charges varied according to the price of corn, calculated on a septennial average for the whole country. Tithe commutation and apportionment of payments took place in Honeychurch in 1838 and in Sampford Courtenay in 1842. In 1838 there were 500 acres in Honeychurch subject to the payment of tithe rent charge, comprising 230 acres of arable land, 40 acres of meadow, 30 acres of woodland and 200 acres of furze and morassy pasture. In 1842 in Sampford Courtenay there were 6,050 acres, comprising 3,160 acres of arable land, 700 acres of meadow and pasture, 90 acres of orchard and garden, 100 acres of woodland and 2,000 acres of moor and furze lands. Subsequent Acts made provision for the liability to pay tithe rent charge to be extinguished by redemption of the charge. The Tithe Act of 1925 transferred tithe rent charges to Queen Anne's Bounty Fund and they were finally extinguished by the Tithe Act of 1936.

Labour and Practices

Apart from the work carried out by farmers and their families, most of the labour requirements on the farms were met by a paid workforce. Servants in husbandry in their teens and early twenties usually lived in the farmhouse. They were hired by the year at local hiring fairs. Men ploughed, harrowed and carted and looked after draught animals, cattle and sheep. Women were involved in dairying, tending to farmyard animals, weeding and various household tasks. Parish apprentices could not move at the end of each year and were invariably used as a means of cheap labour. Some servants remained unmarried and continued to reside on the farm for the rest of their working lives. In 1827 James Badcock was apprenticed at the age of nine to John Dayment of Frankland; he was still unmarried and living at the farm in 1891, by then working for John Dayment's granddaughters. Several of his siblings and his father were also 'parish apprentices'. Normally, farm servants left the household to marry and established themselves in one of the farm cottages. Many of these cottages were still being used for this purpose well into the twentieth century, e.g. Solland Cottages for Solland, and Rebecca's Cottage and Nos. 1 and 2 Shores' Cottages, which belonged to The Barton. In 1808 Vancouver recorded the average hours of work for the farm labourer as from 7.00a.m. to 12.00 noon and from 1.00p.m. to between 5.00p.m. and 6.00p.m. One day's work consisted of:

William Green scything rushes at Lydcott, 1931.

Thrashing of as much wheat, the straw of which when combed into reed, shall make 5 bundles of 28 lbs each; of barley the straw of which shall make 12 bundles of 35 lbs each; of oats 16 bundles of 40 lbs each.

The 'cutting and tying of 100 faggots' of wood was also a day's work, as was the 'spreading of 40 heaps of beat-ashes, lime-mould mixings, dung etc.'

Single-furrow ploughs were drawn by horses or oxen. Oxen did better on stiff, heavy clays, cost less to feed and, when their working life was over, could be fattened for meat. A sale of various items from Langabeer and Incott Farms in 1841 included:

Six prime young plough oxen and two ditto (steers), one useful farm horse, one ditto 5 years old, has been broken to and driven in harness, one handsome 2-year old colt and one 12 months ditto.

At the beginning of the nineteenth century all harvesting of corn and hay was done by hand.

Reaping was done with sickles by gangs of men, with women following behind binding and stacking the sheaves into stooks. According to Vancouver this was carried out:

With practices of a disorderly nature – by eleven or twelve o'clock the ale or cider has so much warmed and elevated their [the reapers'] spirits, that their noisy jokes and ribaldry are heard to a considerable distance.

A custom observed at this time was 'Crying the Neck' at the close of harvest. Richard Pyke remembered this happening in the parish, in around 1880:

From one farm and another, night after night, this strange practice was observed, and we knew that the harvesting was completed when the joyous acclamation came from distant rickyards.

Later in the century scythes were used for cutting both corn and hay; these were faster and it was possible for a man to mow an acre in a day compared to between only a quarter and a third of an acre with a sickle. By the last quarter of the century self-binding reapers had been introduced. In the early years the corn was threshed on the central oaken floor of the threshing barn. It was winnowed by being tossed in a basket, the chaff being carried away in the through draft created by opening both sets of doors. Some of the old threshing barns are still in evidence in the parish. Threshing machines driven by horse power from a roundhouse (wheel-house) were common by the 1820s. On the Tithe Apportionment maps for Sampford Courtenay and Honeychurch, roundhouses are identifiable at many of the farms. In the late 1800s steam-powered threshing was introduced and James Fewings Arscott set up a steam-powered threshing-machine business in the parish (see Chapter Seven). Hay was turned by hand; it was not until the twentieth century that horse-drawn mowers, swath-turners and tedders became common.

Planting of roots and seeds and weeding had to be done by hand or with horse-drawn drills and hoes. All hedge-trimming was done with a billhook. Raising of timber trees and the sale of timber was an important source of income. An advertisement in the *Exeter Flying Post* in 1793 read:

To be sold in one or more lots upwards of 300 fine oak trees fit for the Navy, with their tops and lops at Resland, about one mile from the turnpike road... and about 20 miles from Mortalham and Topsham.

King's College had its own timber yard at the bottom of Green Hill. The sawn wood was used for the repair of farmhouses and buildings.

Local Devon breeds of cattle and sheep were kept; annual fairs were held in Sampford Courtenay on the first Tuesday in July. These took place throughout the nineteenth century. The *Exeter Flying Post* recorded the fair in 1833:

Which was well attended both by buyers and sellers. A good deal of cattle was exhibited and many sales effected. Fat bullocks from 9s. to 9s.6d. per score, sheep from 5½d. to 6d. per pound. Amongst the latter there was a very fine score of ewes, bred and fed by Mr Durant of North Tawton, they excelled everything of the kind we ever saw, considering they had reared their lambs.

Examination of the 1809 King's College survey and the Tithe Apportionment indicates that most of the farms had orchards. Both sources reveal some intriguing field names, probably in existence for many years and which are still in use today. A few are given below:

Glebe Farm, Honeychurch: Great Sanctuary, Kitty Hills.
North Barton: Plashett.
Down's and Aller's Cliston: Carrot Close.
Town Living: Knocker's Hole.
Harvey's in Town: Plundey Field.
Southey: Harry's Plot, George's Garden.
West Trecott: Winnowing Sheet.
West Rowden: Welly Meadow.
Brook: Old Mistress's Orchard, Meadow over the Water.
Higher Dornaford: Daisy Field, Sitting Bottoms.
Webber Hill: Goblet Meadow.
Pitt: Mead behind the Linhay, Smally.
Great Halford: Honey Bog, Higher Sunny Down.
Great Cliston: Hoppy, Blindy Field.

Muriel, Kathleen and Eleanor Hawkins hoeing at Solland, 1920s.

Ewe and six lambs with 'Farmer' Pike, Sampford Courtenay, 1896.

Farming in the Twentieth Century

What fools they were, some years ago,
To work as hard as men did.
I've heard my grand sire say, his dad
Met with some dreadful losses:
No wonder, when they used to work
With those great horrid horses.
From 'Farming in Devonshire' – *Sighs, Smiles and Sketches*
by J.G. Maxwell, 1860.

Dairying

By 1900 little had changed. Each farm had about a dozen or so milking cows which were milked by hand in the shippen using a three-legged stool. Irene Sampson (née Hawkins) remembers milking by hand at Solland in the 1920s. Breeds kept were usually South Devons and Shorthorns. Farm households were larger then and much milk was used at home, together with butter and cream which were made by hand in the dairy. Some dairy produce was sold at local markets. Milking by hand continued until the middle of the century. Mary and Walter Cleverdon milked ten or a dozen cows by hand until the 1950s. The milk was kept cool by standing the churns in a container of cold water in the milk house. By the 1930s the Milk Marketing Board had been created and the transportation of milk by train or lorry to dairy companies was well established. Much of the milk from the parish went to the Ambrosia factory in Lapford. Each farm had a churn stand by the farm gate and some of these are still in existence, e.g. at Glebe Farm, Honeychurch. Some churns in the south of the parish were taken by pony and trap to Sampford Courtenay Station.

Milking bails, which were portable milking parlours powered by stationary engines, were developed in the 1920s. Sam Robertson remembers milking cows on Chapple Moor in around 1960 using a milking bail. For reasons of hygiene bails fell out of favour and by the 1960s and '70s bulk tanks and herring-bone parlours were being introduced. This required a substantial amount of capital investment; the farm had to have a turning place in the yard for the lorry, a suitable driveway and a proper milking parlour rather than the old shippen. Many of the smaller farms therefore left dairying. Electricity was connected to the outlying farms in the 1960s but only farmers with the largest herds could afford to install and run milking machines. Dairy Shorthorns, Ayrshires and Devons were gradually replaced by British Friesians and then by Dutch Holsteins. Following the introduction of quotas in 1984 and the poor prices farmers were getting for their milk in the 1990s, most of the farms in the parish have stopped producing milk; just three (Appledore, Great Cliston and Underdown) have dairy herds.

Beef Cattle

In the early-twentieth century most of the parish farms reared some beef cattle, partly as a by-product of the dairy herd. Nowadays, many of the farms rear bullocks and suckler cows, but the traditional Red Devons have been replaced by other breeds, including Hereford Cross, Limousin, Simmental and Charolais. Many parishioners remember helping to drive cattle along the roads to market at either North Tawton or Okehampton, although from the early 1950s cattle trucks came into use. J.I. Reddaway at Reddaway Farm bred Red Devons and drove many of these to Sampford Courtenay Station from where they were taken to Exeter market. His son, Robert, keeps Charolais cattle at the time of writing. In recent years BSE had a disastrous effect on beef prices; in 2002 and 2003 these have been a little better.

Sale of Red Devon bullocks at Higher Cliston, 1945. Henry Cleverdon is pictured in the centre at the front.

Invoice from Hussey & Son Ltd, Exeter Market, 1930 – purchase of heifers from John Hawkins, Solland.

Left: *Harvesting potatoes at the old rectory (Culverhayes), 1950s.* Left to right: *Fred Coates, Courtenay Johns, Ern Reddaway and Fred Pike.*

Right: *John E. Hawkins of Solland with Devon Longwools, c.1920.*

Above: *J.I. Reddaway with a prize Devon Closewool ram at Hatherleigh Market, 1965. [Western Morning News]*

Above: *Margaret and Robert Reddaway with Devon Closewools at Reddaway Farm, 1957. The sheep won first prizes that year at Instow, Honiton, Okehampton, Dunster, Tavistock and Barnstaple shows. Note the old Okehampton turnpike gate on the left.*

Left: *J.I. and Robert Reddaway with Devon Closewools at Reddaway Farm, 1975.*

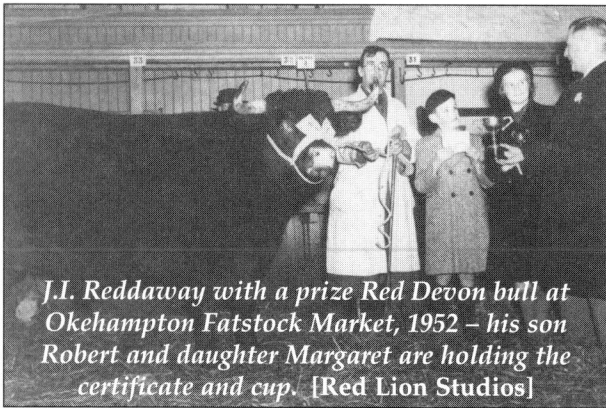

J.I. Reddaway with a prize Red Devon bull at Okehampton Fatstock Market, 1952 – his son Robert and daughter Margaret are holding the certificate and cup. [Red Lion Studios]

John E. Hawkins, whose father Robert farmed Beerhill, set up on his own at Solland in 1894 when he bought four steers at Hatherleigh Fair for £44. His farming accounts book for the first three decades of the twentieth century recorded the prices he realised for cattle sold over this period:

1902 Mr Madge N. Tawton – 2 fat steers at £19 each £38.0s.0d.
1917 Messrs. Callaway & Co. – 2 steers Oke'ton Fair (less comm.) £85.15s.8d.
1920 4 steers @ £55 each (less comm.) £218.3s.4d.

Roots

Large quantities of potatoes were grown in the parish during the nineteenth century and well into the twentieth. Children were often kept home from school to help with both planting and harvesting. John Hawkins sold to various people locally: '1910 Culley & Co., Oke'ton Camp – 14 bags potatoes @ 4s.6d. £3.3s.0d.'

Bert Coates in the 1930s and '40s, in common with most of the farms, grew several acres of roots each year, some for animal feed. The Barton grew 3–6 acres of swedes, 3–4 acres of mangolds and 1–1½ acres of potatoes. Any surplus was sold locally. Potatoes had to be harvested by hand but could be planted mechanically using a plough. The seed potatoes were placed on the edge of the furrow and then ploughed in. Mechanical potato diggers were available from the 1950s. In recent years the growing of potatoes in the parish has gradually died out, particularly in the last ten years. Irene Sampson remembers growing mangolds at Solland. These had to be cut up for animal feed using a root-cutting machine, which was turned by hand. In the 1960s Irene's nephew, another John Hawkins, was still feeding mangolds to his cattle and remembers: 'There's nothing like the sound of a long line of cows chewing mangolds.' They are rarely grown nowadays, having disappeared in the 1960s and '70s, as they were too labour-intensive. Most of the farms were growing swedes until the 1950s and a few are still grown today. In the earlier part of the century weeding the fields of roots was done by hand. Nowadays swedes are precision drilled, sprayed and not touched until harvest.

Unfortunately the supermarkets insist on vegetables of a uniform size so many have to be discarded and used as animal feed.

Sheep

Sheep numbers increased significantly in the parish through the course of the twentieth century. There has also been a change of breeds kept by farmers. Since the Second World War public taste has moved away from mutton in favour of lamb. Indoor lambing in recent years has improved stocking and lambing rates. When the UK entered the EEC in 1973, the import tariff on New Zealand lamb resulted in expansion of the home market but in recent years selling prices fell, primarily as a result of the strong pound and oversupply. Post foot-and-mouth disease, prices have improved.

John Hawkins of Solland, in the early part of the century, kept Devon Longwools and was a recognised authority on the breed locally. The sheep are very large and no longer in favour; smaller lambs (30/40lb) are now the requirement. In 1894 John Hawkins bought his first sheep for Solland, which included: 'Mr Isaac, Belstone – 26 two-teeth hogs £54.10s.0d.' Subsequent entries in his accounts book indicated sale prices:

1916 Mr Knight – 30 hogs 1929 lbs at 1s.0½d. per lb £100.9s.0d.
1928 30 Ewes Oke'ton Market – 10 @ 72s.6d., 10 @ 71s.6d., 10 @ 67s.6d. (less comm.) £105.15s.0d.

J.I. Reddaway and his son Robert at Reddaway Farm bred and showed Devon Closewools and Exmoor Horns. The former is a North Devon breed which is not very common today as the sheep get rather fat. The meat of both breeds, unlike that of a Suffolk, for example, is marbled with fat; people now prefer leaner meat. J.I., between the 1950s and '70s, exhibited both breeds of sheep at Devon shows as well as at Smithfield and won many prizes. He was a show judge at Smithfield in 1971 and was chairman of the Okehampton Show for seven years from 1970, being responsible for resurrecting it after it had been discontinued for five years. Most farms in the parish now keep the leaner breeds, such as Suffolk, Suffolk Cross, Poll Dorset or Texel.

The sale of wool until recent years provided a useful source of farm income. John Hawkins' accounts book recorded prices realised in the early part of the last century:

1901 Mr Paddon, North Tawton – 2730 lbs wool at 4½d. per lb £51.3s.6d.
1917 Messrs Shaw & Sons. Wool for War Office – 2396 lbs @ 1s.3d. (Payt. rec'd by draft from War Office) £149.15s.0d.
1928 Mr Anstey, Upcott – pack 33¾ wool (less 5 lbs @ 1s.3d.) £460.18s.0d.

With the introduction of man-made fibres, wool has fallen out of favour and prices obtained for the fleeces, now taken to the wool factory at South Molton, are much reduced. Sheep were initially sheared with hand shears; these were replaced by mechanical clippers that required another person to turn the handle. Irene Sampson, Bert Coates and others remembered using mechanical clippers before electrically-powered equipment was introduced. Sheep-dipping took place at Hole Down Farm in Exbourne and The Barton in Sampford Courtenay. Farmers came from miles around, from Honeychurch and even Withybrook, to use the specially constructed concrete pits. In recent years sheep-dipping has almost ceased due to worries about the side-effects of organo-phosphates.

Pigs

A few pigs were kept at the farms but not on a large scale. In the early part of the century some of the cottagers, including Becky and George Horn at Hammett's Hill, were still keeping a pig or two. The 'pig-sticker' came round to kill the pig; the procedure

Mary Green (née Madders) of Lydcott as a young child feeding chickens with her mother, 1914.

was quite barbaric. The animal, which for many months had been cosseted and admired, was hoisted up onto a rough bench and its throat cut. The job was often bungled and there was always a great deal of squealing. Bert Coates remembered that when killing one of their pigs, they would shut one of the dogs in the farmyard to create a lot of barking to drown the noise. At Frankland an old carcass roller still exists where the pig was hung up. John Hawkins at Solland, however, took his pigs to Butcher Glanville at Exbourne for killing: '1923 Mr Glanville, Exbourne – 3 pigs 41 sc. 8lbs @ 18s. (less killing) £36.17s.8d.'

The home killing of pigs stopped in the 1950s when use of the humane killer became compulsory.

Poultry

Most farms had a few chickens for home use but eggs and chickens for meat were also sold. The female members of the family looked after the poultry. Over the years there have been one or two larger poultry enterprises in the parish. At the time of writing turkeys for the Christmas market are reared at East Town, Honeychurch.

Invoice from F. Glanville & Son, Exbourne, 1922 – pigs purchased from John E. Hawkins of Solland, less household meat, etc. supplied.

Titan tractor at Lydcott, late 1930s.

Power

Tractors were available in the 1920s and '30s, and at first towed implements from a draw bar; in the 1940s and '50s power take-off and three-point linkage made them much more adaptable for a variety of uses. From the 1960s tractors have had weather cabs and have become increasingly sophisticated and expensive. The biggest impact of the tractor has been the reduction in labour requirements. Most farms in the parish did not change to tractors until the 1940s or '50s and many people in Sampford Courtenay remember working with horses. The Hawkins family at Solland in the 1920s and '30s had three or four horses and a pony, but they had a Blackstone engine to drive the threshing machine and reed comber. The horse-driven threshing machine in the roundhouse had disappeared by 1900. Bert Coates' father, Sydney, had seven Shire cart-horses at The Barton in 1936, including two stallions that were taken around the district by a groom. The family showed some of the horses but, after Sydney died in 1946, Bert and his brother Harold kept a show mare for another year or two and then gave up, mainly because summer shows clashed with farming activities. The first person to acquire a tractor in Sampford Courtenay was Will Sanders of Beerhill in 1925. The Coates bought their first tractor during the Second World War – it was a 12hp Farmall made by International, which ran on tractor vaporising oil. It had iron wheels with lugs or cleats which had to be covered with iron bands for road use. Their next tractor was a Fordson with rubber tyres but they had to keep their horses until they could afford to buy new machinery to use with the tractor. They were then able to change to a two-furrow plough, halving ploughing time. Mary Cleverdon remembers the Fordson doing 11mph, 'which was a tremendous speed in those days'. The Barton had a Hornsby stationary engine for operating machinery in the threshing barn – a thresher, a reed comber, a winnowing machine, a chaff-cutter, a kibbler (for breaking down maize), a corn-mill for grinding corn for pigs and poultry and a saw bench. Bob Johnson used horses at Great Cliston until after the war; the farmer, Bill King, did not buy his first tractor until 1951. Myrtle Hunkin (née Hawking) remembers her family acquiring its first tractor, a Fordson with metal wheels, at Glebe Farm, Honeychurch, during the war in order to plough extra ground as part of the war effort.

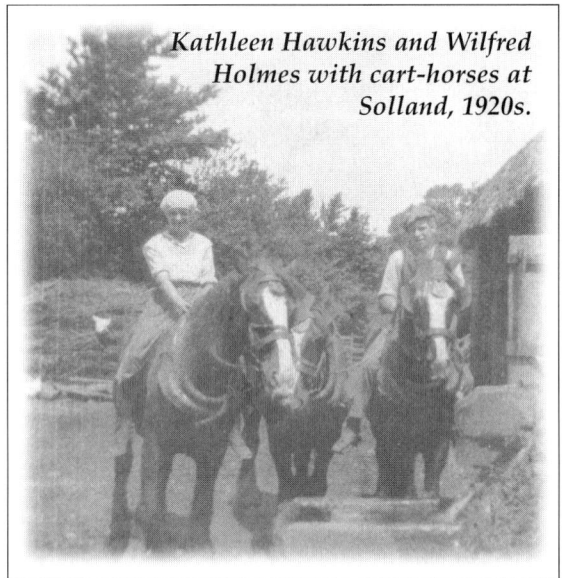

Kathleen Hawkins and Wilfred Holmes with cart-horses at Solland, 1920s.

Left: *Fleetwood Green on a Case tractor at Lydcott, 1940s.*

Haymaking at The Barton, 1937 – with Ivy Reddaway on the left.

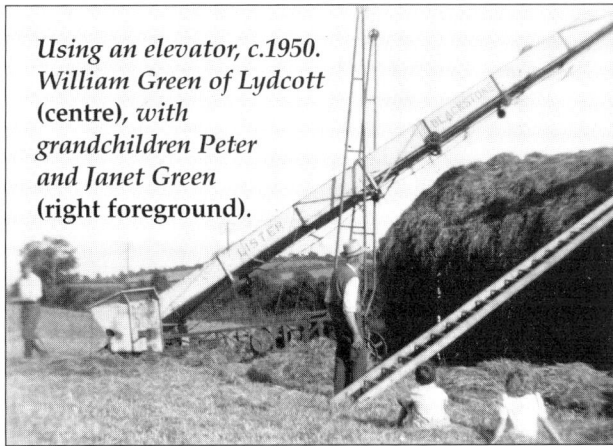

Using an elevator, c.1950. William Green of Lydcott (centre), with grandchildren Peter and Janet Green (right foreground).

Horse-drawn mower at Lydcott, c.1930.

Harvesting, late 1950s. Left to right: Peter Green, Dick Hinton, Janet Green, Fleetwood Green, William Green.

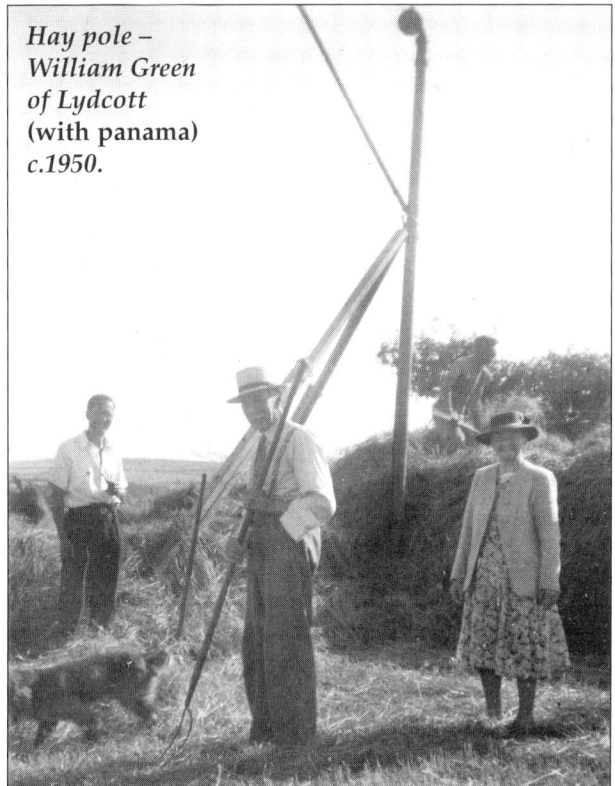

Hay pole – William Green of Lydcott (with panama) c.1950.

Hay

At the beginning of the century grass was still being cut by hand with scythes, but by the First World War, horse-drawn mowers were being introduced. Tractor-trailed mowers continued into the 1950s and were gradually superseded by tractor-mounted cutter-bar mowers. It was not until the 1980s that the rotary mower was commonly used. Initially, hay was turned and raked by hand and pitchforked onto the hay cart. Horse-drawn swath turners and tedders were soon introduced and horse-drawn hay sweeps gathered the hay beside the wagon, which was then taken to the stack. The hay was lifted onto the stack using a structure called a hay pole or hay grab. The pole was placed in a hole in the ground, about 2 feet deep, and secured with stays. A horse operated a wire rope and pulley system which pulled a grab of hay to the top of the stack, which was then released with a lever. Many people in the parish, including Irene Sampson, Bob Johnson and Valerie Hawking, remember the arduous task of leading the horse up and down many, many times during the course of the day. Elevators were available by the 1910s/'20s. The ricks were built outside, on beds of faggots, and thatched with straw. Hay had to be cut out of the rick with a hay knife and 'it would take a strong man to do it'. A hay tester (a long tool with an eye) was used to test the quality of hay in a rick and to ensure that the centre had not overheated. Grass was also cut for its seed which was called 'eaver'. According to Bert

Coates, turning grass for eaver was like handling eggs and had to be done by hand. By the 1950s tractor-drawn turners and tedders, and stationary balers, followed by pick-up balers, speeded up haymaking. In recent years advances in equipment, such as grabs for loading several bales of hay at a time and the introduction of large bales, have improved production times still further. Some silage has been made in the parish in recent years.

Baling hay in Higher Meadow, Frankland, 1996.

James Fewings Arscott junr (on reaper-binder) *and Bill Paddon* (in Chevrolet car) *cutting corn at Sampford Chapple, 1930s.*

Below: *The Cleverdons reed combing at Higher Cliston, late 1940s.* Left to right: *Ken and Leslie Cleverdon, Courtenay Sanders* (in background), *Walter and Henry Cleverdon.*

Below left: *Richard Weeks combining in Gratton, West Barton Lane, 2001.*

Arable

Wheat, barley and oats were traditionally grown in the parish. In the early years seed was sown with horse-drawn drills but Irene Sampson can remember a seedlip or 'fiddle' being used for casting seed around the field edges. Horse-drawn reaper-binders were in use but some scything was still carried out, particularly around field margins, within living memory. Freddie Johns remembers learning how to use a scythe, which was not that easy – 'you had to keep the heel down and the toe up.' During both world wars more land was ploughed up for corn; in the Second World War Chapple Moor was commandeered by the Ministry and ploughed with huge caterpillar tractors. Some rye and oats were grown. After the war the Coates family continued arable production on the Moor for a few years, but cultivating the heavy clay proved so much work that they sold the land to Farmer Playford of West Trecott who kept a dairy herd there in summer for a while; by around 1969/70 it had been sold to the Forestry Commission.

The sheaves of corn were gathered behind the reaper-binder and stacked into stooks which were left to dry out for about 14 days. The sheaves were collected by horse and wagon and built into thatched ricks; these were threshed during the winter. Several farms had their own threshing machines; others used Arscott & Paddon (see Chapter Seven). Reed combers were used for processing the straw for thatching. As a general rule King's College did not allow their tenants to sell hay or straw 'to prevent the holding being deteriorated by a careless tenant.' However, if the farm was well managed and the rent paid up, a reasonable amount could be disposed of

with the prior permission of the college. John Hawkins sold 'nitches of reed' locally for thatching: '1923 Messrs Rawlence & Squarey: To 50 nitches reed @ £8.10s. per hundred £4.5s.0d.' A nitch of wheat straw was a large bundle weighing 28lb. Ten nitches would thatch a portion of roof 10 feet square. John Hawkins also sold thatching spars made from hedge parings.

Cutting the corn and threshing were great events in the parish and farmers helped each other on both occasions. This continued until the 1950s and '60s when combine harvesters were introduced. (See Chapter Twelve for a description of 'threshing day'.) Many members of the parish, who were children at the time, remember the excitements of the harvest field. Les Beer's father and brothers would help locally and one of the perks was the plentiful supply of rabbits that ended up in the centre of the field. The introduction of combines dramatically reduced the man-power required but also took away the camaraderie and community spirit that had existed for centuries. Bert Coates' first combine was driven by its own engine but had to be pulled with a tractor. Modern combine harvesters process 40 acres of corn a day and the large bales of straw are handled mechanically. Grain dryers are used on the larger farms. Grain was originally ground at the manor mills at Rowden or at Sticklepath but, by the twentieth century, Newland Mill in North Tawton was being used, as identified in John Hawkins' accounts book: '1927 Mr Tavener, Newland Mills – 404 bushell wheat at 7s.3d. £147.18s.0d.' In the earlier years wheat was grown for human consumption, but most now is used for animal feed and is sold to Risdon Mill or West Devon Farmers.

Orchards

As mentioned above, practically all the parish farms had orchards in the mid-nineteenth century. There was a pound-house (for pressing apples) opposite Harvey's in Town, but this had disappeared by 1885. Cider was made on many farms until well into the twentieth century; Bill King at Great Cliston and John Reddaway in Honeychurch had cider presses in living memory. Picking the apples was labour-intensive and orchards became uneconomic, their use gradually dying out after the Second World War. However, Bert Coates took trailer loads of apples to Inch's Cider at Winkleigh until the 1970s. Almost all the old orchards in the parish are now gone, although in recent years many of the fields at Solland have been planted out with apple trees.

Rabbits

Before myxomatosis, which arrived in the early 1950s, the catching of rabbits provided a useful source of income for the farmers and trappers alike. In later years it came to be regarded as more of a sporting event. A bag of 50 to 100 rabbits a day was customary. John Hawkins' records gave an indication of the numbers caught at Solland and sold to butchers:

Mr H.C. Isaac, Winkleigh:
3.12.1902 98 rabbits on rail at S.C. Station £2.9s.0d.
5.12.1902 68 rabbits on rail at N.T. Station £1.14s.0d.
12.12.1902 36 rabbits on rail at S.C. Station 18s.0d.
15.12.1902 100 rabbits on rail at S.C. Station £1.10s.0d.
16.12.1902 40 rabbits to Winkleigh £1.0s.0d.

Some went by rail to destinations outside Devon.

Len Piper remembers rabbiting in the 1940s/'50s, when rabbits were flushed out by beaters and shot; if they went to ground, ferrets were sent down one end of the burrow and nets placed at the other end. Ern Reddaway and Alfie Day, who both lived in the village, were rabbit trappers and would buy the rights to trap rabbits from local farmers. The rabbits continued to be sold to local butchers such as the Glanvilles at Exbourne or dispatched by rail from Sampford Courtenay Station for sale in the towns. Other parishioners, including Bert Coates and Les Beer, remembered rabbit-shooting parties as more of a social occasion; the day's sport was followed by a meal and a game of nap. Henry Johns, who was a farm worker at Halford, was accidentally blinded by a shotgun when out rabbiting.

Produce of the Hedges

The picking of blackberries, whortleberries and rosehips, to provide additional income, was practised until after the Second World War. Many people remember as children in the 1930s and '40s picking bucket loads of blackberries and taking them to Billy Hearn at Sampford Station. He bought them by the pound and sent them by rail for jam making. Freddie Johns, Len Piper and Bob Johnson all remember blackberry picking as young boys during the war for extra pocket money. With the advent of flail hedge cutters, numbers of blackberries and rosehips are now much reduced. The hedges were cut by hand until the 1950s, but finger-bar cutters, followed by flail cutters, have made the job many times less arduous. Some hedges have been grubbed out in recent years to provide bigger fields for the larger machinery now used.

The Sale of the Manor

An agricultural depression commenced in the mid-1870s and lasted for about 20 years. This was owing to bad seasons, poor harvests and low prices because of the increasing import of grain. This, together with the increased use of machinery, meant fewer jobs for farm labourers and many drifted away from the land into the towns; some left the country and emigrated to Canada, Australia and New Zealand. By the second decade of the twentieth century farming was more prosperous but in the 1920s and '30s the UK was in a severe general depression. At about this time the bursar of King's College, John Maynard Keynes, decided to divest the college of its outlying estates in favour of other forms of investment. Some of the farms and cottages were sold to the tenants by private treaty but, between 1920 and 1929, the remaining properties were auctioned off, most being purchased by the existing tenants. Few lots exceeded their reserves. In 1929 Rawlence & Squarey, who were handling the sale, wrote to the bursar:

We regret to commence by saying that our task has been made very difficult owing to the following facts:
1. Mr Lang of Barton Farm has just purchased the best red land field on Fullaford Farm at the rate of £20 an acre.
2. A red land holding of 200 acres on the Sampford Courtenay/North Tawton road, let at £50 a year, has just been put up to auction and the only bid obtained was one of £400.
These facts have been thrown at us by the tenants and made it somewhat difficult for us to argue with them as to values.

Most of the farms sold for between £1,500 and £3,000 each; Solland, with 134 acres and two cottages, at £4,100 and The Barton, with 316 acres and five cottages, at £5,600, achieved the best prices, while the cottages sold for between £60 and £100 each. The cessation of the college's control, which had lasted for 350 years, marked the end of an era and changed the farming way of life. In the 1990s, an operation called

Sale of the residue of Sampford Courtenay Manor Estate by King's College, 1929.

Manorial Auctions approached the college with a view to selling the lordship of Sampford Courtenay Manor on their behalf. However, King's College, because of the long association, decided to retain the lordship on a permanent basis.

By Order of the Provost and Scholars of King's College, Cambridge.

THE RESIDUE OF THE
SAMPFORD COURTENAY MANOR ESTATE
DEVON.

Situate amidst perfect Devon scenery, and within easy reach of Sampford Courtenay Station (S. Rly.), and within five miles of the important Market Town of Okehampton.

Particulars, Plans & Conditions of Sale
of the

Valuable Freehold Agricultural
and Sporting Property

embracing

Three excellent mixed Red Land Farms, and sundry Small Holdings; A Smithy; Accommodation Lands; many picturesque Devon Cottages; also Two Valuable Reversionary Interests of Leasehold Properties,

having a total area of about

667 ACRES

Messrs. Rawlence & Squarey

are instructed to offer the above for Sale by Auction in convenient Lots (unless previously disposed of), subject to the General Conditions of Sale of the Law Society of 1925 (1928 Edition) and certain Special Conditions, at

THE WHITE HART HOTEL, OKEHAMPTON,
ON THURSDAY, THE 18th JULY, 1929, at 3 P.M.

Particulars, Plans and Conditions of Sale may be obtained from:—

The Solicitors:
Messrs. JAMES & SNOW, The Close, Exeter, or

The Auctioneers and Land Agents:
Messrs. RAWLENCE & SQUAREY, Sherborne, Dorset; Salisbury, Wilts; 4 The Sanctuary, Westminster, S.W.1; and 5 High Street, Southampton.

Particulars

LOT 1
(coloured Pink on Plan).

THE VALUABLE MIXED FARM

known as

"Solland Farm"

situate midway between Sampford Courtenay and Exbourne on the Red Land soil, and approached by good roads. It is watered by permanent streams, and contains in all an area of about

134 a.   1 r.   4 p.

as detailed below.

THE FARMHOUSE

contains:—

ON THE GROUND FLOOR:—Front Hall; Large Drawing Room, about 17ft. x 15ft. 6in.; Dining Room, about 19ft. x 17ft. 3in., with open hearth; Kitchen; Dairy, Store Room; Pump House and E.C. in garden.

ON THE FIRST FLOOR:—Bedroom, about 17ft. 6in. x 15ft. 3in., with fireplace; Bedroom, about 17ft. 6in. x 12ft., with fireplace; 3 smaller Bedrooms, and Box Room.

THE FARM BUILDINGS

conveniently situated around the Yard, comprise:—

At Solland:—Potato House with loft over; Mangold House with loft over; Stable with loft over; large Barn; Cattle Shed; Engine House; lean-to Cattle Shed; 7-stall 2 Piggeries; open Linhay with loft over; Calves House; 10-ties Shippen with loft over; Root House; 10-ties Shippen with loft over; Pony Stable; 3 Piggeries; Ashhouse; Shippen with loft over; Granary; on the opposite side of the road:—4-bay Cart Linhay and Trap House.

At Lower Solland :—Implement Shed; Poultry Houses.

2 WELL BUILT COTTAGES, each containing:—Living Room, Scullery with copper, and 3 Bedrooms.

King's College sale catalogue, 1929 – Solland Farm.

parish caused by FMD. Foot-and-mouth disease was reported in Devon at the end of February 2001 at Beaworthy. The subsequent weeks brought the disease ever nearer. In April a case was reported at Walson Barton, Broadwood Kelly, just north of

Farming Today

Over the last 100 years, apart from during the two world wars, arable production in the parish has reduced in favour of permanent grass. Nowadays most of the land is used for keeping sheep and beef cattle, although wheat, barley and some oats, oil-seed rape, flax, forage maize and swedes are grown. Consolidation of the holdings has continued and the number of working farms has fallen from the 90 holdings in existence in 1570 to under 30 in 2003. Many of the old farmhouses have been sold, with a few acres, to private residents. Some diversification has taken place into bed-and-breakfast accommodation, horse breeding, rearing of rare-breed sheep, pheasant rearing/shooting and large-scale orchards. Some of the larger establishments still employ a few staff, although mostly on a part-time basis, but since the middle of the twentieth century the class of farm labourers has all but disappeared. Farming families mostly manage themselves or rely on contractors to do tasks requiring expensive equipment. In the 1960s a family could earn a decent living on a farm of 100 acres, but in recent years incomes have fallen considerably.

BSE has dealt a severe blow to those with beef cattle and 2001 was a further dreadful year for the whole

Honeychurch and ten days later animals in Honeychurch were slaughtered on suspicion (although the relative test results subsequently proved negative). This was followed by contiguous culls of most of the animals in Honeychurch. Flocks of sheep that had been bred over many years were lost. Luckily Sampford Courtenay and Honeychurch avoided the awful pyres that had to be endured by surrounding parishes but the dead animals were left in situ, some for as long as eight or nine days. The whole operation was hopelessly mismanaged by MAFF (now DEFRA) but eventually the carcasses were removed by lorry for rendering. Some of the Sampford Courtenay farms also lost animals in contiguous culls. A considerable knock-on effect was felt in the parish as a whole; all social activities were cancelled and many farmers were virtually imprisoned in their farms. Farmers who did not have animals slaughtered were possibly worse off as they could not move or sell their stock. The cleansing and disinfecting operation, for all concerned, was a long and tedious process.

In 2003 farming is dominated by the demands of the supermarkets, from whom 70 per cent of the nation's food purchases are made. The use of pesticides and fertilisers is commonplace and the introduction of genetically modified crops is threatened. Profits from the production of milk and meat are squeezed by the need for retailers to increase their margins. Farmers are reliant on the various Government subsidies available on stock and grain. Bureaucratic requirements are a further burden. Locally arable farms are breaking even, but corn prices of around £60 per tonne are half those of a few years ago. Labour is increasingly scarce; youngsters today are not inclined towards farm work. Diversification into other forms of farming such as organic production is an option but start-up costs are high.

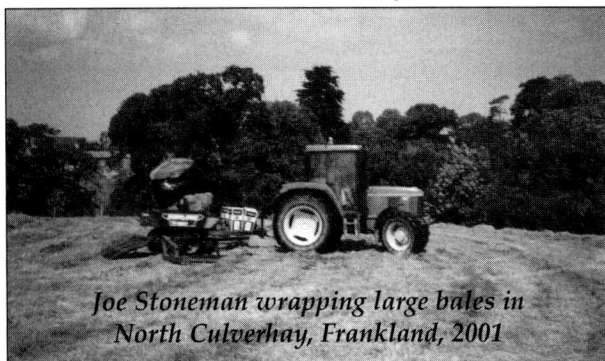

Joe Stoneman wrapping large bales in North Culverhay, Frankland, 2001

Chapter Six

THE VILLAGE SCHOOL

There, in his noisy mansion, skilled to rule,
The village master taught his little school;
A man severe he was, and stern to view;
I knew him well, and every truant knew;
Well had the boding tremblers learned to trace
The day's disasters in his morning face.
From 'The Deserted Village' by Oliver Goldsmith, 1770.

Before 1876

The first record of a possible school in Sampford Courtenay is in the overseers of the poor book for 1704: 'Paid Mary Potter for scoolinge of poore children 7s.6d.' This suggests the provision of some form of teaching in the parish; Mary Potter may have been running a dame's or common day-school in which a local matron provided crèche facilities plus some basic elementary instruction. There is stronger evidence of the establishment of a school in 1720, when an application for a schoolmaster's licence, endorsed by the rector and parish officers, was made to the Bishop of Exeter by Thomas Cleary. Cleary wrote as follows:

There being in Sampford Courtny an antient and convenient school house and place convenient for keeping school and the parishioners being destitute of a fit person for instructing of children, sent for your aforesaid petitioner... desiring him to accept of that imployment and there being a prospect of many children to be instructed not only of persons of sufficiency but also of the poorer sort by subscriptions for a charity school of which there are a considerable number your aforesaid petitioner agreed to accept of that imployment and commenced his habitation accordingly. Therefore your petitioner humbly prayes your Lordships lycence to keep a school within the said parrish of Sampford Courtny.

The application was endorsed by the rector (William Downe), the churchwarden (Henry Shaxton), and 12 other gentlemen, presumably of some standing in the parish, as follows:

We... being well satisfied and assured that Mr Thomas Cleary the petitioner... is a person well skilled in reading, writeing and arithmetick and well able and

willing to instruct children and others as a school-master, and the said Mr Thomas Cleary being a person of a sober life and conversation, and in all things conformable to the Church of England, and for the encourrageing of the pious education of poor children; here being a charity school, likewise agreed upon and subscriptions to that purpose, humbly pray your Lordship's lycence whereby the said Mr Thomas Cleary may be allowed and lycenced to keep a school within our said parrish.

The survival of the document suggests that the bishop approved the application; the convenient schoolhouse was almost certainly Church House. At this time, as well as religious instruction, pupils probably would have received teaching in basic literacy and numeracy only. Until well into the nineteenth century, many considered education of the working classes to be undesirable and that it should be sufficient only to equip them to discharge the duties of their station.

There is no further record of the existence of a school in the parish for almost another 70 years. However, between 1786 and 1868, both in the Manor Court roll book and the churchwardens' accounts, there are numerous references to the schoolhouse or school chamber, for example in 1823:

To Robert Folland for labour repairing the school chamber stairs 11s.8d.
To ditto for stones for ditto and procuring other stones and sand 6s.2d.

This confirms that the school was situated in the upper 'court room' of Church House. The churchwardens' accounts also recorded the payment (from 1809 to 1837) of an annual salary of £9.10s.10d. to Humphrey Parish for the clerkship (Parish Clerk) and the schooling of six poor children. Humphrey Parish died on 20 September 1839 aged 78 and his headstone in Sampford Courtenay churchyard is inscribed:

Underneath are deposited the remains of Humphery [sic] Parish who for nearly 40 years had discharged with credit the offices of parish clerk and schoolmaster. He was a man of truth and integrity...

This would indicate that he was teaching in the village from around 1800. It appears that Humphrey Parish had not always led such a blameless life. In 1795 he fathered 'a base-born child of Mary Rapson, a single woman of the parish.' He was bound by a bastardy bond to the parish officers; the condition of his obligation was that he paid:

The sum of twenty shillings towards Mary Rapson's laying-in and the further sum of one shilling per week and every week until the said child shall arrive to the age of seven years if the said child should happen so long to live.

Today we would think that he got off lightly!

Ann Palmer's diary (see Chapter Eleven) recorded that between 1809 and 1812 Ann received instruction in reading, writing and arithmetic from the Parish Clerk, 'a respectable man of the old school'. This was obviously Humphrey Parish. Soon after this, 'she used to resort to the parish school, the master of which shewed great attention and kindness to her.' There were therefore two schoolmasters at the same time. It is not clear if they were at the same school, if there were two schools or if Parish partially retired at some stage just retaining the instruction of the poor children. The provision of education to a poor child was recorded in the poor book of 1811 and gave some indication of the costs involved at the time: '27.10.1811 To schooling of Susan Jones, 2 November 1810 to

Michaelmas 1811. Paper and ink included 17s.6d.'

Following the establishment of the Okehampton Union in 1836, the two under rooms at the south end of Church House ceased to be used as a poorhouse and Revd George Richards, at his own expense, fitted them out as the school. John Pyke probably took charge of the school at some time between 1837 and 1839. In the 1841 census, John Pike [sic] and Simon Fewings were described as schoolmasters. By 1851 John Pyke was 'an invalid, formerly a schoolmaster' and the school was being run by his wife Elizabeth and daughter Anna; Simon Fewings and his wife Mary Ann had moved out of the parish to run Farringdon School near Exeter. In 1857 *Billing's Directory* recorded:

The National School is held in a large room belonging to the Church Houses (the remainder being occupied by poor families rent-free); it is supported by subscriptions and the children's pence. Number of scholars 80. Elizabeth Pyke Mistress.

In 1811 the Church of England had formed the National Society for Promoting the Education of the Poor in the Principles of the Established Church. Affiliation to the society provided financial benefits including building grants and cheap textbooks.

At some stage during the second half of the nineteenth century, Church House Cottage became the head teacher's home. By 1866 Simon and Mary Ann Fewings had returned to Sampford Courtenay and were running the school. Following the Forster Elementary Education Act of 1870, *Kelly's Directory* recorded that in 1874 a School Board of five members was established for the united district of Sampford Courtenay and Honeychurch 'with Belstone contributory with two members'. In 1878 the Board comprised: Revd Edward Theed (chairman), Thomas Sloman (vice-chairman), William Kelland, John Cook, Henry Drew, John Langmead and Edward Endacott, with R.W. Fulford as the clerk. The Board ran two schools, one at Sampford Courtenay and the other at Sticklepath. Pupils allocated to Sampford Courtenay came from as far south as Westhill, Lydcott, Honeycott, Withybrook, Rowden and Halford. During 1877 and 1878 there appeared to be a rival dame's school in the village, run by a Mrs Ellis.

Sampford Courtenay village green, c.1892. Left to right, standing: William Manuell (village schoolmaster 1876–93), ?, Thirzena Manuell (née Ash), ?, Eliza Ash, Edwin Ash, William Ash senr, William Ash junr; sitting: Harold, William and Percival Manuell.

1876–93

Although a requirement of Lowe's Revised Code of 1862, the Sampford Courtenay school admissions registers and logbooks did not appear to commence until January 1876 when William Manuell became schoolmaster. Mary Ann Fewings was still schoolmistress; Simon Fewings by then was Parish Clerk and secretary to the Old Age Benefit Society. The Code laid down that the head teacher should keep a bare record of events and that 'no expressions of opinion' were to be entered; fortunately for the local historian, this ruling was largely ignored. The logbooks thus provide a comprehensive record of the conditions and interesting events at the school and in the surrounding parish for the next 70 years. Finance for the Board School comprised Government grant, voluntary local rates and children's pence (until replaced by fee grant in 1891). The weekly fee paid for each child varied according to the financial circumstances of the parents and was brought to the school by the child each Monday morning. In May 1877 the scale of fees was:

Farmers 6d. each child [reduced to 4d. in January 1878], tradesmen and artisans 2d., labourers 1d. and children attending the infant class 1d. Where more than two children of the same parents attend the school at the same time, each child above that number to pay one half of the above scale.

In 1876 William Manuell was only 21 and the prospect of being responsible for over 100 children (56 boys and 59 girls in 1882/3) must have been daunting. At first Manuell lodged with George and Mary Snell at Middletown but in 1881 he married Thirzena, the daughter of the local builder William Ash, and they soon took up residence in the schoolmaster's cottage. Manuell was to face many problems during his 17 years as schoolmaster. The Government grant was based on two factors only: attendance and the results of an annual test of reading, writing and arithmetic conducted by a visiting inspector. Part of Manuell's salary, at the discretion of the Board, would have been directly proportionate to the level of grant earned. He was plagued by the all too frequent non-attendance of his pupils and many of his lamentations relate to the absence of what on numerous occasions amounted to nearly half the school. Under an Act of 1876, school attendance had been made compulsory from the ages of five to ten years, and half-time (a most unsatisfactory arrangement) from then to 13, unless a child achieved exemption by passing Standard IV. There were six standards roughly corresponding to age. Although a locally appointed attendance officer made regular checks, at Sampford Courtenay (in common with most of rural Devon) compulsion remained a fiction throughout the rest of the century.

One of the main problems was that the children, particularly the older ones, were kept at home to assist their parents with farming activities – hay and corn harvests, planting and digging potatoes, etc. Labourers' wages were very low and the small amount of extra money that could be brought into the household was all important:

30.6.1876 Average attendance for week very small owing chiefly to sheep shearing and the hay harvest.
7.4.1881 Attendance today very bad. The excuse given by nearly every child that has been absent is that they are kept at home to assist in tilling the potatoes.

The vast majority of children would have had to walk to school, some as far as three miles. Although they were kitted out with stout boots, the distance and any inclement weather took their toll, particularly on the younger children:

14.11.1887 Several children absent with sore feet.
8.12.1887 Attendance today bad owing to the rain. Only a few country children present.
10.3.1891 Snow storms still raging. Impossible for children to attend school. Closed school for the week.

Outbreaks of illness played their part too, but it was not always the ill health of the child that led to non-attendance, especially where those from 'long' families were concerned:

24.7.1877 Re-admitted Mary Ann Hill who has been absent for several months on account of the death of her mother.
2.12.1879 Certificate from Dr Deans stating that Ann Harris must be kept home occasionally in order to help in nursing the baby who is in a dangerous state of health.

Major epidemics of measles, whooping cough, scarlet fever and diphtheria often closed the school completely and some cases ended in death:

27.6.1892 Over 40 children away, 25 of whom are prevented from attending owing to sickness of some kind or another. Diphtheria at Treecott. One case terminated fatally on Thursday evening last.

Absences were not always the result of economic necessity or illness. Various events on the social calendar, within a fairly wide radius, appeared too great a temptation to resist:

7.7.1876 Average attendance for week very small owing to its being Fair Week.
9.11.1876 School closed. Sampford Courtenay and Honeychurch annual ploughing match.

1.3.1877 Attendance today very small, chiefly owing to Lord Portsmouth's meet of foxhounds at Sampford Chapple.

9.5.1877 Attendance today rather small on account of Wombwells' Menagerie being at North Tawton.

22.12.1881 Attendance exceedingly small owing to the Christmas market at North Tawton.

There were many other reasons for absence and school closure, including:

10.10.1877 Several children absent, excuse sent for absence 'Mother sent them to pick blackberries'.

14.10.1891 School closed this afternoon for the Church Harvest Festival Tea.

The continuing problem of non-attendance drove Manuell to distraction; he exhausted his supply of suitable adjectives – attendance was successively: wretchedly, shockingly, dreadfully, miserably and frightfully bad! He complained that compulsory powers were badly wanted in order to make satisfactory progress in the school and he regularly gave the attendance officer lists of names of children who never attended. Although their parents were warned, the situation did not improve: '28.1.1892 The attendance is getting worse every day. Number present this afternoon 69 out of a possible 115.'

Several children were kept at home until well beyond the statutory starting age of five: '25.9.1876 Admitted William Hill from Honeychurch, 12 years old and unable to read, write and cipher.'

Manuell also had problems with his staff. He had two assistant teachers – a mistress who taught needlework and the infants, and a monitor or a pupil-teacher who helped with the younger children. There were numerous critical comments by H.M. Inspector, who urged the provision of a properly trained teacher to take charge of the infants and needlework instruction. Much importance was attached to needlework skills, which could gain a girl a good job as a domestic servant; she would also need to make and repair her own clothes and eventually those of her family. Following illness, Mrs Fewings disappeared from the logs in 1879 and her place was taken by Emily Potter who appeared competent but soon left to be married. The next two mistresses proved unsatisfactory, although each retained the position for four or five years.

Pupil-teachers were teenagers, usually former pupils, who were indentured for four or five years, receiving one and a half hours' daily instruction from the headmaster in addition to giving their own teaching. They worked at the same time for their annual examinations and for the Queen's Scholarship, the passing of which could earn them a place at training college. Some of the daily instruction at Sampford Courtenay was given during the lunch break. William Avery, aged 14 and son of George Avery the Sampford Courtenay tailor, was taken on in 1877 and left in 1883, eventually progressing to an appointment as head teacher at Sticklepath Board School from 1889 to 1893. Charles Page, the 15-year-old youngest son of Richard Page of Great Cliston, was the next pupil-teacher. He did not do so well. In 1887 H.M. Inspector commented: 'Charles Page has passed so bad an examination that my Lords have been unable to consider him as part of the school staff for the past year.'

Page nevertheless struggled on until early 1889, when Frank Richards, the 13-year-old son of Thomas Richards, a railway labourer, took his place, initially starting as a monitor because of his young age. Richards did well and in 1894 he was helping with the upper classes. He took and passed the Queen's Scholarship and 'was presented with a leather travelling writing case subscribed for by the teachers and scholars' when he left the service of the Board in June 1894. Richards went to Exeter Training College and, from 1898 until 1939, was the well-loved and respected headmaster of Sticklepath School.

The Code of 1862 made H.M. Inspector an arbiter in matters of grant and his authority was virtually unchallengeable. The children were examined annually and the resultant report had to be copied into the logbook by the head teacher, which must have proved a great humiliation on many occasions. The local inspector, from 1875 until his retirement in 1899, was Henry Codd, 'a tall frock-coated, top-hatted, saturnine figure'. He had a habit of rapping on school windows from horseback to announce his arrival and must have inspired terror in children and teachers alike. Richard Pyke, who attended Sampford Courtenay School from 1877 to 1885, recalled in *Men and Memories*:

We were examined in this book [Goldsmith's *Deserted Village*] *by a pompous inspector. He asked what was meant by 'And every pang that folly pays to pride'. One of us got full marks through illustrating this profound observation by a reference to tight corsets.*

Not all of Codd's comments were critical and there is much praise in his reports, particularly on the level of discipline. Perhaps he was responsible too for the provision of a new school building:

15.8.1878 The present premises are very unsatisfactory. The lighting is not good. There is no ventilation except through the windows and the office arrangements [lavatories] *are as bad as can be. The present lime-ash floor should be replaced by a wooden one.*

The reference to a lime-ash floor would seem to indicate that the schoolroom continued to occupy the lower floor of Church House. By July 1879, new buildings were in the course of being provided and, in September 1880, the school moved into the new premises. H.M. Inspector remarked on his next visit:

*11.7.1881 In such hand-
some and commodious
buildings, the school
has, as might have
been anticipated,
made progress. The
discipline is good and
much of the instruc-
tion very creditable.*

A conveyance dated
25 May 1880 indicated
that King's College had
granted the site for the
school 'freely and volun-
tarily and without any valuable consideration' to the
Sampford Courtenay and Honeychurch Board. The
new building consisted of three classrooms. One of
the larger rooms had a gallery for the infants, which
was removed in 1912. There were separate entrances
and playgrounds (divided by iron railings) for boys
and girls.

In February 1893 Manuell became ill; entries in the
logs were minimal and in a different hand. The annual
report from H.M. Inspector received in August,
referring to a visit made earlier in the year, recorded:

*Considering that the Master has been unable to attend
to his duties for the last three months in consequence
of sickness, which has now, I regret to learn, terminated in death, the work appears to have suffered very
little if at all.*

William Manuell died on 15 June leaving his widow
Thirzena with three young sons. He was only 38.
Richard Pyke wrote a more fitting epitaph for him:

*The Board School which I attended was fortunate in
having an excellent headmaster. He died while still
young, and many of the boys and girls shed tears as
they sang 'Jesu lover of my soul' by the graveside.
He was a a strict disciplinarian, a rather bigoted
churchman with little sympathy for dissenters: but he
was never unjust... I think his teaching must have
been excellent: at any rate I was grounded well
enough in the subjects taught to pursue my studies
alone, without any confusion of mind.*

1893–98

Samuel Challice, like William Manuell, was in his early
twenties when he commenced duties as headmaster in
August 1893. From September 1891, elementary
education had become free. In 1893 the school-leaving
age was raised to 11 and, by the end of the century, to
12. In both Manuell's and Challice's time, a member of
the Board, usually the rector, made regular visits to the
school to check the registers and ensure all was
running smoothly. By the late 1890s the formal

*The Village Hall, 2001. The building
was the village school from 1880 until 1947.*

examination in the 'three
Rs' by H.M. Inspector
was changed to a system
of two 'annual visits
without notice', which
proved more construc-
tive and much less trau-
matic for head teachers.
The diocesan inspector
also made an annual
inspection of religious
instruction in the
school but, unlike the
Government inspector,
his comments were
invariably complimentary. The local ladies' sewing
committee, in Challice's time represented by Mrs
Manuell and Mrs Sloman, made regular checks on the
standard of the girls' needlework.

Challice was to suffer the same problems as
Manuell – inadequate staff and low attendance by
pupils. He was even more vociferous:

*14.8.1893 Due to fine harvest weather, only 71 out of
117 children on the books attended.*
*22.12.1893 The attendance of late has been
abominable. I have on more than one occasion
written to the Board, calling their attention to the
matter. 'Compulsory attendance' here is a farce.*
*12.7.1894 Attendance very low. Without a monitor
to assist me, I find it absolutely impossible to do
the work.*
*19.9.1894 The attendance is still no better.
Irregularity almost invariably prevails in the
upper standards. Working as I am, almost
single-handed, it is impossible to do efficient work.*
*27.9.1894 Tested the work of Standards I and II, the
result being a miserable failure in all subjects, as
might be expected considering that the Monitor
does not seem to take the faintest interest in his
work. It is most unfair that I have not more
assistance for a school this size.*

The monitor in question was 13-year-old Frank
Sanders, son of Henry Sanders, the publican of the
Courtenay Arms. He did little to obtain Challice's
approval:

*14.1.1895 I have had cause today to complain to
Sanders, who is again a candidate on probation,
about the manifest indifference he exhibits about
his home lessons. 'Scampering' his written work
was the chief ground of complaint.*
*31.5.1895 Tested the work of Standards I and II.
Geography very weak, which might be reasonably
expected considering that the Monitor has not even
the vaguest conception of what the sea, a ship or a
boat is like, having never seen either. Impressed
upon him the advantage of extending his travels.*

One wonders if Sanders had the means at his disposal to do this. He left the school in early 1896 after less than two years. H.M. Inspector supported Challice's complaints about his staff: '27.7.1894 A high order of efficiency cannot be looked for with such a feeble staff.'

Low attendance continued with inclement weather and illness partially contributory. In 1895, during an outbreak of diphtheria, two younger scholars died and measles closed the school for four weeks. Two years later, Challice remarked: '12.2.1897 The average attendance for the week is very low due in part to sickness, the weather and indifference – especially the latter.'

Three more female assistant teachers came and went, but by 1895 Ellen Davey had been appointed as the infants' and sewing mistress; she was to stay for eight years and appeared very competent. Annie Lang was pupil-teacher from 1896 until 1899, when she left through ill health. By October 1897, Challice presumably had persuaded the Board at last to take tougher action against parents of children who did not make regular attendance. The attendance officer, Henry Arscott, had sent out 19 notices threatening prosecution if irregularity continued. This seemed to have the desired effect, but the Government report in November was not favourable: 'The school does not make satisfactory progress' and, in February 1898, Challice resigned his appointment to take up a situation in a boys' school in Hastings. The Government report in July 1898 noted:

The late Master must have neglected his work... The work of the upper standards is very unsatisfactory though there are signs of a better state of things under the new Master.

Revd Thomas Little wrote to Charles Grant, the bursar of King's College: 'Challice, our very unsatisfactory schoolmaster, has beyond all our hopes got another appointment and resigned his post here. So now we hope for brighter things.' One wonders how much of Challice's inability to satisfy stemmed from his harassment of the School Board for provision of better staff and a firmer stance on the enforcement of compulsory attendance. Also, the burials register records the death in August 1895 of 25-year-old Mary Challice at 'The School House'. It seems that Challice had to cope too with the death of a near relative, his wife or sister perhaps, during his time as schoolmaster.

1898–1921

When Orman Reynolds took charge in February 1898, the number of scholars had reduced to about 95. He was in his early thirties and lived, with his wife and family, in Church House Cottage. Unfortunately, he was to experience some of the problems of his predecessors. Epidemics of illness occurred frequently and sometimes closed the school for weeks at a time. Bad weather kept away all but the village children. However, instances of the older children taking time off to help in the fields gradually lessened.

Following the Balfour Education Act of 1902, in 1903 Sampford Courtenay School came under the jurisdiction of the Local Education Authority and became a Council School with a Board of Managers.

Sampford Courtenay School, c.1900.

Sampford Courtenay School, 1909. Pictured are: Edwin Hawkins (back row, third from left), Eleanor Hawkins (third row, first left), Kathleen Hawkins (third row, far right), Clifford Hawkins (front row, second from left) and Muriel Hawkins (front row, third from left).

Later the 1918 Education Act raised the school-leaving age to 14. Visits continued on a regular basis by one of the managers (usually the rector and, for many years, Robert Hawkins), the local attendance officer and the ladies' sewing committee. By the end of the nineteenth century, the curriculum had become more varied and equipment, such as kindergarten apparatus, had been acquired. H.M. Inspector criticised a lack of physical training in 1897, which had received attention by 1898 and in 1902 there was mention of drilling in the playground (popular following the Boer War). In 1908 the teaching of the making of Honiton lace was introduced, the teachers being Mrs Pease and Miss Trissie Knight, the daughter of Samuel Knight the bootmaker. Four girls were selected to receive instruction: Eleanor Hawkins, May Reddaway, Annie Hill and Beatrice Sloman.

The school continued to close for local events, such as church and chapel teas and harvest festivals, club walks and agricultural shows. Children still stayed away to enjoy other local excitements, including meets of the local foxhounds, cricket matches, cattle fairs, the travelling menagerie and flower shows. In 1906 the Education Committee promised certificates for perfect attendance and in May 1907 Elsie Northam was recorded as having achieved this distinction. Those who made at least 98 per cent of attendances included Lena Reddaway, May Reddaway, George Lake, Hugh Piper and Andrew Ash. In 1909, 98 per cent attendance was achieved by Eleanor Hawkins, Herbert and Hugh Piper and Tom Reddaway.

During Reynolds' headship, there was a high turnover of monitors and assistant teachers – 14 in total plus three or four supply teachers, all apart from one (Beatrice Easterbrook, who remained for four years) only staying for between one and three years. The Government report of 1910 reflected Reynolds' problems:

The several changes in the staff during recent years have interfered with the general progress. Discipline continues to be somewhat unsteady, especially among the older scholars... The supplementary teachers are approved with some hesitation.

The two supplementary teachers in question, Mrs Chappell and Miss Clarke (mother and daughter), suffered from frequent ill health and by early 1913 had both resigned. The reports on religious instruction, however, continued to be favourable:

16.12.1912 The little ones were keenly responsive and eager to show their knowledge of the simple truths of Christianity so carefully imparted to them.
20.9.1916 There was a devotional atmosphere about the opening of school and it was gratifying to find the children spend a few moments in silent prayer each day at noon.

By 1906 the number of pupils had fallen to 75 and by 1913 to 60. In 1913 Revd Burnaby praised the wonderfully improved tone of the school, but the report from H.M. Inspector read:

The children generally are well behaved and attentive. The value however of orderly marching in and out of school and of occasional smart physical exercises seems to have been overlooked.

The school was heated by two Tortoise stoves, run on coke, and an open fire in the small room. These did not appear very efficient. In 1900 it was thought desirable to acquire a thermometer and adverse temperatures were subsequently recorded, very often between 33 and 37 degrees Fahrenheit. In 1911 the Government inspector reported:

Both rooms are terribly cold and the children certainly suffered and could not possibly have done any work to the best advantage. Of course, it is an exceptionally cold day, but naturally such a day is a real test of the adequacy of the heating arrangements. Snow was actually falling in the infants' room this morning!

Nothing was done to remedy this and low temperatures continued. Irene Sampson (née Hawkins) remembers having to wear 'masses of warm clothes' to school. Other inadequacies, such as a lack of dry earth, for use in the 'offices', and fresh drinking-water were mentioned by the medical inspector. From 1914 children were weighed and measured and from about 1917 were examined by the head or 'nit' nurse. (Visits from the school dentist commenced in 1924.) The first indication of an outing to the seaside (to Exmouth) was in June 1901 and a chapel outing was mentioned in August 1914. Empire Day on 24 May (Queen Victoria's birthday) was regularly celebrated at the school. The children sang 'Rule Britannia' and the 'National Anthem' and saluted the school photograph of the King. There were a few references to the war – in May 1916 Miss Olive Shears, the assistant teacher, was absent to visit her brother who was proceeding to the Front. Unusually, the school closed for two weeks in July 1918 'to allow children to help with the hay harvest' and one afternoon in September for blackberry picking. On 11 November 1918, the school log recorded: 'Received telegraphic news this afternoon of Germans signing armistice, school watched hoisting of Union Jack, cheered, sang patriotic songs and dismissed.'

Irene Sampson has many memories of the school in Orman Reynolds' time. All the girls wore white pinafores and the children sat two at a desk. Irene and her brothers and sisters took their lunch to school but would go to Annie Piper's cottage in the village to eat it and for a cup of cocoa. She remembers the cane being used. During the war, the children gave a concert to raise money for the soldiers and Irene remembers: 'I was dressed as a fairy, a silk frock and some wings, and Clifford [her brother] was dressed as a soldier.' She also remembers the dreaded school inspector:

We didn't know he was coming. He would say something and then he would point at someone to answer a question. You had to be on your toes, because you never knew who he was going to ask. The teachers were more afraid of him than the pupils.

In later years, Mary Cleverdon (née Bolt) recalls Reynolds falling off his seat. Apparently he regularly attended nap parties (see Chapter Ten), which invariably continued into the early hours, so the next morning possibly found him a little the worse for wear.

By 1916 pupil numbers at Sampford Courtenay had fallen to 53, which in 1917 led to a consequent reduction in staff from three to two. In 1919 the number of children on the register stood at 46. The Government report received in February 1920 was fairly critical on a wide range of issues, including discipline and a lack of training in habits of cleanliness. Even the report on religious instruction was less favourable that year. In January 1921, in an

Sampford Courtenay School, c.1920. Mary Bolt is pictured fourth from left in the back row.

Sampford Courtenay School, 1922. The teachers are: *Doris Horn* (on left), *Grace Hill* (on right, standing), *Ellie Hill* (on right, crouching). *Note the shed in the school grounds in which Grace Hill kept a loom.*

Sampford Courtenay School, 1925. Left to right, back row: *Doris Horn (teacher), Kenneth Snell, Eleanor Harris, Len Hodge, Dorothy Phare, Gwen Newcombe, Mary Bolt, Ellie Hill (headmistress)*; third row: *Courtenay Lake, Courtenay Johns, Wallace Lake, Harold Harris, Roy Hawking, Wilfred Smith, Gorwyn Arscott, Maurice Horn*; second row: *Myrtle Luxton, Yvonne Arscott, Ron Snell, Ron Hodge, John Reddaway, Alice Phare, Gwennie Jones, Nova Stevens*; front row: *Ivy Reddaway, Martin Snell, Phil Reddaway, Evelyn Cole.*

Left: *Sampford Courtenay School, 1926.* Left to right, back row: *Ellie Hill (headmistress), Ron Hodge, Ken Snell, Eleanor Harris, Gwennie Jones, Myrtle Luxton, Yvonne Arscott, Maurice Horn, Mary Bolt, Doris Horn (teacher);* third row: *Harold Harris, Roy Hawking, ?, Nova Stevens, Ernie Wooldridge, Ivy Reddaway, Alice Phare, Ron Snell, Gwennie Newcombe, Courtenay Sanders;* second row: *Courtenay Johns, Joan Reddaway, Myrtle Hawking, Florence Luxton, Marion Reddaway, Phil Reddaway, George Stevens, May Lake;* front row: *Bill Newcombe, Wallace Lake, John Reddaway, Miss Hill's dog, Martin Snell, Wilfred Smith.*

Sampford Courtenay School, 1927. Left to right, back row: *Nova Stevens, Courtenay Sanders, Harold Harris, Ernie Wooldridge, Gwennie Newcombe, Alice Phare, Ron Hodge, Roy Hawking, Wallace Lake, May Lake, Doris Horn (teacher);* middle row: *Myrtle Hawking, Courtenay Harris, Martin Snell, Frank Horn, Bill Newcombe, Eleanor Harris (standing), Courtenay Johns, Wilfred Smith, John Reddaway, Evelyn Cole, George Stevens, Ivy Reddaway;* front row: *?, Joan Reddaway, Winnie Horn, Marion Reddaway, Phil Reddaway, ? Goodwyn, Courtenay Lake, Pearl Lake, Joyce Newcombe, Daisy Lake, Nancy Snell, Francis Snell.*

Sampford Courtenay School, 1934. Left to right, back row: Mary Skinner (teacher), George West, Ivy Lake, Audrey Reddaway, Barbara Jones, Valerie Squire, Phyllis Joslin, Marjorie Kelland (headmistress); middle row: Megan Jones, Noel Phare, Horace Hawkins, Bert Piper, Ethel West, Nova Lake, Pearl West, Eric Johns, Arthur Sleeman; front row, kneeling: Len Piper, Desmond Hawkins, Philip Jones, Lily Lake, Ron King, Ruby Jones, Nancy Arscott, Rodney Ash, Fred Reynolds.

Left: *Ivy Reddaway, monitress at
Sampford Courtenay School, 1934–36.*

Below: *Sampford Courtenay School, 1935. Left to right, back
row: Heber Harris, Clarice Lake, Barbara Jones, Nova Lake,
George West, Marjorie Kelland (headmistress); third row:
Ivy Reddaway (monitress), Bert Piper, Valerie Squire, Ivy Lake,
Phyllis Joslin, Audrey Reddaway, Ethel West, Arthur Sleeman;
second row, kneeling: Horace Hawkins, Nancy Arscott,
Pearl West, Lily Lake, Noel Phare; front row, sitting:
Philip Jones, Len Piper, Desmond Hawkins, Megan Jones,
Ruby Jones, John Reddaway, Maurice West, Ron King.*

*Sampford Courtenay School, 1936. Left to right, back row: Eric Johns, Ethel West, Barbara Jones,
Horace Hawkins, George West, Gladys Mounsden (headmistress); third row: Ivy Reddaway (monitress),
Arthur Sleeman, Bert Piper, Nova Lake, Valerie Squire, Audrey Reddaway, Pearl West, Ivy Lake, Nancy
Arscott, John Reddaway, Noel Phare; second row: Fred Reynolds, Megan Jones, Ruby Jones, Mary
Sleeman, Barbara Sanders, Lily Lake, Ivy Johns, Patsie Johns, Ron King, Len Piper; front row: Rodney
Ash, Bert Johns, Freddie Johns, Desmond Hawkins, Maurice West, Basil Goodman, Len Harris.*

unusually shaky hand, Orman Reynolds wrote: 'Have this day given up charge, being transferred to Ottery St Mary'. He was 54.

1921–47

The year 1921 was to mark a permanent change to female head teachers and assistants; this was common in rural schools across the country. There were many different teachers over the next 26 years. Early in 1921 Revd Burnaby wrote in the school log: 'Visited the school... and found Mrs Gridgeman in charge and a kind of peace almost indescribable, and all hard at work and interested.' By April 1921, Ellie Hill was headmistress, briefly assisted by her sister Grace. In 1925 Agnes Lethem took over from Miss Hill as the head. She was an older lady who lodged with Mrs Paddon at Thornbury Cottage. Doris Horn, daughter of Bert Horn the blacksmith, was appointed monitress in 1922 and became the assistant teacher in 1925 (at a salary of £35 per year). She left to be married in 1929 and her place was taken by Marjorie Kelland who lodged with Mrs Ward at Higher Town. Although fairly young and inexperienced, Miss Kelland took over as head in 1932 with Mary Skinner as assistant. Miss Kelland gave piano lessons to

pupils in the lunch hour and Myrtle Hunkin (née Hawking) remembers paying 6d. for 20 minutes' tuition. Mary Bolt, as monitress, covered Mary Skinner's absence on several occasions between 1931 and 1934. Mary Skinner left in 1934 to teach at another school. Ivy Reddaway, who was later to marry Bert Coates of The Barton, was monitress for two years until 1936. Marjorie Kelland left to marry Harold Cornelius the bootmaker in 1936 and they moved to North Tawton. Gladys Mounsdon became headmistress with Evelyn Ball as assistant, both lodging at Higher Town. When Miss Ball transferred to Whiddon Down School in 1938 her place was taken by Mollie Clarke. Both Miss Mounsdon and Miss Clarke left in September 1940.

The period between the world wars appears to have been a happy and peaceful time for Sampford Courtenay School. Between 1921 and 1932, the number of children on the register varied between 26 and 44. The 1918 Education Act had replaced elementary schools with separate junior and senior establishments, although these were not common until after 1926. The division did not come to the parish until February 1932 when the senior scholars (those who were 11 years of age on 1 April) transferred to North Tawton Senior School, leaving 23 pupils at Sampford Courtenay. The older

Above: *Church fête at Culverhayes, 1971 – the two ladies with hats are Becky Horn and Mollie Clarke (former teacher).*

Top picture: *Sampford Courtenay School – craft work under the elm tree, 1927.*

children, from Sampford Courtenay, Bondleigh, Spreyton and Bow, were taken to their new school by bus. Between 1932 and 1940, pupil numbers fluctuated between 22 and 33, sometimes being temporarily augmented by visiting gypsy families.

Various practical work was introduced, such as woodwork, gardening, leather and cane work. The Government inspector commented in 1932:

The children are making steady progress in all the ordinary subjects and their lives are brightened by the excursions and other out-of-school activities organised by the Mistress [Marjorie Kelland] and financed mainly through her efforts.

It was Agnes Lethem who, in 1928, had set up a school fund to finance Christmas parties and annual trips to the seaside, money being raised from open days, sales of work and concerts given by the children. The annual seaside trip, documented from 1926 to 1939, to Teignmouth, Exmouth, Paignton or Dawlish, was taken one Friday in July. On 20 July 1934 a trip to Exmouth was supported by 80 adults and children. Phil Reddaway, who attended the school from 1924 until 1932, remembers: 'The outing was the highlight of the year; the only time anyone got to the seaside.' The children would ride to the

station in horse-drawn wagons and parents would walk there or ride bicycles. In later years charabancs were used and Phil recalls one trip to Paignton when Mrs Cleverdon and her children (from Cliston) went. The coach got back as far as Newton Abbot when somebody said: 'Mrs Cleverdon isn't on the bus' and it had to return to Paignton to pick them up.

The smooth running of the school during the 1920s and '30s must have been partially due to the cessation of the problem of non-attendance:

22.12.1922 The old half days' absence for pleasure etc. have practically disappeared and the children are keen on attending regularly. Mr Robert Hawkins has helped in this as he offered three prizes for the best attenders throughout the year. They have been gained by Harold Cornelius, Mary Bolt and Ronald Snell.

It was not all work and no play, however. Time off was allowed to attend local fêtes, agricultural shows, etc., and the teacher often took the children at playtime to see the hounds meet. On one occasion, however, according to Myrtle Hunkin, the children had gone without permission to see the hounds at the New Inn. Unfortunately it was a day when the school inspector called. The children were severely

Sampford Courtenay School, 1939. Left to right, back row: *Gladys Mounsdon (headmistress), John Reddaway, Barbara Sanders, Nancy Arscott, Hazel Pike, Horace Hawkins, Mollie Clarke (teacher);* third row: *Desmond Hawkins, Fred Reynolds, Ivy Johns, Patsie Johns, Monica Scoble, Mary Sleeman, Ron King, Len Piper;* second row: *Eddie Hodge, Len Harris, Eric Pike, Peter Reddaway, Bill Weeks;* front row: *Freddie Johns, Victor Hodge, John Hodge, Chris Gill, Douglas Hodge.*

reprimanded: 'Some of the boys got the cane, which was hidden away in a little hole in the back of the piano.' Lessons appeared much more enjoyable over this period and in summer were often held out of doors. There was nature study in the lanes and occasional sports in a nearby field. The school had its own garden from 1927; the younger children planted bulbs and wallflowers and the boys received instruction in pruning fruit bushes. In the 1920s, for the Christmas concerts, the children made everything themselves: 'The girls are doing fairy frocks, the boys cardboard work, programme printing etc.' Needlework, including lace-making, continued throughout these years. Myrtle Hunkin remembers making lace with a pillow and bobbins; it was very difficult and needed a lot of patience: 'It would take months just to make a handkerchief.'

Government and diocesan reports throughout the 1920s and '30s were complimentary. In 1938 the Government inspector wrote:

The Headmistress [Gladys Mounsdon] *has put this school on an admirable footing... Both she and her assistant* [Evelyn Ball] *have the interests of the children very much at heart and a note of genuine humanity marks all their dealings with them. The effect of these happy relationships on the children is one of the school's outstanding characteristics.*

From 1920 until 1941 most of the inspections of religious instruction were conducted by Herbert Hawkins. Sampford Courtenay School appeared to be a special favourite and, in 1937, following a visit to China, he presented the school with 'a beautiful collection of moths and butterflies'.

Until 1940, the celebration of Empire Day was regularly recorded in the school logs:

24.5.1922 It is Empire Day and the children have had a short address on their responsibilities and privileges as members of the British Empire. We all saluted the Flag. [The flag-pole stood near the smithy.]

Phil and Audrey Reddaway recall the demise of the flag-pole, probably in the 1950s or '60s. It blew down and another pole was cut from the plantation at Chapple Moor. The pole eventually fell down again and 'they didn't bother to put it back up'. Armistice Day was also observed:

11.11.1936 The silence at 11 o'clock was observed. A simple talk stressing the need for a better understanding between the nations of the world was given by the Head Teacher. [If only!]

There were, of course, a few problems. Many children still walked fairly long distances each day. In the 1930s Arthur and Mary Sleeman had to walk in from Withybrook; they would cross the railway at Green Lane Bridge and walk across the fields past Southey to the village. They sometimes arrived too late for their mark, which is hardly surprising as they had 2½ miles to travel. Myrtle Hunkin and Valerie Hawking (née Squire) remember walking from Honeychurch: 'We got wet a few times, and hot, because we had to wear loads of clothes.' Bad weather and the usual childhood illnesses kept children away and occasionally closed the school. As many ex-pupils remember, heating the building was always difficult. In January 1922 the headmistress reported: 'This week... the temperature at 9a.m. has been below 40 degrees. There is ice inside the infants' classroom now on the window ledge at 10.30a.m.' Neither electricity nor a water-supply was ever connected to the school. Oil-lamps were used for lighting and bucket lavatories and portable wash-basins were across the open yard. Water had to be brought each day by the caretaker, Becky Horn, collected from the standpipe near the carpenter's shop. Becky, helped by husband George, had the job too of emptying the lavatory buckets into a large pit in the school grounds. There were doors at the back of the lavatories to extract them. According to Len Piper, some naughty boys would poke stinging nettles through to disturb other children: 'There was a heck of a do once because it was the teacher in there!'

The first signs of the approaching war were documented in October 1938, when air-raid wardens visited and gave instructions on the use of gas masks. In July 1939 the school managers submitted a plan for a trench to be dug in the school grounds to provide an air-raid shelter in the event of war breaking out. Several ex-pupils recall the trench and shelter being constructed, with their assistance. By the end of 1939 four unofficial evacuees (relatives of people in the village) had moved into Sampford Courtenay and registered at the school. There were then 31 on the register. The beginning of 1940 saw heavy snow-storms and a measles epidemic. On 10 May the school closed for the Whitsun holiday but on 14 May 'reopened owing to War news and a letter from the Secretary stating that the Board of Education had ordered all holidays to be cancelled.' On 24 May the children celebrated Empire Day as usual. On 13 June 30 evacuees from a London school, with their two teachers, arrived in the village and on 17 June the teachers, Miss Rayner and Mrs Lloyd-Jones, commenced duties with their pupils at the school premises. The teachers and children were billeted with families nearby. Initially it was thought that the two schools would operate independently but, by July, the two sets of children merged into one school, with a total of 63 on the books. The teaching arrangements were: Miss Mounsdon – head teacher, Standard IV and Seniors; Miss Rayner – Standard III and Lower IV; Mrs Lloyd-Jones – Standards I and II; and Miss Clarke – Infants and under fives. Although the school officially closed on 1 August for the summer holidays, it remained open for children who wished to attend to do war work. This appeared to consist of raising money by various means, such as a concert and whist drive and the picking of whortleberries and blackberries.

On 7 September Gladys Mounsdon and Mollie Clarke left the school. From then onwards there were few entries in the logbooks and the school arrangements appeared rather disorganised. There followed a succession of different teachers for short periods of time, six in all between September 1940 and March 1942. By September 1940 pupil numbers had reduced to 44; 23 of these were evacuees. The two London teachers had gone by October 1941, but it is not clear when the evacuee children left. In April 1942 Miss Grose took charge and ran the school on her own until she left in November 1946. The diocesan inspector reported:

She has no easy task in dealing with a group of children with such a wide age range. Fortunately she has had a good deal of experience and she is tackling the problem with success.

The annual summer outing to the seaside stopped. The holiday club, presumably for war work, was opened during school holidays but, on each occasion, attendance was nil. Miss Grose had no cover; supply teachers were never available and whenever she was absent the school had to close. January 1945 saw more blizzards and another outbreak of measles, with a resultant low attendance. By April there were only 15 pupils at the school. Two days' holiday, on 8 and 9 May, was given to celebrate the Victory in Europe. There appeared to be some confusion as to the length of the holiday as on 10 May: 'Three absentees, due to North Tawton Senior School children declaring that they had three days' holiday

and remaining in the village.'

The supply teacher who took over from Miss Grose in December 1946 did not give her name in the logbook, but it was possibly a Miss Carr. Presumably because of low pupil numbers, the likely closure of the school was being discussed, and in March 1947 Miss Carr recorded: 'Saw Education Officer, school is definitely to close this term.' Her last remarks in the log were somewhat bitter:

20.3.1947 Pathway between school and children's lavatories very messy, should have been concreted years ago. One of the reasons for poor attendance is I believe through children having to cross in open, all weathers, the distance between school and wc, roof [of which] leaks.
21.3.1947 Class very trying this morning, the children seem more stupid than ever.

The last entry was on 26 March. There were only nine children at the school, who presumably transferred to North Tawton. The school building remained empty until 1951/2 when it was purchased by the village from Devon County Council for use as a Village Hall. In more recent years the building fulfilled its original purpose as a school on two separate occasions. In January 1989, Blyth School opened at Sampford Courtenay providing kindergarten and preparatory facilities (for three- to seven-year-olds). However, there were various operational problems, including the difficulty of keeping the classrooms warm in the winter, and the school closed in July 1991. From April 1993 until July 1994, the building was used as a temporary base by Exbourne School whilst extensive building work was carried out at their own premises. The head teacher described it as 'a lovely setting in which to teach'. Possibly it was a mild winter!

The New Inn, 1971 – old implements, the fire-engine and wagon wheels.

The Wool Industry

Throughout the centuries, the main occupation of the inhabitants of Sampford Courtenay has been agriculture (see Chapter Five). However, for many years the woollen-cloth industry would have employed a significant number of people in the parish. In the Middle Ages there were many fulling mills along the small streams of Devon to which the country weavers would have taken their cloth to be fulled. Fulling was one of the last processes – the cloth was cleaned, shrunk and thickened in water and then brushed or 'felted' until smooth. In Devon fulling was also known as tucking; the earliest record of fulling or tucking mills in the county was in Sampford Courtenay parish in 1294. During the fourteenth century more and more wool was being woven into cloth, the greatest part by people in their own homes. Initially the cloth was made for the local market, but by 1500 Devon was contributing ten per cent of cloths exported from this country. Cloth making, particularly of serge, flourished until the mid-eighteenth century. However, by then the woollen trade in general had begun to deteriorate

Devon Longwool lamb at Solland, c.1915.

because of continual wars destroying the export market. Devon also lost out to competition from other parts of the country, such as Yorkshire, where cloth production became highly mechanised. The Napoleonic Wars, at the beginning of the nineteenth century, were the deathblow. The Sampford Courtenay book of the overseers of the poor for 1815 recorded the payment of poor relief 'to twelve women weavers on account of the scarcity of employ'. Spinning too had been carried out in the home by farm labourers' wives. Vancouver, in his 1808 report on the agriculture of Devon, commented that this important source of income for the peasant family had all but ceased over the previous 15 years because of the introduction of spinning machinery.

However, serge was still being produced by the Pearse family at Cleave Mill in Sticklepath until the 1850s and its manufacture, although much reduced, continued in North Tawton until the mid-twentieth century. The 1851 census returns recorded about 60 people in the parish, mostly in Sticklepath village, employed or formerly employed as wool combers, sorters, spinners, carders, slopers or serge weavers. There was a small group of serge weavers in Sampford Courtenay village, centred around the cottages on Rectory Hill; presumably they worked for the North Tawton mill. It is thought that the Harvey family at one stage were involved in the organisation of the wool out-workers in the north of the parish. In the late-eighteenth and early-nineteenth centuries the overseers of the poor books recorded John Harvey being paid for teaching paupers to weave. By 1881 there were only two people in the parish employed in the cloth industry; they were both clerks in a woollen manufactory, probably at North Tawton.

Corn-mills

There were several corn- or grist-mills along the River Taw, most of which were in Sticklepath, but two were further north, one near Halford and one at Peckets Ford. Halford Mills were situated about halfway between Halford Manor and Taw Green, where the road turns a sharp right angle and then runs close to the river. Little detail of these mills exists other than brief references to them in various parish records between 1685 and 1831, when they probably belonged to the Snell family of Halford Manor. John Palmer, from 1780 until 1798, was possibly the last miller. The mills had certainly ceased operation by 1837, from which time the property on the site became known as Little Halford. The buildings disappeared many years ago.

The ownership of Rowden Mills at Peckets Ford passed to King's College on their acquisition of the manor in 1570, although mills probably would have existed here well before this time. The college's survey that year recorded Richard Slowman as the tenant. In 1759 Richard Frost was the miller, but by 1765 he had died; his widow Honour Frost obviously did not manage the business successfully because she was in arrears for both land tax and poor rate. In 1767, at the Manor Court, the mills were reported as

being out of repair and quite useless. By 1769 Honour Frost was on poor relief and the contents of the mills had been sold off. In 1774 it was reported at the court that she had died and the mills thus reverted to the college. In 1809 'Rowden Mill plot' was still in the lords' hands, but between 1814 and 1816 the mills were rebuilt and by 1837 run by the Rattenbury family. George Hooper appeared to be the last miller at Rowden in about 1914. The old mill buildings are now two tied cottages attached to the Institute of Grassland and Environmental Research at North Wyke in South Tawton parish. The course of the old mill leat is still in evidence near the cottages and ran from a tributary of the River Taw joining the River Taw itself just south of Peckets Ford Bridge.

Public Houses and Inns

Low lies that house where nut-brown draughts inspired,
Where grey-beard mirth and smiling toil retired,
Where village statesmen talk'd with looks profound,
And news much older than their ale went round.
From 'The Deserted Village' by Oliver Goldsmith, 1770.

There were, at various times, five public houses in the parish (excluding Sticklepath) – the Courtenay Arms, the Chapple Inn, the Courtenay Railway Hotel, the New Inn and the Countryman. Strangely the King's College survey in 1809 listed Glebe House in the village as a public house, but maybe there was some confusion between this property and Albury which lies almost opposite and was certainly an alehouse known as the Courtenay Arms by 1841. John Hammett (who was also a butcher) was the victualler of the Courtenay Arms in the 1840s and '50s. Thomas Seawood and Thomas Ellis in the 1860s, followed by Henry Finning Sanders (who was also described as a cattle doctor or farrier) in the 1870s and '80s, ran the business, but by 1891 the alehouse had closed.

The Courtenay Railway Hotel, 1947.

The New Inn with landlord Samuel Hill by the mounting-block, c.1902. Note the old footbridge and the stream across the road. [Beaford Photographic Archive]

The Chapple Inn at Sampford Chapple had a relatively short life as a public house. The property (which included a malt-house) and the adjacent cottages were built during the first half of the nineteenth century. In 1851 the *Exeter Flying Post* advertised the sale of:

All that dwelling house and malthouse with courtlage, stabling and large garden, late in the occupation of Mr John Heathman... The above premises are situate at Sampford Chapple... and are well adapted for carrying on an extensive malting trade.

There were numerous publicans over the next few decades, including various members of the Sanders family and the wheelwright Richard Brealey. From about 1910 until the pub's closure, Henry Reddaway was the victualler. At some stage the business was acquired by the Heavitree Brewery Company, who dispatched beer by rail from Exeter to Sampford Courtenay Station. Phil Reddaway remembers his grandfather Henry collecting it with a horse and cart. Between 1930 and 1945 the Government decided that there were too many public houses in the country and many were closed under a compensation scheme. The Chapple Inn was identified as one of the 'redundant' pubs and closed in 1930. Compensation was paid by the Devon Compensation Authority – £217 to Heavitree Brewery and £43 to the tenant. In 1931 the inn was sold to the tenant Henry Reddaway for £250. The inn is now a private house but the old malt-house was demolished in 2001. Another malt-house in the village, next to the Old Forge on Rectory Hill, had been converted into a cottage by 1809.

The Courtenay Railway Hotel, on the Okehampton to Crediton road at Sampford Station, was also in existence for less than 100 years. Its origins were recounted in a letter from Rawlence & Squarey (the King's College land agents) to the bursar of the College at the time of the sale of the property in 1929:

In regard to the reversion of the Railway Inn, so far as I understand it, the little old shanty was originally leased to the brewery company and they made a sort of shack where they used to sell liquor to the navvies when they were making the railway; this was on a strip of waste. Then later on they took a lease of a larger piece of waste on which they built the present Railway Hotel.

As the railway station opened in January 1867, the 'shanty' must have been erected in the 1860s. A 99-year lease was taken out by the brewery company, Messrs Starkey, Knight & Co., in 1888 at £5 per annum ground-rent. In 1929 the reversion was purchased from the college by the brewers for £150. There were many changes of innkeeper over the years; the hotel was probably not very well patronised. When the station finally closed in the 1970s, the Railway Hotel closed too. Les Beer remembers that by then 'only the locals used it; you would get about a dozen in there on a Saturday night, but the bar wasn't very big so it would seem full up.' The hotel's licence was transferred, by the owner Stanley Cave, to the Countryman nearby. The hotel is now a private house and the hotel stables and the shanty have been converted into modern bungalows.

The Countryman in the 1940s and '50s was a small cottage with rough scat walls and asbestos roof where Miss Timms and Miss Ames sold cigarettes and sweets. A larger premises was built around and over the old cottage in the 1970s and has traded since as a public house and restaurant.

The New Inn on Sampford Courtenay cross-roads dates back to the early-sixteenth century. In 1570 Robert Ellis owned the copyhold of Ninecotts, of which the inn formed a part. The Manor Court rolls in the 1790s and the King's College survey of 1809 refer to the premises as the 'Holsworthy Inn' or the 'Holdsworthy Arms', with John, followed by George, Huxtable as the tenants. However, by 1829 the court roll book referred to 'the house of George Huxtable known by the sign of the New Inn'. From the 1840s to '60s John Snell was the landlord, followed by Samuel Hill from about 1870 until the early 1900s. Both also were recorded as farmers. By 1910 the wheelwright Richard Brealey had moved from the Chapple Inn to the New Inn. When the inn was sold by King's College in 1928, Cornelius Sellers was the tenant; he was ex-Royal Navy and married to Rose Cooper, Becky Horn's sister. The business was purchased by Heavitree Brewery for £1,250 and the property included a garden (now the car park near North Town) and a linhay (now gone) adjacent to South Town. Various other tenants followed, including Thomas Curtis who was tragically shot dead in the pub in 1965 by another villager Cecil Ash (a diagnosed schizophrenic), who then turned the gun on himself and also died. Mike and Rosemary Spiers ran the New Inn during the 1980s and '90s, but trade suffered after the Okehampton bypass opened in 1987. Following Rosemary's death in 2000, Mike retired in 2001 and in 2003 the inn is run by Steve Tickner and his wife Lyn.

Mike Spiers, landlord of the New Inn, c.1990.

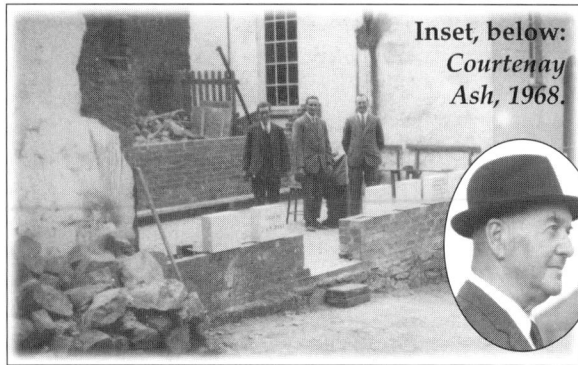

Above: *Building the Methodist chapel Sunday school, 1933.* Left to right: *Fred Reynolds, Herbert Piper, Courtenay Ash.*

Inset, below: Courtenay Ash, 1968.

Above: *William Ash & Sons workmen, 1960s.* Left to right: *Hugh Piper, Len Piper, Phil Reddaway, Bert Piper, Ray Pinwill.*

William Ash & Sons

The building business established in Sampford Courtenay by William Ash & Sons was for many years the major employer in the northern part of the parish. The origins of the enterprise can be traced back over several generations. During the first half of the nineteenth century Robert Ash and his two sons, Robert junr and William, were stonemasons in the village. They carried out most of the regular building works on the church, the church rooms, the parish bridges and, probably by this stage, on the college farms and cottages in the parish. Robert junr had moved to Sticklepath by 1851, but William remained with his father in Sampford Courtenay. In 1851 William Ash's name first appeared in the churchwardens' accounts when he repaired the font in St Andrew's Church at a cost of 3s. Robert senr died in 1869 aged 83 and Robert junr retired back to Sampford Courtenay village in around 1880 and died in 1892 aged 77. Following his father's death William took over the business; by 1871 he employed eight men including Robert junr's sons, John and Thomas.

By 1881 William's sons, Edwin aged 21 and William junr aged 18, were working with their father. His daughter Thirzena, aged 22, was soon to marry William Manuell, the young village schoolmaster. In *Kelly's Directory* of 1893 the business was described for the first time as William Ash & Sons, but by the end of that year Edwin had died unmarried. Younger son William married Elizabeth, the daughter of Samuel Hill, who was the landlord of the New Inn and farmed Yondhill. William senr died in 1905 aged 85 and William junr in 1929 aged 68. William Ash junr's eldest and third sons, Edwin and Courtenay, worked in the business; his second and fourth sons, Andrew and Cecil, became farmers. Edwin joined the Army during the First World War and on his return his father bought him into Blatchford Ash & Co Ltd. (builders and furniture retailers in Okehampton). Younger son Courtenay ran the Sampford Courtenay business for many years. The two firms, in Sampford Courtenay and Okehampton, acquired the quarry in

North Road, Okehampton, (now Fahey's) where they established a brickworks; this produced most of the red bricks in the area at the time.

William Ash & Sons built many local properties, one of the most notable being Broomford Manor in Jacobstowe, constructed by William Ash senr in 1871–73. The house was designed in the Tudor style by the architect George Devey for Colonel Sir Robert White-Thompson. William Ash junr built The Old Rectory at Honeychurch in 1895/6 followed by The Barton threshing-barn shortly afterwards. Between the wars the firm expanded and employed over 30 workmen, some from the village and some from North Tawton. Young men in the village either went to work on the farms or for William Ash & Sons. The main builder's yard was next to No.3 Shores' Cottages with another yard next to the Ash family home at Glebe House. The firm also built the new village shop and Post Office in 1925, the council-houses at Sampford Station in 1926 and at Four Acres in 1927, the Methodist chapel Sunday school in 1933 and Hazelwood at Beacon Cross (for Thomas Lang), also in the 1930s. In 1930 Courtenay built Ridgeway for himself and his wife Effie in the garden of Glebe House, using bricks from the Okehampton brick-works. It was one of the first houses in the village to have electricity and a telephone. William Ash & Sons continued to carry out maintenance work on the church and built barns and shippens in the area before steel-fabricated buildings were introduced. From the late 1930s the carpentry work was carried out at the single-storey building near Harvey's in Town, since converted into a bungalow. The firm also made all the coffins for the village.

Bert and Len Piper, following in the footsteps of father Herbert and grandfather William, worked for William Ash & Sons, as did Phil and Peter Reddaway. All his ex-employees remember Courtenay as being a good boss, although apparently he stuck to the old-fashioned ways of doing things by hand. One of his other workmen, when asked by the Inspector of Works where the cement-mixer was, answered: 'You're looking at him!' In later years the business gradually wound down. Courtenay retired in 1967 and the firm closed. Two of the former workmen, Len Piper and Peter Reddaway, both set up their own building businesses locally.

As well as running the family firm and being a director of both Okehampton Brickworks and Blatchford Ash & Co., Courtenay Ash was involved in many parish activities. He was rector's church-warden and treasurer of the Parochial Church Council from 1936 until 1986, a governor of both Sampford Courtenay and Sticklepath schools and served on the committees of the Village Hall, the flower and produce show and Britain in Bloom. In his younger days he played cricket for the village, for Exbourne and for Okehampton. During the Second World War he was an ARP warden in the village. Courtenay died in 1988 aged 86 and his funeral service at the village church was conducted by his great friend David Bickerton. In giving thanks for a truly Christian life, Revd Bickerton said: 'The end of an era has been reached: to many people Mr Ash was in effect 'Mr Sampford Courtenay'.'

Arscott & Paddon

Although threshing machines were introduced in the early-nineteenth century, the Arscotts towards the end of the century were the first recorded commercial threshing machine owners in Sampford Courtenay parish. In 1881 James Fewings Arscott was operating as a 'skam thrashing machine proprietor', living with his brother William at Lower Trecott. The threshing machinery was kept at the King's College timber yard at the bottom of Green Hill. By 1891 James Arscott had married and was living at Yondhill with his wife and two young children, three-year-old James Fewings junr and one-year-old Eva. By 1901 he had moved to the Old Forge on Rectory Hill and had had two more children, Ellen and Henry.

At first James Arscott used a stationary engine for threshing. This was steam powered using Welsh steam coal (from Gregory's in North Tawton), carried in a bunker behind the engine. The engine drove a belt which operated the threshing machine. There was also a water cart; using a pump on the engine, water was pumped from a nearby stream or well. All three items of equipment were pulled from farm to farm by horses provided by the farmer being visited. The arrangement was that each farmer acquired a supply of coal and on each trip James Arscott arrived with a full bunker and left with a full bunker. The operator of the engine had to rise early in the morning to light the fire to achieve a sufficient head of steam. The whole procedure was extremely labour-intensive. As well as the threshing of grain, clover hulling (separating clover seeds for sowing) was carried out.

By 1901 the stationary engine had been replaced by a traction-engine which travelled at two miles per hour. This engine needed more water to move between the farms and the driver had to keep stopping to fill up; finding enough water was always a major problem. James Arscott senr ran the business until about 1910 when it was taken on by his son James junr. Henry, the younger son, died in his twenties in an influenza epidemic. James junr's sister Eva married William Paddon in 1922 and the latter went into partnership with his brother-in-law. James senr, who became the first clerk to the new Parish Council in 1895, died in 1938 at the age of 87.

During the First World War farmers had to grow more grain; there was plenty of threshing to be done and the business did well, taking on additional work in South Devon. However, Arscott & Paddon was short of labour so Eva often drove the steam engine. John Morris, James Arscott senr's great-nephew, remembers hearing from William (Bungie) Jones, who was James Arscott's nephew, about the time

James Fewings Arscott senr clover hulling at Iddesleigh, c.1880s. [**Beaford Photographic Archive**]

Left: *King's College timber yard on Green Hill, c.1900. Left to right: William Lake and J. Coombe (estate carpenters), John Ward (King's College steward) and James Fewings Arscott senr.*

Second from top: *James Fewings Arscott senr reed combing, c.1900.*

Above: *Arscott & Paddon sawing timber at Iddesleigh, 1920s. Left to right: James Fewings Arscott junr, Bill Paddon, Bill Bird.*

Right: *James Fewings Arscott senr, aged 84, with Rhona Cooke and Phil Reddaway, 1934. [Western Times]*

Above: *Arscott & Paddon with travelling saw bench sawing elm timbers, 1920s.*

Right: *Arscott & Paddon, 1920s.* Left to right, on the truck: *Bill Bird, Eva Paddon, Bill Paddon, James Fewings Arscott junr;* leaning against the truck: *?.*

Right: *William (Bungie) Jones of Lower Trecott, 1960s.*

Below: *The Paddons' steam engine at Umberleigh Rally, 1966.* Left to right: *John Morris, Bill Paddon with Anthony Morris, Eva Paddon with Patrick Morris.*

when, in 1914, Bungie walked most of the way (apart from taking the train from Bovey Tracey to Newton Abbot) from Lower Trecott to Stokeinteignhead where his uncle was threshing. Unfortunately he arrived just as work had finished.

Between the wars there was an agricultural depression and Arscott & Paddon spent a lot of time sawing wood. Some was processed in the village timber yard (purchased from King's College in 1932) using the steam engine, but the firm also had a travelling saw bench and cut up felled timber at the farms. Another job was making sleepers for the Halwill–Torrington railway line. The business did well again during the Second World War but by the 1950s had contracted and was mainly involved in reed combing; the threshing machine was by then driven by a Marshall tractor. James Arscott junr never married and the Paddons had no children, so, as there was no one to take on the business, Arscott & Paddon did not venture into combine harvesters which were then being introduced. The business gradually wound down and finally folded in 1958. One of the old steam engines was kept for several years and was entered in local rallies.

Blacksmiths

The forge was once the nucleus of every rural community. The smith was both a farrier who specialised in shoeing horses and a blacksmith who worked black metal for a variety of different purposes, including the maintenance of farm machinery and vehicles and the manufacture of tools and implements. There would have been blacksmiths in Sampford Courtenay for hundreds of years, but little is known of them until the early-nineteenth century. In 1809 there were two blacksmith's shops in the village, one at Harvey's, probably run by John Heathman, and one at the Old Forge on Rectory Hill, where Simon Fewens (or Fewings) was the blacksmith. The Fewings family ran the business on Rectory Hill for many more years but it had ceased operation by the early 1880s. At some stage between 1809 and 1842, the forge at the other end of the village was moved down the hill to a site opposite Wood's Cottages; the new premises had a single storey and was built of stone. By 1841 Solon Heathman had taken over from his father John and, like his father, also farmed about 50 acres. Living with him at this time was Thomas Counter aged 20, described as an apprentice agricultural labourer. Counter must have soon turned his hand to work in the forge as by 1856 he had taken over the business from Solon Heathman, remaining the village blacksmith until his death in 1896. He had two men working for him, one of whom was his son William. Thomas Counter's friendship with Edward Theed, the son of the rector of Sampford Courtenay, was recalled some years later by Fred White:

I was with him [Theed] *once when he went to Sampford Courtenay. Tom Counter the blacksmith, who was a boy with him in Sampford Courtenay, came along, just as he was, hearing of his visit. I was made to feel that to be introduced to him was an honour and it was borne in upon me that, by hastening up from the forge in his workday, Tom Counter had paid a much greater compliment to Edward Theed than if he had changed into his Sunday best. To be sure, it was 'Tom!' on the one side and 'Sir!' on the other, but essentially it was just the meeting of a couple of firm Devonshire boy friends who, in growing up, had not grown out of their mutual affection.*

Isaac Finch, with assistant Richard Bolt, ran the forge for a short time, but in 1912 Bert Horn took over, moving with his family from Okehampton into Forge Cottage. In later years, his sons Len and Maurice helped at the forge; his son Ernie was a mason for William Ash & Sons and his daughter Doris taught at the village school. In 1929 Bert bought the forge and cottage from King's College for £250. On two days a week Bert and Len would travel to Taw Green to do shoeing work. Apart from shoeing (mostly farm horses), the Horns spent much of their time repairing agricultural implements and, during and after the Second World War, they concentrated more on this side of the business. New farm machinery was unavailable; there was more repair work, therefore, to be carried out on existing implements and second-hand items were in demand. The Horns bought in old machinery and restored it for resale. Bert Horn died in 1953 and Len and Maurice ran the business until the 1960s, although shoeing work had dwindled as tractors gradually replaced horses. Len married Joyce Ward, the daughter of John Ward the King's College steward. Joyce died in 1984 but Len, in 2003 at the age of 94, still lives in the parish.

In the early 1980s the forge was converted into a cottage with a second storey and is now called Forge House. The old tyring platforms, or bonding plates, consisting of large circular pieces of granite with holes in the centre with the tyre benders behind, are still in evidence at both the old village forges. It was on these that the iron 'tyres' were made for the wooden wagon wheels.

The Horns outside Forge Cottage, late 1920s.

LOT 7

(coloured Yellow on Plan).

A Block of Four Highly Picturesque Devon Cottages

formerly known as

"Harvey's in Town"

together with their Gardens, numbered 1731b and 1759c on Plan, situate in the centre of the Village, and containing an area of about

0 a.   3 r.   18 p.

COTTAGE (in occupation of Miss E. Brealey), let on a monthly tenancy, contains:— Living Room and 1 Bedroom, E.C.

COTTAGE AND GARDEN (in occupation of Mr. W. Mills), let on a monthly tenancy, contains:—Living Room, Kitchen, Pantry, Boxroom, 2 Bedrooms, together with E.C., Carpenter's Shop and Timber Shed.

COTTAGE AND GARDEN (in occupation of Mr. J. Stevens), let on a quarterly tenancy, contains:—Living Room, Kitchen, 3 Bedrooms, E.C., Pigstye and Linhay.

COTTAGE AND GARDEN (in occupation of Mr. S. Knight), let on a monthly tenancy, contains:—Living Room, Back Kitchen, Shoemaker's Shop, 2 Bedrooms, together with Woodshed with loft over, and Pigstye.

SCHEDULE.

No. on Plan.	Description. In Sampford Courtenay Parish.			Area A. R. P.
		...		2 8
				1 10
1731b	Four Cottages and Gardens	...	...	
1759c	Garden	...	...	**A. 3 18**

Outgoings:— Commuted Tithe Rent Charge, 4s. 0d.

As to Tenant's Fixtures, see Notes and General Remarks.

N.B.—A Right of Way is reserved to the owner of the Cottage now occupied by Mrs. Ward, as now used, across No. 1731b into No. 1730, and also the right of user by the Rector as now enjoyed.

———

LOT 8

(coloured Green on Plan).

SOLD TO TENANT

The Very Valuable Smithy

together with

Forge, Shoeing Shop, Cottage and Garden

embracing in all an area of about

0 a.   1 r.   4 p.

THE SMITHY commands nearly all of the Smith's work in the district, and contains:— Forge, Shoeing Shed with loft over, and Yard.

THE COTTAGE comprises:—Living Room, Back Kitchen with sink, Sitting Room, 3 Bedrooms.

Above: *Inside the forge, 1981.*

The forge (right), 1981.

Above left: *King's College sale catalogue, 1929 – Harvey's in Town and the smithy. Note the carpenter's and shoemaker's shops at Harvey's.*

Above right: *The New Inn, c.1990.* Left to right: *David Bourne, Rosemary Spiers and Len Horn.*

The old tyre bender, Forge House, 2000.

Wheelwrights and Carpenters

Three families operated as wheelwrights and carpenters in the village in the nineteenth century. The Heathmans (Thomas, William and John) were in business for most of the century and the Brealeys (several generations all called William, George or Richard) from the 1820s onwards and continuing into the twentieth century until the beginning of the First World War. The Wards (George, George junr and William) were in operation from about 1830 to 1880. From the 1880s until the 1920s William Ward's son John was the college carpenter and steward, operating at Carpenter's Barn near Higher Town where he lived. James Potter & Sons, during the second half of the nineteenth century, were agricultural implement makers, wheelwrights and machinists at Sampford Chapple. George Chastey was a wheelwright and carpenter at Tongue End from the 1870s until the 1890s. By 1891 William Mills, aged 20,

was apprenticed to George Brealey his grandfather and Richard his uncle. When Richard died in 1916, William ran the business until the 1930s (possibly until his death in 1938). He was the last wheelwright in Sampford Courtenay. The sites of the wheelwright's/carpenter's shops are unclear. The one at Sampford Chapple was probably at Dartmoor View, where a workshop was recorded in the King's College survey of 1809. It is possible that both the Heathmans and the Brealeys used the Harvey's in Town workshop. William Mills is remembered as living in No.2 Part Harveys and using this workshop in the 1920s and '30s. It was subsequently taken over by William Ash & Sons for their carpentry work and is now a bungalow called The Barn. However, the Brealeys were in operation at the same time as the Heathmans for most of the nineteenth century and initially may have been operating from a workshop behind the Alberries cottages.

Carpenter's Barn, 1994.

Above: *North Town and South Town, looking south, c.1900. Note the farm wagon on the right.*

Right: *Carpenter's Barn, 1975.*

The carpenter's shop (now 'The Barn'), 1985.

The carpenter's shop, 1981.

Rectory Hill with old Post Office on the right, c.1907. The ladies in the background are Mrs Rebecca Cooper and Mrs Stone; the two girls outside the Post Office are the Reddaway sisters. [Beaford Photographic Archive]

The Village Shop and Post Office

... in his zeal for trade,
He has his shop an ark for all things made;
And there, in spite of his all guarding eye,
His sundry wares in strange confusion lie
Delightful token of the haste that keeps
Those mingled matters in their shapeless heaps.
From 'Barnaby the Shopman' by George Crabbe, 1834.

During the first half of the nineteenth century Isaac, followed by John, Yeo kept a shop on Rectory Hill in a block of cottages (now gone) between the Old Forge and Fairview. In 1852 John Yeo's shop took on the role of Post Office. During the seventeenth and eighteenth centuries letters from Sampford Courtenay would have been taken privately or by the local goods carrier to Crediton or Exeter to be put into the general postal system. A letter dated 27 October 1715 is known to have been dispatched from the village via Exeter to Chudleigh. From around 1810 to 1856 letters would have been taken to North Tawton to pick up the provincial penny post service to Crediton or direct to Crediton to enter the general post service. Initially letters were charged by weight and distance but in 1840 Parliament introduced the standard penny post, which enabled the poor to communicate with loved ones from whom they were separated. From Post Office records it would seem that Sampford Courtenay was issued with its first postmark hand stamp in June 1852. A sub-office opened at Sampford Courtenay Railway Station in the early 1880s.

John Yeo was the sub-postmaster until his death in 1877; Mary Ann his widow then took over, followed by Robert and Mary Fewings. The Post Office remained on Rectory Hill with Robert ('Buck') Fewings in charge until 1910. Eva Paddon (née Arscott), who lived next door in the Old Forge, worked at the Post Office as a young woman and served the first old-age pension in Sampford Courtenay in 1908. (The Old Age Pensions Act provided between 1s. and 5s. a week to people over 70 on incomes not over 12s.) In 1910 Herbert Ash took over the village shop and Post Office, probably from that date operating from Langford Cottage opposite Glebe House. The block of cottages on Rectory Hill incorporating the old Post Office must have disappeared shortly after this time.

Herbert Ash was born in Sampford Courtenay on 29 December 1880 and lived with his mother and grandparents in the village. After leaving the village school, he trained as a stonemason with his uncle, William Ash senr, and cousin, William junr. His early life was somewhat problematic, as described in 1897 by Revd Thomas Little in a letter to Charles Grant, the bursar of King's College:

I am writing to you about a house in the village – of which until lately Mrs Robert Ash who died some months ago, was the tenant. You probably know that she

111

Above: *Fund-raising for the local Conservative Association, 1950s. Left to right: Herbert Ash, Gwen Watts, Percy Smythe-Osborne, Jim Searle, Mary Cleverdon, Clara Weeks, Ada Ash.*

Right: *King's College sale catalogue, 1929 – the village shop and Post Office.*

SCHEDULE.

No. on Plan.	Description. In Sampford Courtenay Parish.				A.	Area R.	P.
1725d	Cottage and Garden	...	...	...			10
1759a	Smithy and Yard	...	...	...			13
1759h	Garden	...	...	...			21
					A.	1	4

No. 1759h of this Lot is let to Mr. S. Northam on a quarterly tenancy. The remainder is let to Mr. B. G. Horn on a quarterly tenancy.

Outgoings:—
Commuted Tithe Rent Charge, 6d.

As to Tenant's Fixtures, see Notes and General Remarks.

N.B.—A Right of Way is reserved, as now used, over the Yard, No. 1759a of this Lot, to the back premises of Lot 9.

LOT 9
(coloured Pink on Plan)

The Village Shop and Post Office
together with
Private House and Garden

Numbered Pt. 1759b on Plan, and situate in the centre of Sampford Courtenay Village.

THE SHOP, recently and substantially built, has a large Store Room over. Adjoining the Shop is the House, which comprises:—Hall; Kitchen; Back Kitchen; 3 Bedrooms. There is a leanto Shed in the Yard, also a Pigsty and Oil House.

The area of the whole comprises about

0 a.   0 r.   27 p.

This Lot is let to Mr. H. Ash on a Quarterly tenancy.

Outgoings:—
Commuted Tithe-Rent Charge, 9d.

As to Tenant's Fixtures, see Notes and General Remarks.

With this Lot is sold a Right of Way over the Yard of the Smithy adjoining as at present enjoyed.

The village shop and Post Office, 1990s.

The village shop and Post Office with Herbert Ash in the doorway, late 1920s.

has a most unsatisfactory daughter [Eliza] unmarried with four illegitimate children, varying in ages from sixteen to two. She is at present the occupier of the house; but this is a very unfitting state of things... she is... quite untrustworthy as a householder in all respects. A week or two ago she broke open her eldest boy's money-box and took out his quarter's wages which had just been paid and spent it in a preposterous manner.

The Ashs tell me that the woman has no money except the burial money received for her mother which is fast disappearing and there will be nothing for her but the workhouse. But plainly it is to the interest of the Parish that her term here as a free woman should be as short as possible: on the other hand, while she has a house over her head, she cannot be taken to the Union. Could you investigate what security you have for your Lady Day rent and act accordingly if you find there is none.

Aerial view of the village from the church tower, late 1970s. Note the village shop with the forge behind it.

Eliza Ash's 'eldest boy' was Herbert. By 1901 he was living with his Uncle William at Glebe and his brother Hedley was working for William Lang at The Barton. Eliza and her two younger children had left the parish. An Eliza Ash was working in Okehampton as a domestic servant in 1901; this was probably Herbert's mother. By 1910 Herbert had married, given up masonry work and had taken on the vacant position of sub-postmaster.

Herbert was to keep the village shop and Post Office for many years. The Post Office opening hours in 1910 were 8.00a.m. to 7.30p.m. on weekdays (a long day for the postmaster) and 9.00a.m. to 10.00a.m. on Sundays. There were numerous requests by the Parish Council to the Post Office authorities for telegraph facilities in the village from 1909 onwards; they were not met until some stage during the First World War. In 1924 the council wrote to Rawlence & Squarey asking if the college would kindly supply the Post Office with better accommodation and by October 1925 a new building (the present Post Office) had been provided. Mary Cleverdon remembers the grand opening ceremony with dancing to a band from North Tawton. Interestingly, there are plans in the college archives, drawn up in 1887, for a much larger two-storey building (including a shop) on the site. For some reason, the college never went ahead with this project, opting for a much more modest building in 1925. In 1929 Herbert Ash bought the shop and adjacent cottage from King's College for £500.

Herbert's shop, which included an upstairs storeroom, stocked everything. There was such a vast amount of merchandise, in jars, sacks and boxes cluttering almost every square inch of floor surface, it was extremely difficult to enter the shop; this was only possible down a very narrow aisle in the centre. Herbert sold all the usual grocery and greengrocery items plus a wide variety of other goods, including cigarettes and tobacco, bootlaces, soap, hardware, cartridges, paraffin and there was even a small library. It was a wonder he could find anything. Irene Sampson remembers going to the shop in the 1920s or '30s and there appeared to be nobody there. She called out: 'Is anybody here?' and a voice answered: 'Yes I'm here!' and Irene spotted him. He had clambered up over some sacks and was bending over them with just his feet protruding. The abundance of comestibles obviously attracted the odd rodent or two and several of Herbert's former customers recall hearing scurrying sounds amongst the boxes. Herbert would cough discreetly to hide the noise.

Until the 1950s, the post was delivered from Sampford Courtenay Post Office on foot partly via the old green lanes and footpaths. Bert Coates remembered Herbert delivering some of the letters before he opened the shop each morning. John Reddaway recalls hearing that Samuel Knight the shoemaker

did the Honeychurch post round in the 1920s, both delivering and collecting and blowing a whistle to let everyone know when he was emptying the box. The original Victorian postbox still survives in Honeychurch. During the Second World War John Reddaway himself helped with postal deliveries before going to work in North Tawton. In later years two of Herbert's sons, Noel and Rodney, assisted their father with the business, Rodney doing the post round. Herbert ran the shop until he was in his seventies. He retired in the 1950s, but died soon afterwards. After he retired, the post was collected and delivered by van from Okehampton.

Numerous other couples ran the shop and Post Office over the next 30 years, including the Drabbles, Pipers, Talbots, Normans, Sims and Peels. However, in the 1970s an International supermarket opened in Okehampton and takings immediately went down. Subsequent owners tried to make a go of it, the last being Stan and Denise Stimson who bought the business in 1985. For about a year they experimented with various ideas without success and, although they still operate the Post Office, they also now run an estate agents from one part of the premises and let the other part as an office for Lamisell Ltd, who are involved in the manufacture, design and sale of laminated timber building frames and structures.

Tailors

William Parsons the village tailor, 1933.

Although many items of clothing would have been made in the home, tailors are known to have existed in Sampford Courtenay as far back as the early-seventeenth century. The Heathmans ran a tailoring business in part of Church House during most of that century. From 1677 until 1841 parish records contained many references to several generations of John Palmer who were tailors in the village, the last of whom was the father of Ann Palmer, whose story appears in Chapter Eleven. In later years the Palmers lived at Higher Mount Ivy, a cottage (now gone) just north of Cricket Farm. Items made included breeches, waistcoats, frock-coats, and women's gowns. Richard Saul was a Sampford Courtenay tailor in the second half of the eighteenth century. By 1841 John Palmer at Mount Ivy, who was by then 75, had a young apprentice, George Avery aged 17. Over the next three decades Thomas Fewings, James Babbage, John Yeo, George Avery and George Dimond were all recorded as tailors in the village. Thomas Fewings, followed by James Babbage, possibly worked from Green Cottage, then called Palmer's Cottage. John Yeo, who also ran the Post Office, was on Rectory Hill; the tailor's shop was probably at Fairview. By the late 1870s it would appear that George Avery had taken over the business from John Yeo at Fairview. George Dimond was also still listed as a tailor, but by 1883 George Avery was the only tailor in the village.

By the early 1890s William Beer Parsons, aged 30, was running the tailor's shop at Fairview. He was still recorded as the village tailor in 1939, but he died in 1943 aged 79. William Parsons, or 'Billy Snip' as he was known, moved to Sampford Courtenay from Bristol. In his youth a fall from a horse left him badly crippled. Several parishioners remember him sitting on a table, which was situated in his cottage window, to do his tailoring work. From this vantage point, he could watch the world go by and, being the secretary of the local branch of the Foresters' Friendly Society, keep an eye open for members going about their business when they were claiming sick benefit and should have been at home. William married Maria, George Avery's daughter. The couple were Methodists and Irene Sampson remembers Maria as a very happy person, who was always smiling. She would sit on a front seat in the chapel and the preachers used to say what an inspiration she was. 'Billy Snip' was the last of the Sampford Courtenay tailors.

Over the years there were many dressmakers recorded in the parish, mostly single young women. In 1881 there were seven such, one of whom, Mary Coombe, lived at Martinmas with her sister Elizabeth and Uncle Henry who was a butcher. Becky Horn could remember a 'penny shop' here, where haberdashery items were sold, probably run by this family.

Boot- and Shoemakers

Until the 1920s and '30s everyone, including small children, wore laced boots. Country people walked everywhere and the parish lanes had not as yet been tarred. Boots were 'cuted', i.e. reinforced with steel around the toes and heels, to make them more durable, particularly for farm work. In the 1851 census returns, Thomas Brook at Shores', William Reid on Rectory Hill, Thomas Piper at Alberries and John Bowden at Sampford Chapple were all recorded as shoemakers. By the late 1870s there were three shoemakers – John Bowden, George Brook at Plumtree (now Brook) Cottage and Samuel Knight. In 1893 *Kelly's Directory* listed just George Brook and Samuel Knight and by 1901 Samuel Knight was the only boot- and shoemaker in Sampford Courtenay.

Samuel Knight was in business for many years, from the 1870s until he died aged 82 in 1933. He was also for many years the clerk for the parish church. The shoemaker's shop was in No.1 Part Harveys and several people remember him there. Samuel Knight's young grandson, Harold Cornelius, spent much of his childhood with his grandfather and in 1923, aged 14, joined the business, taking over the shop when

Samuel died. Harold continued in Sampford Courtenay for a short time, marrying village school teacher Marjorie Kelland, but in 1936 closed the shop and moved to a premises on Fore Street in North Tawton. John Reddaway from Fir Cottage, then aged 16, went to work for him for 6s.6d. a week. The two men worked together for over 38 years until Harold's retirement in 1974.

Sampford Courtenay Station Abattoir

An abattoir was established in the station yard at Sampford Courtenay by the London & South Western Railway, probably at the end of the nineteenth century, and was run by John Easterbrook. Local farmers drove animals along the roads to be slaughtered there, many of the carcasses going off by train to Smithfield market. In about 1920 Will Knight took over the business, but during the 1940s, because of new wartime regulations, the abattoir closed and never reopened.

Other Village Trades

Robert, followed by John, Folland were stonemasons in the village from the 1820s until the 1880s. There were probably thatchers in Sampford Courtenay for many years; those in the nineteenth century included Richard and Simon Stoat in the 1850s and William Heathman in the 1840s, followed by his son Thomas from the 1850s until the '70s. Jonathon Jones in the 1880s and '90s was the last thatcher resident in the village.

Two members of the Sanders family were variously described as veterinary surgeons, cattle doctors or farriers, firstly William in the 1850s followed by Henry Finning Sanders from the 1860s until his death in 1903.

There was a butcher's shop at the bottom of Rectory Hill at the end of the eighteenth century. John Hammett, at Alberries, was listed as a butcher in the 1850s and Henry Coombe at Martinmas (then known as Longfield or Shores') in the 1880s. Henry Coombe had moved to Sampford Chapple by 1901.

In the late-nineteenth and early-twentieth centuries, John Stentiford, possibly operating on Rectory Hill, was variously described as a fellmonger (dealer in hides) or a whip and thong maker. There are thought to have been general or grocer's shops during the same period at Little Hilly and Green Cottages; these were run by John and Mary Reddaway and Mary Ann Reed. Samuel Northam (just before and possibly during the First World War) was the last shopkeeper in the village apart from Herbert Ash.

For a short period a café, petrol pumps and adjoining bungalow existed near Sampford Station at Moorcroft Caravan Park. Sampford Bridge Tea

Sampford Bridge Tea House, 1960s.

House was built in about 1960 by Mr and Mrs Carr and groceries and other items were also sold from the premises. There were several subsequent owners but, after the bypass opened in 1987, trade deteriorated and the café closed. In the early 1990s the café and bungalow were demolished and The Beeches complex of bungalows erected on the site of the park. Another caravan park at Culverhayes closed in recent years. Culverhayes was run as a residential home for the elderly during the 1980s and '90s. In 2003 approval was granted for the building of a conference centre in the grounds of the property. Following the closure of William Ash & Sons in 1967, Len Piper, subsequently assisted by his sons David and Adrian, ran a building business firstly from the village and then from Sampford Chapple. His work in the parish included the conversion of old buildings at Southey and Forge House and the construction of Lendor House. From 1989 he gradually wound down and he retired in 1995.

Working farms and farm-related enterprises excepted, there are now few trades based in the parish. Apart from the Post Office and Lamisell mentioned previously, Marshall Joinery at Sampford Station and Clayton Cabinets at Langdale both make furniture, R.L. Taylor Ltd are hauliers based at Station Farm and Peter Reddaway and Mark Hedges are builders.

Chapter Eight

THE ROADS, RAILWAY AND OTHER PUBLIC SERVICES

The Roads

Ye winding lanes of Devon, how I love ye all the year!
How many a joy your wild flowers bring,
how many a memory dear!
And though, like life, you're sometimes dark,
with uphill roads and rough,
You've breaks to let the sunshine in, and pathways smooth enough.
From 'Devonshire Lanes' – *Sighs, Smiles and Sketches*
by J.G. Maxwell, 1860.

By the middle of the fourteenth century, the immense network of roads in Devon was already in existence. The devious course of many roadways and tracks often may have been due to a short-term policy of expediency. Old paths hugged hedgerows leading approximately in the right direction and avoided trampling crops or opposition from local landlords who did not want more direct routes crossing their fields. Until Tudor times, the maintenance of the local roads devolved upon the landowners or the manor. Under Elizabeth I, however, responsibility was transferred to the parishes, from which gradually evolved the present arrangements. All roads until the end of the eighteenth century were hazardous – strewn with boulders, fallen trees, mud and deep potholes. Few travellers from outside the county wished to repeat their first experience of Devon lanes. Most goods traffic went by packhorse until after 1800, with the heaviest loads being dragged on a type of sled by horses or oxen. The first passenger service from London to Exeter at the end of the seventeenth century took about four days but by the end of the eighteenth century this had been cut to 32 hours. The 'Quicksilver' in 1835 managed the journey in 16½ hours. The improvement was achieved because of better-surfaced roads, better-designed coaches and rapid and frequent changes of horses. The journey, however, must have been decidedly uncomfortable. Local services linked with Exeter from most of the other towns in Devon.

The introduction of turnpike trusts helped the situation; the Okehampton Trust began in 1760. A turnpike was originally the gated entrance of a walled town where the way through was of sufficient width for the sentry to 'turn his pike' horizontally to halt and carefully scrutinise visitors. A group of trustees, usually local businessmen, raised the money to improve the road; this was recouped by the imposition of tolls and the payment by any parish through which the road passed of a 'composition' sum as a contribution to expenses. A turnpike road passed through Sampford Courtenay parish from Okehampton to the White Hart at Bow. Two of the old Okehampton turnpike gates are still in existence, one at Reddaway Farm and one at Webber Hill. The Okehampton Trust also converted an old track through Sticklepath known as the 'Black Road' into a turnpike road in about 1770. Although little used at first, this became the main western thoroughfare (the old A30) until the 1980s.

In 1555 the Highways Act required that a surveyor of the highways, or waywarden, should be appointed by warrant in each parish at Easter. The office was unpaid and filled by rotation. The surveyor's duties included inspecting the roads at least three times a year and organising the statute labour. Each able-bodied householder or tenant was obliged to provide four days' labour a year (from 1691 this became six), to provide a substitute or pay a fine. Other parishioners were required to supply carts and horses to assist with road repairs. Highway rates imposed on property owners were introduced at the end of the seventeenth century. The parish waywarden remained in charge of local highways until the General Highway Act of 1835. The Justices were supposed to supervise the system, but generally did not become involved and the condition of the roads became worse every year. Occasionally, however, defaulting parishes were indicted or presented and ordered to improve their roads, and there were several occasions when this happened in Sampford Courtenay and Honeychurch. At Honeychurch:

1765 Paid for taking of two presentments from the hayways whene p'sented by Esquire Buller £5.10s.8d.

Paid the expences for two Justices to vew the rodes and respite and jorney to Exon the Counsellor and journeys fee £2.16s.6d.

Allowing the parish roads to fall into disrepair was obviously an expensive burden for Honeychurch. In the earlier part of the eighteenth century, Honeychurch paid 'Bridge Money' to the hundred constable, but this was incorporated within county rates paid from 1740 onwards. Apart from the purchase of warrants and other legal expenses, Honeychurch records contain no other references to work on the roads; presumably labour and materials were provided locally.

With Sampford Courtenay being such a large parish, two waywardens were appointed, one to cover the north 'side' and one the south 'side', and these changed each year. In the early years Sampford Courtenay spent very little on maintenance of the roads; the total disbursements for 1768/9 were £1.19s.1½d. At first funds were raised with the poor rate but from 1771/2 the parish was imposing a separate highways rate and the expenditure was recorded in a waywardens' accounts book. Initial costs mostly covered maintenance of the parish picks, purchasing furze and stones for the road surfaces and repairing various bridges in the parish:

1700 Pd towards the repairinge of Jacopstow bridge and Bundleigh bridge 14s.4d.

1762 Wm Langmead for mending and righting of the parish picks 8s.2d.

1768 Pd for stones and furze about the highway at Chessicott Wood Gate 10s.9d.

1770/1 Pd for 24 seams of stons at 2d. pr seam for mending the Town bridge 4s.0d.

Pd for ale for the workmen 4d.

1771/2 Pd Josef Denaford for breaking his ground to have stons to round the roads 7s.0d.

The last entry referred to extraction of stone from Frankland Quarry; Joseph Dennaford was the tenant of Frankland at this time. Other sources of stone were Beerhill, Solland, Beer, Agistment and Appledore in Sampford Courtenay, and Frankland Hill and a site near Slade in Honeychurch. Stone cracking was one of the poorest-paid jobs and very often was carried out by old men or by those on parish relief. Even by 1840 the day labourers on the local roads were only paid between 8d. and 1s.2d. per day.

Peckets Ford Bridge near East Rowden must have had heavy traffic, no doubt due to the frequent delivery of corn to the manor mills, for its maintenance featured on numerous occasions: '1698 Pd Symon Ffewins for walling up the claper to Pecketsford with staks and binders 8s.0d.'

In 1704 a new bridge was built at a cost of £5.9s.2d.; materials included 'attree for the claper, 20 ffoot of timber ffor realles and 10 iron spookes.' Later in the century an indictment had been imposed on the parish in respect of Peckets Ford:

1777/8 For making the wear at Pecketsford £15.0s.0d.

For respiting the indictment on Pecketsford twice £1.11s.6d.

For taking of the indictment, drawing brieffs and counsels ffees £5.15s.6d.

For three journeys at Exeter 7s.6d.

Above: *View of St Andrew's Church from Weirford Lane, 1950s.*

Peckets Ford Bridge, 2002.

The total cost of £23.14s.6d. represented about two-thirds of the parish expenses for the year. Subsequent years saw continued expenditure in connection with the maintenance of the bridge and weir. In 1783 the local Justices, who each year examined and verified the waywardens' accounts, made the comment:

It is not at all surprising to the justices that you have so many indictments on your parish as the small sum of money laid out on your parish fully explains the cause.

The annual expenditure at that time averaged around £30 to £35. The following year saw a sharp increase to a total expenditure of £79 and many of the parish roads saw significant improvement. However, there appeared to be three indictments on the parish plus some disagreement with the Okehampton Turnpike Trust and the legal costs that year were considerable, the parishioners footing the bill in their rates. In 1785, at a total cost of £33.15s.7½d., a new more substantial bridge was built at Peckets Ford. The bridge being situated on the boundary between Sampford Courtenay and South Tawton parishes, Articles of Agreement were drawn up by the two sets of waywardens, in which the two parishes agreed to maintain the bridge at their joint expense. Thereafter the bridge, which is still in use in 2003 and carries a roadway only 8½ feet wide, caused little trouble.

The parish paid an annual sum, initially £4 and subsequently £10 per year, to the Okehampton Turnpike Trust. However, by 1798 considerable amounts of money were being paid (raised from the local rates and from a loan of £100 at interest) to repair the Trust road; it would appear that this was relative to an indictment. By 1812 the Trust owed Sampford Courtenay parish nearly £300, which was eventually repaid in instalments. By this time the annual expenditure on the parish roads had risen to between £75 and £100; the roads maintained included some that are now green lanes, such as Weirford Lane, Shoalgate Cross to Ratcombe and Piecegate to Cliston hamlet. The majority of the roads were by now repaired on a contract basis; between 1813 and 1819, Thomas Fewings & Co. appeared to acquire most of these contracts.

The parish was responsible for fencing any quarry workings and compensation for 'damages and trespass' was paid to the relative landowners:

1802/3 *To Mr Legg and John Dayment to damages for quarries one year* [Beerhill and Frankland] *10s.8d.*
1816/7 *To fencing Frankland Quarry including plants and labour 19s.0d.*
1819/20 *To John Dayment in recompence for damage done to his horse by falling in the quarry in consequence of the same not being properly fenced out £1.0s.0d.*
To plants for fencing out Frankland Quarry £1.10s.6d.

Perhaps this was not enough compensation or there was another similar incident:

1823/4 *To John Dayment recompence for damage done to his horse by falling into the quarry £3.0s.0d.*
To Joseph Cockram for ten seams of plants for fencing Frankland Quarry £2.0s.0d.
To a summons and expenses relative to John Dayment's horse 9s.0d.

The old footbridge at the New Inn.
[Beaford Photographic Archive]

Between 1815 and 1825 the annual expenditure on the parish roads varied between £200 and £300, although it fell to an average of about £180 in the nine years to 1834. In 1823/4 a new road bridge was constructed at 'Brook Water commonly called Stock Bridge' at a cost of £54.17s.6d. Over the years there was much timber work repairing the parish footbridges, including 'Town Bridge' and 'Frankland Ford'. (It was not until 1873 that a road bridge was built at Frankland Ford.) In spite of all the additional work and expense, Sampford Courtenay managed to acquire a further indictment in 1830/1, this time on Fullaford Moor Road; the cost of legal advice alone for this was £16.3s.6d.

In the early part of the nineteenth century, two of the heaviest burdens the parish had to bear were caused by the condition of the roads and the large increase in the numbers of unemployed and mostly unemployable poor. It was thought sensible to try to make the two problems solve one another by employing pauper labour on the roads. Between 1822 and 1827, entries appeared in the Sampford Courtenay overseers of the poor books for 'Order Men', two teams being employed, one on the north 'side' and one on the south. The rates paid were extremely low, varying from 1d. to 1s. per day, but mostly 4d. or 6d. Generally this scheme failed to work. According to the Webbs in *The Story of the King's Highway*: 'The dissolute idleness of the little groups of able-bodied paupers on the roads became notorious.'

By various Acts between 1832 and 1894, parochial autonomy on the roads was destroyed. Sampford Courtenay waywardens' books from the 1840s survive; they recorded work by day labourers at local quarries, contract work on the roads, charges by local landowners for horse-and-cart hire and rent of pits and quarries. The development of railways in the 1870s caused a widespread decline in road use and the turnpike trusts were eventually driven out of business. In 1888 the upkeep of the 'disturnpiked' or 'main' roads was transferred to the county councils. The Local Government Act of 1894 finally removed all remaining parish authority to the new district councils.

New Inn Bridge

It was a long time before anything was done to construct a road bridge over the stream near the New Inn. By 1900 the Parish Council was calling the attention of Okehampton District Council to the 'unsafe condition of the two foot bridges' and in 1908 Robert Hawkins proposed, and Charles Bolt seconded, 'that it would be of great advantage to the public to have a bridge over the water on the main road to North Tawton.' Unfortunately the cost of a bridge appeared to pose something of a quandary; the Parish Council felt the expense should be borne by the County Council, as an improvement would benefit the neighbourhood rather than the parish, but the County Council obviously thought otherwise.

Above and below: Building the new road bridge at the New Inn, 1931.

Several more requests were made, but were unsuccessful until 1929. An article in the *Western Morning News* of 5 May 1931 recorded that at last the bridge was being constructed. However, it seemed to be a no-win situation for the Parish Council as the article was headed: 'Scheme villagers dislike: Sampford Courtenay beauty spot spoilt.' The 'massive white bridge' was considered far too large for so small a place and it was felt that it would destroy the village's 'quiet rusticity'. It was claimed that the stream had not posed much of a problem except to 'people pushing perambulators, who were obliged to walk through the stream because of the insufficient width of the footbridge.' Apparently, the stream did sometimes flood; in 1872 the water had lapped the top steps leading to the New Inn and lifted barrels out of the cellar. One resident commented: 'They have perfectly ruined the whole of the most picturesque part of the village. The general feeling here is wrath at the waste of money.' The stone for building the bridge was extracted from Honeychurch Quarry.

Road Travel

Various carriers and coach services operated in the parish during the nineteenth century; initially these passed through Sticklepath, but by the 1880s a carrier was operating daily from Hatherleigh to North Tawton (presumably passing through Sampford Courtenay village) and another from Hatherleigh to Exeter on Thursdays returning Saturdays. From the 1880s Coles

Below: *Glebe House, c.1920. Note the two different modes of transport – horse and rider in the background and Cecil Ash's motorcycle in the foreground.* [Beaford Photographic Archive]

Above: *John E. and Hannah Hawkins with pony and trap, 1919.*

Left: *John E. Hawkins of Solland with a new Chevrolet, 1922.*

Below: *Mary and John Reddaway and their relatives from London with motor bike and side-car outside Fir Cottage, 1930s.*

Sampford Chapple crossroads, early 1930s. The two cottages in the right foreground were demolished, c.1955, to improve road visibility. In the 1920s the privy belonging to the right-hand cottage was in the garden opposite, to the left of the picture.

Left: *Sampford Courtenay crossroads, 1930s. Note that the New Inn linhay* (behind the signpost) *has a galvanised roof.*

omnibus ran from Sticklepath to Okehampton on Saturdays. By the 1920s all the carrier services had ceased but Devon Motor Transport Co. Ltd were operating regular omnibuses from Okehampton to Exeter through Sticklepath. By the 1940s a Southern National bus was running from North Devon through Exbourne to Okehampton, but a request by the Parish Council for a diversion through Sampford Chapple was turned down. During and after the Second World War there was one bus each week to Exeter on Fridays. Bus services through Sampford Courtenay village improved in the 1950s. At the time of writing, apart from school buses, several 'Devon Bus' services (with financial support from Devon County Council) operate from the village. From Monday to Saturday, there are seven buses a day to North Tawton, eight to Okehampton and four to Exeter.

Richard Pyke recalled the state of the parish lanes at the end of the nineteenth century:

They were covered with sharp stones, which were slowly worn in by the hoofs of horses or the iron bands of the cartwheel. When the bicycle was introduced, the rider had to thread his way along the narrow cart track... Pneumatic tyres were useless. It was an adventurous ride and when both bicycle and rider were pitchforked into a gutter there was little pity for him... A Devonshire lane sounds poetical: but in those days it was a path with deep ruts and abundant mud.

In November 1907 the rector, William Surtees, wrote to the bursar of King's College: 'The countryside is in a delightful state of mud. I went to Langbeer to see Will Newcombe and I think the mud there was quite record breaking.'

The Parish Council minutes in the 1920s mentioned the bad state of many of the parish roads, some of which were almost impassable for cars, and it was suggested that the stone from Honeychurch Quarry should not be used as it was too soft and soon turned to mud. Several parishioners remember when local men looked after the parish lanes in the 1920s and '30s. A supply of stone from the quarry was kept on the verge between Fir Cottage and Bank Cottage. There were requests to the District Council in 1930 and 1931 to tar the Sampford Courtenay roads, but this did not take place until later in the 1930s. Unfortunately there were several subsequent references to the continuing unsatisfactory state of the highways. Following a complaint to the District Council in 1950, the Divisional Surveyor said that all available money had been spent on road repair in Sampford Courtenay – a familiar excuse!

Until well into the twentieth century many of the inhabitants of Sampford Courtenay never ventured very far outside the parish. Richard Pyke recollected:

It was an event in my life one day when he [the village schoolmaster] asked us in turn how far we had ever gone from home. One after another could claim to have travelled as far as Okehampton, a journey of five miles. I was eager for my turn to come, and was proud to claim that I had been all the way to Bridestowe, four miles farther. 'A great traveller!' was his unsatisfactory comment.

There was little change until after the Second World War, although bicycles were much used for local journeys. Distance travel was accomplished by train from Sampford Courtenay Station. Bert Coates remembered that when he came to The Barton in 1936, there were only five cars in the village; today almost every household has at least one vehicle.

The New A30

The possibility of a bypass for Sticklepath, as a result of increased traffic and the relative danger to pedestrians, was first brought up in 1958 and in 1962 a petition was sent to the Ministry of Transport. The reply was that such a scheme would be of substantial cost and unlikely to be put in hand for some years to come. By the 1970s, the two other main roads through the parish – the B3215 and the A3072 – were being used in the summer months as alternative holiday routes instead of the A30 through Sticklepath. Traffic on the A3072 through Sampford Courtenay was so congested and it became so difficult to emerge from side roads that in 1985 Devon County Council suggested a one-way system through the village, but thankfully this was never implemented. However, by the 1980s there was more positive progress on the provision of a bypass across the south of the parish. The new dual carriageway (now the A30), running north of Sticklepath and south of Reddaway and Willey, was opened in 1987. Sticklepath was effectively cut off by the road from the rest of the parish and it separated from Sampford Courtenay and formed its own parish in May 1987. The traffic on the other two main roads has since lessened, although Rectory Hill, due to its narrowness and poor visibility, has proved to be a continuing problem which has, to this day, not been satisfactorily resolved. There have been several accidents on the hill and buildings have been struck by vehicles. A variety of possible solutions has been suggested and some have been implemented. The present arrangements of a mini-roundabout on the crossroads and 30mph speed restrictions with warning lights have partially alleviated the problem. Unfortunately, Sampford Courtenay crossroads, due to the various road-widening schemes over the years and the loss of some of the cottages there, has lost much of its previous charm.

The Railway

The London & South Western Railway Company reached Sampford Courtenay in 1867. The station, which opened on 8 January, was initially called Okehampton Road and for almost five years, until the railway progressed to Okehampton, was the busiest on the line from Exeter. There were six trains each day and passengers and goods completed their journey to Okehampton by horse and wagon. Contemporary accounts of the passenger 'bus' described it as 'an old and dilapidated wagonette'. After Okehampton Station opened in October 1871, Okehampton Road was renamed Belstone Corner and less than three months later it became Sampford Courtenay. The station buildings on the up side, compared to the imposing structures at North Tawton and Bow, were rather modest and comprised a booking-hall and office, a waiting-room, porters' room and toilets. There was also a small waiting-shelter on the down platform but, to get to it, passengers had to cross the road bridge or the railway track near the signal-box. A stationmaster's house and six cottages for railway employees were provided by the railway company. The water-supply for the station and cottages was from a well. Electricity was never connected to the station; oil-lamps were used until it closed and even the signals (arm type) were operated with oil-lamps. With Okehampton open, Sampford Courtenay Station became less used and for much of its life thereafter was one of the least busy stations on the line. In 1930 the number of tickets issued was 2,689 with 3,243 collected, about a quarter of those at North Tawton. When the railway line was constructed in the 1860s, the section of track from Sampford Courtenay to Okehampton involved much heavy construction work with rock being blasted from the deep cuttings and used to build the embankments. In 1878 the line was doubled between North Tawton and Sampford Courtenay and between Sampford Courtenay and Meldon in 1879. A short distance west of Fullaford Bridge in Sampford Courtenay parish there is evidence of the start of a line to Bude via Hatherleigh. This was never continued and eventually a link with Bude was made from Okehampton via Halwill Junction.

William Gallop was the first stationmaster, but by 1923 the station was run from North Tawton with the duties being carried out by two porter-signalmen. There was a small goods shed (with a two-ton crane) in the station yard as well as an abattoir. These were both LSWR wooden structures. The latter provided much of the traffic leaving the station. West Devon Farmers and Murrins of Monkokehampton, both grain merchants, had depots there. John Reddaway remembers Murrins making two trips a day from Monkokehampton to the station by horse and wagon. Rectory Hill was too steep for the horses and the wagons had to pass through Sampford Courtenay village past the school. Animals for Exeter market (including ponies) were loaded onto the train. In the 1930s J.I. Reddaway, in order to catch the early train in the

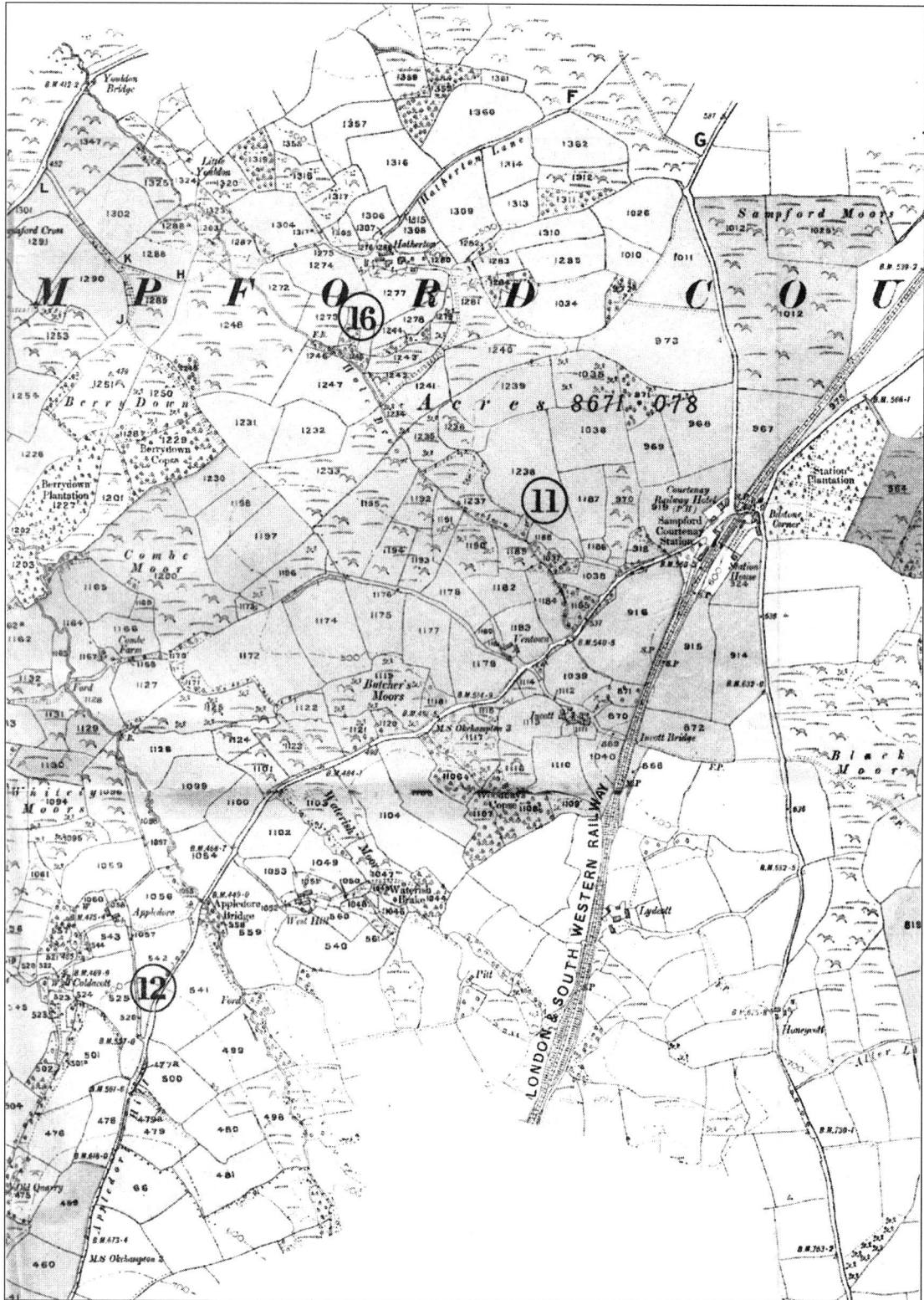

*Map showing the route of the London & South Western Railway
and Sampford Courtenay Station, 1928.*

wintertime, would drive cattle along the road from Reddaway in the dark using lanterns. Round and sawn timber and churns of milk were also forwarded from the station. Les Beer, who has lived nearby for most of his life, remembers crates of rabbits (20 or 30 per crate) and barrels of blackberries (for jam) being dispatched. Some local children used the train to go to school in Okehampton. Les' father Robert was a ganger on the railway and was based at Sampford Courtenay from just after the First World War until he retired in the 1960s. He was in charge of a gang of men who looked after the Sampford Courtenay section of the track. Les remembers walking along the line with his mother during the snow of 1947 to take food to his father who was working to clear the track.

British Railways came into existence in 1948 and the line from Exeter westwards was part of the Southern Region or the Western Region at various times. The first diesel locomotives appeared on the line in 1958 but some steam engines continued until 1965. The goods yard at Sampford Courtenay Station closed in 1961 and, following the Beeching Report, in 1964 the signal-box was closed and the station became an unstaffed halt. The section of the line between Coleford Junction and Okehampton was finally closed to passenger trains in June 1972, along with the four stations at Bow, North Tawton, Sampford Courtenay and Okehampton. A bus service between

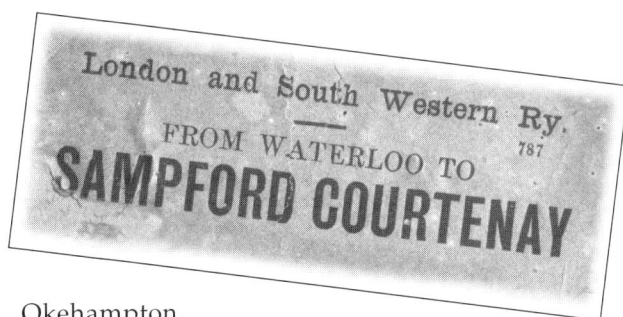

Okehampton, Sampford Courtenay and Exeter was introduced to replace the railway, subsidised by the National Bus Co., British Railways and the local authorities. The railway line, now singled, is still used by Meldon Quarry. The station buildings, by then derelict, were demolished in 1984. In recent years Devon County Council, West Devon Borough Council and Dartmoor National Park have redeveloped the Okehampton site as a Youth Hostel and in 1997 the Dartmoor Line from Exeter to Okehampton was reopened. The Dartmoor Railway Company expects to reopen Sampford Courtenay Station as part of this project. The station yard was briefly used by Shiptons of North Tawton as a store and in 2003 is occupied by Marshall Joinery.

London and South Western Ry.
——
FROM WATERLOO TO
787
SAMPFORD COURTENAY

Sampford Courtenay Station, looking towards Okehampton, 1971. **[Bernard Mills]**

Dartmoor ponies at Sampford Courtenay Station yard, 1929.

125

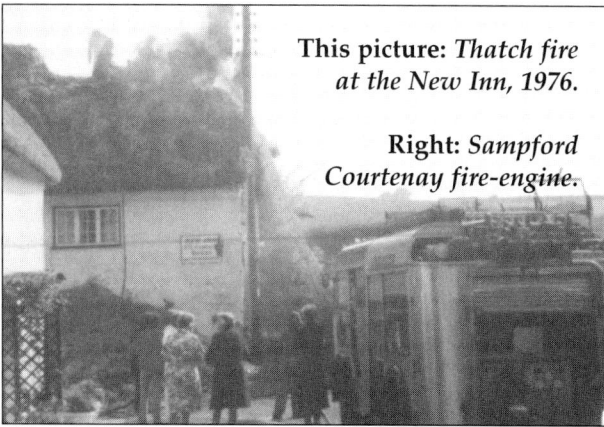

This picture: *Thatch fire at the New Inn, 1976.*

Right: *Sampford Courtenay fire-engine.*

Fire Fighting

The provision of a fire service in Sampford Courtenay left much to be desired until the mid-twentieth century. Thatch fires were fairly frequent and little could be done to deal with them, apart from raking off the thatch from adjacent buildings to curtail the spread. The difficulty of obtaining water accentuated the problem. The *Exeter Flying Post* gave accounts of two fires in the parish during the nineteenth century, one dealt with successfully, one not:

> 1.5.1845 *Sampford Courtenay – shortly before noon on the 15th inst. a fire broke out at Wood Farm in this parish, one of our engines was immediately dispatched to the scene of the conflagration, but proved of no service owing to the want of water. The dwelling house and the whole of the outbuildings were speedily reduced to a mass of ruins, a portion only of the furniture being saved.*
>
> 13.5.1887 *Sampford Courtenay. Yesterday morning an outbreak of fire occurred at Beerhill Farm, the residence of Mr Hawkins, the Sampford Courtenay Fire Brigade which was dispatched for, being soon on the spot. Its services, however, were not brought into requisition as willing hands had extinguished the flames by stripping a portion of the roof and using a plentiful supply of water. It is thought that a spark from an engine which works a machine for grinding corn, ignited the thatch of the house.*

In March 1886 there was a fire in the village which destroyed four houses, a shop and a barn. It is not clear where this occurred – possibly at the Alberries cottages. The Wood Farm blaze was probably dealt with by the Okehampton Fire Brigade, using a horse-drawn engine, but at Beerhill the services of the Sampford Courtenay Fire Brigade were employed. Sampford Courtenay's fire-engine initially belonged to King's College, but it is not known when the village brigade was established. The red engine, used in the late-nineteenth and early-twentieth centuries, is still in existence and is displayed at the Okehampton Museum of Dartmoor Life, but this may have replaced earlier

equipment. The existing engine is a Shand Mason & Co., c.1890, for manual drawing only. It was the smallest model, described as an eight-man, and could be used for drawing water out of a well by suction. A cistern was incorporated within the machine.

The fire-engine has had an interesting history. In 1912 the Parish Council declined any responsibility for expenses incurred by Okehampton Brigade, the college having a fire brigade of their own, although by the 1920s it appeared that some support was available from Okehampton. When the college sold the remaining parts of the manor in 1929, it was proposed that the parish should take over the engine and appliances and pay the college 10s. a year for housing it. The engine was at this time kept in a shed at Higher Town, which was still in the ownership of the college. In March 1930 a new fire brigade was established and consisted of: Courtenay Ash (captain and in charge of the key – presumably to the shed), William Mills (vice-captain), J. Snell, B. Horn, L. Horn, H. Cornelius, E. Reddaway, J. Seward, P. Smith, H. Piper, D. Ash and N. Ash.

In 1935 new lengths of hose were needed for the engine. The Parish Council agreed that the expense would be heavy and that it would be more satisfactory to rely on the Okehampton fire-engine if available. In March 1936 details of Okehampton's charges were given:

> Engine turning out £5.5s.
> Pumping first hour £1.10s.
> Pumping each hour after £1.5s.
> Standing by per hour £1.1s.
> Journey per mile 2s.
> Firemen, 9 at 3s. per hour £1.7s.
> Captain, 5s. per hour 5s.

In April Mr Paddon was asked to put the Sampford Courtenay engine in working order, so presumably Okehampton's terms were considered too expensive and were consequently declined. At the same time the council asked King's College for a reduction in rent from 10s. to 5s. a year for housing the engine as 'five shillings was quite enough in view of the size of the house and the state of repair.' The college refused.

In 1938 the Fire Brigades Act transferred the power to operate brigades from parish councils to rural district councils in country areas, although private brigades were still permitted. In March 1940 Sampford Courtenay was instructed to call on North Tawton, who had recently replaced their horse-drawn engine with a new motorised vehicle. However, the Parish Council decided to keep the Sampford Courtenay engine but to ask the District Council to take over responsibility and pay the housing fee. This was arranged and in April 1941 Revd Burnaby, in his capacity as captain of the local Home Guard, took charge of the engine. In 1944 Higher Town was sold by the college and Rawlence & Squarey asked what was to be done with the engine. By then all fire appliances had officially been taken over by the National Fire Service (until 1947 when they reverted to the local authorities) but in 1945 this organisation declined to do so. The District Council suggested that the villagers might themselves take it over. It would appear that the college presented the engine to the village, but it was subsequently offered for sale. By March 1946 only one reply had been received to the advertisement from a lady who wanted it for watering the garden! Two further offers were made for the engine but it was not sold. For some years it was kept out in the open, at first near Harvey's and for many years outside the New Inn. In 1974 the engine was on the point of being put up for sale again, when luckily the Finch Foundry Trust at Sticklepath Museum gave it a good home. Although still in the ownership of Sampford Courtenay, the engine was moved to Okehampton Museum in February 1990. The North Tawton Brigade, with back-up from Okehampton, now covers Sampford Courtenay parish.

Electricity

Before the 1930s Sampford Courtenay had to manage with candles or oil-lamps for lighting purposes and cooking was done on the open fire, in the bread oven or kitchen range or with paraffin stoves. Electricity arrived in the village in 1932; it is likely the power was produced by Christys of North Tawton, who offered four lights free if you signed up with them. Although some of the farms had their own generators, it was not until the early 1960s that power was connected to most of the outlying areas such as Sampford Chapple, Sampford Station, the Clistons and Honeychurch.

Street lighting, presumably using oil-lamps, was first suggested for Sampford Courtenay village in 1897 by Revd Thomas Little. He proposed it to the bursar of King's College as a possible project to celebrate Queen Victoria's diamond jubilee, but the scheme was never implemented. Although the provision of street lighting was raised by the Parish Council from the 1950s until the 1970s, nothing

happened until the 1980s. By 1984 lighting of the A30 through Sticklepath was operational, but Devon County Council informed Sampford Courtenay Parish Council that, as funds were very limited, they did not foresee a scheme for the A3072 unless Sampford Courtenay provided it at their own expense. At the end of 1987, the installation of some lights on the A3072 was being considered. In March 1988 a letter was sent to the County Council, accompanied by a petition of some 120 signatures, asking for street lights to be provided throughout the village, including the approach road to the Village Hall, as well as on the A3072. In 1988 five lamps were installed on the A3072 and, towards the end of 1989, six further lanterns were erected in the village street. Between 1989 and 1992 additional lamps were provided to cover the areas as far as the council-houses at Four Acres and northwards as far as The Barton. A further lamp was installed, at the Parish Council's expense, in 1995 and three more were provided in 1996. Although in 1995 the County Council promised the provision of street lighting for Sampford Chapple the following year, if funding were available, and for Sampford Station within four years, this has not taken place at the time of writing.

In 1977 the electricity and telephone cables in the top half of the village (near the church) were re-laid underground as part of a SWEB amenity scheme, but the unsightly cables in the lower part of the village persist. A request to the relative authorities to lay the remaining cables underground in 1994 met with no success. In 1998/9, South Western Electricity put forward plans for a new 132,000-volt overhead power line running from Alverdiscott to North Tawton through Sampford Courtenay parish. There was strong local opposition, which included the formation of a local action group, and a petition (featuring 253 signatures) and 64 letters of objection were lodged with the Department of Trade and Industry. The objection was based on lack of proven need for the line, visual intrusion in a conservation area and the possible health risks attached to high-voltage lines near residential property. South Western Electricity claimed undergrounding the whole stretch of line would be far too expensive. At the time of writing they have suggested an alternative route just clipping the parish boundary. Interestingly, the undergrounding of the remaining overhead cables in the village had been offered as a trade-off if the initial project had gone ahead.

Water-supply and Drainage

Until the 1870s water for household use was provided by wells. Each of the farms and probably some of the village properties had their own wells, although most of the village water would have been obtained from the well at the bottom of the village green, hence the name of the Water Path which ran to it from the village square. In 1877 a piped water-supply, from a reservoir in one of The Barton fields above the village near Piece (now Peace) Gate Cross, was constructed at a cost of £50 paid for by King's College. The supply fed The Barton and several standpipes in the village. In 1898 a further piped supply was installed from Wellspring near Trecott and fed a village tap and horse trough on the crossroads near the New Inn. When King's College sold the manor, arrangements were made with Okehampton Rural District Council for the latter to take over responsibility for the two water-supplies to the village. This took effect in June 1929; a water rate was levied on consumers and Robert Hawkins and John Snell undertook to act as caretakers for the first 12 months. During the next two decades, various problems were encountered with the reservoir. In 1932 corroded pipes had to be replaced and in 1933 a shortage of water led to the supply being turned off at night-time. In 1938 the Parish Council brought to the attention of the District Council that 'the water sometimes was not fit to drink and nothing had been done to cleanse the reservoir for years.' The fencing around the reservoir, apparently, was inadequate to keep out cattle. Contractors were appointed to carry out the work; it is not clear if this was done as in the 1940s there were further complaints that the water was dirty and the reservoir had not been maintained.

Local residents remember the old standpipes which were situated outside The Barton, at Alberries opposite the church, outside the forge, at the carpenter's shop and at Rebecca's Cottage. Ridgeway, built in 1930, had its own water-supply pumped from the Water Path well. The rectory, too, built in 1870, had its own water, piped from a well and provided by two pumps in the kitchen which had to be operated manually each morning. The inhabitants of Sampford Chapple, including the occupants of Thornbury Cottage, collected their water from a well-house next to Dartmoor View. In Honeychurch Freddie Johns remembers Bertha Hunkin, the housekeeper at East Town Farm, having to carry all the washday water in buckets from Honeychurch well.

By 1950 the prospect of a mains water-supply was first mentioned in the Parish Council minutes and in 1953 the Parish Clerk wrote to the District Council suggesting that a supply be brought to Sampford Courtenay by the North Devon Water Board based in North Tawton. In May 1955 the Board was due to start work as soon as the local authorities

granted approval, so presumably this took place soon after. Mains water was connected to the south of the parish in 1959 and reached the other outlying areas, including Honeychurch, by the early 1960s. Some properties, however, still rely on boreholes. The water-supply to the crossroads ceased to run in 1961 although the tap and trough were re-sited in 1963 following road widening. There is no longer a supply of water to the trough. Its reinstatement was considered in 1988/9 but was judged to be impracticable.

The question of drainage for the village was first considered in 1896. The Parish Council decided it was not practicable or advisable to attempt a general system of drainage: 'In the country sewage was to be disposed of in other ways.' All properties had earth closets in privies outside the house and night-soil was disposed of in the garden. Although the Parish Council in 1902 drew the attention of the District Council to 'the sewage of Sampford Courtenay which empties itself into the village green', no one remembers there being a sewerage system until about the 1920s when a septic tank was constructed under the village green to serve a few of the premises nearby. In the 1930s this was extended to accommodate more of the village. The provision of a better drainage system was discussed by the Parish Council in the 1950s and eventually new sewage works were installed in 1961. These are situated east of Lower Middletown and were altered and updated in 1992. Although numerous representations have been made for the provision of mains drainage facilities at Sampford Courtenay Station these have not been provided to date.

The majority of the outlying farms in the parish still rely on private drainage systems; septic tanks began to be introduced in the late 1940s. However, it was not until the 1960s that some properties in the parish acquired indoor flush toilets and bathrooms. Several people remember having to use tin baths in front of the kitchen fire and outside privies. At least one privy in the parish was some distance from the cottage it served. When a garden at Sampford Chapple (immediately south of the telephone box) was sold by King's College in 1928, the owner of Frankland Farm claimed a right to the use of the closet therein. Stanley Pike, who had purchased Frankland in 1925, had also bought the cottage (now gone) opposite the garden on the other side of the road to Okehampton, presumably for one of his farm workers, and this was the privy belonging to it.

Opening the sewage works at Sampford Courtenay, 1961.

Village street with Hammett's Hill Cottage and Virginia Cottage on the left, 1930s. In the late-nineteenth century Virginia Cottage was the police station.

In 1980 public conveniences were provided for the village by West Devon Borough Council at a cost of £14,000. After some initial disagreement as to where they should be sited, they were built on land purchased from the Village Hall. By 2002 the toilets, along with various others in West Devon, were under threat of closure. However, it was subsequently agreed that they would stay open with the Parish Council funding 30 per cent of the cleaning costs.

Law and Order

In the Middle Ages it was the responsibility of a locality to attend to its own law and order with a high constable in each hundred and, under him, petty constables in each tithing. This arrangement continued through the Tudor period, when the parish Vestry appointed a constable who assisted the local Justices in maintaining the King's Peace, as well as carrying out various other duties such as the apprenticing of pauper children, the supervision of vagabonds and beggars, the collection of maintenance from the fathers of illegitimate children and the training of local militia. The militia was responsible for dealing with any widespread disturbance or insurrection. In the eighteenth century, in many parishes, property owners clubbed together in societies to which they paid subscriptions to be used as a fund for the prosecution of felons. A document detailing an arrangement of this type was drawn up in Sampford Courtenay in 1761 and signed by the rector, John Heath, and 18 farmers. It read:

Diverse robberys, burglarys, housebreakings, felony, larceny and thefts have lately been committed within the parish of Sampford Courtenay... to the great danger

and damage of the inhabitants of the said parish... But the offenders by reason of the great charge and expence attending prosecutions in such cases have gone either intirely undiscovered or have been but seldom brought to justice and punishment.

The document went on to arrange that any future detection and prosecution costs would be met in equal shares by all parties.

In 1808 Vancouver reported an 'inordinate disposition to thievery in Devon', which included sheep stealing and even neighbours robbing each other of potatoes. By the early-nineteenth century over 200 crimes incurred the death penalty. At this time, Sir Robert Peel introduced his 'peelers' or 'bobbies' in London and in 1839 the County Police Act enabled Justices of the Peace to establish paid police forces in rural areas. However, it was not until 1856 that every county had its own police force. The 1861 census listed a police constable, James Pearce, living in Sampford Courtenay village. By 1871 the county police station was at Virginia Cottage. William Kemp, John Bidgood, John Cox and Alfred Hill successively were the village constables, but by 1910 there was no longer a resident policeman.

The Parish Council

The Local Government Act of 1894 established parish councils of elected members in rural areas with a population exceeding 300. The small parish of Honeychurch, therefore, united with Sampford Courtenay and the inaugural meeting of the new council took place on 3 January 1895. Revd Thomas Little was elected chairman, the other members being:

J.I. Reddaway at Reddaway Farm, 1970.
He was a parish councillor for 42 years.

William Charles Horn, Parish Clerk 1899–1928.

Thomas Sloman, Samuel Hill, George Sanders, George Snell, William Reddaway, William Knapman, Albany George Finch, Richard Yeo, William Ash junr and Edwin Hill. Long-serving members over the years include Albany George Finch for 50 years (from 1895 until 1945), Robert Hawkins for over 30 years, J.I. Reddaway for over 40 years, Roy Hawking for over 25 years and Ralph Squire, who is still a parish councillor, in 2003, having joined in 1973. The longest-serving clerks were William Charles Horn of Ball Farm (subsequently Webber Hill Farm) from 1899 until 1928 and Ralph Finch from 1930 until 1969. Initially, meetings were held on a fairly irregular basis but in recent years the council has met monthly.

Other Services

The telephone arrived in the parish in the late 1930s. At first few people had the service installed and, in the early years, lines had to be shared with other users. There is a mains gas supply along the B3215, which was installed in the mid-twentieth century.

It seems unlikely that there was ever a resident doctor in Sampford Courtenay; the services of the North Tawton doctor, Samuel Budd, were certainly being employed in the northern part of the parish at the beginning of the nineteenth century.

Chapter Nine

IN TIMES OF WAR

What passing bells for these who die as cattle?
Only the monstrous anger of the guns
Only the stuttering rifles' rapid rattle
Can patter out their hasty orisons.
From 'Anthem for Doomed Youth' by Wilfred Owen, 1917.

By the Middle Ages, each county was obliged to raise a local militia from the civilian population to supplement the regular Army in times of war. Muster-rolls were compiled, listing all men available to serve. In the Tudor period, the hundred and parish constables were responsible for raising the required levies. All able-bodied men between 16 and 60 were liable for service and formal inspections or general musters were held at least once every three years. Certificates of the muster, with the names of the men and their equipment, were returned through the Lord Lieutenant. The 1569 muster-roll for Devon is one of the most important to have survived for any county from any period. For each parish, details were given of sworn presenters (the most important parishioners), of providers of equipment (the richer yeoman in the parish) and of all able men. For 'Sampford Cortnye Parrishe the presenters sworen' were: Richard Facye, Lewes Besset, John Hortoppe and Simon Hortopp. The providers of armour and weapons included: Thomas Ellyce, John Newcomb, William Tickell, John Ellice, John Westwaye, Robert Newcomb and William Arscot. The 'habell menne of the parishe' were made up of archers, harquebusiers, pikemen and billmen and included: William Hethman, Gilbert Westway, John Beare, Simon Wekes, Henry Ellice, Pascowe Quycke, Christopher Hethman, William Denford, John Drewe, William Aller, Hugh Canne and Richard Newcombe.

The Militia Act of 1672 established a statutory, rather than a feudal, system of military service; the Act of 1757 removed the liability from individuals to the parish. Men were chosen by lot and compelled to serve for three years or to provide £10 for a substitute. Legislation in 1758 and 1759 permitted the raising of volunteer companies; these were finally disbanded at the conclusion of the Napoleonic Wars in 1816.

There were various references in parish records in connection with the administration of the local militia. Bounties were paid by the parish to militia volunteers:

> *1760 Pd Mr Arscott for receiveing the Militia Money 1s.0d.*
> *1779 Mr John Lacey: bounty money as a militia man £4.4s.0d.*
> *Henry Stott: do £4.4s.0d.*
> *William Ash: do £4.4s.0d.*
> *1786 Pd four men for a journey to Holsworthy to be sworn in the Militia 10s.0d.*
> *1814 To the Petty Constable for duty under the Local Militia Act 12s.6d.*

There were many instances of the relief (paid out of the poor rates) of disbanded soldiers and sailors, presumably returning from battles and passing through the parish:

> *1687 Pd eight souldiers marching to their colours 1s.6d.*
> *Pd to sick souldiers who had a certificate from the Hospitall 6d.*
> *Pd to a maser of a ship who had 17 in his company and a lawfull pas 2s.6d.*

Prior to the twentieth century, little is known of the participation of the men of Sampford Courtenay in the various wars. The West Country played a significant role in the Civil War; few parishes in Devon would have escaped involvement during almost continuous campaigning between 1642 and 1646. The less disciplined of the forces on both sides would have resorted to pillaging livestock, fodder and other provisions. In 1644, the two armies certainly passed through Sampford Courtenay parish and there was an engagement on Hatherleigh Moor. When the war with the French began in 1793, there was no conscription; men for the Navy and Army were acquired by the bounty system. Nothing is known of any

Edwin Ash, 1917.

Herbert Piper, aged 18, at the beginning of the First World War.

Private Edwin Hawkins, Somerset Light Infantry, 1918.

members of the parish fighting in the Boer War, although the school logbooks recorded a half-day's holiday granted in March 1900 to celebrate the relief of Ladysmith and a whole day in May that year in honour of the relief of Mafeking. A further half day was awarded when peace was declared in June.

The First World War, 1914–18

The First World War was seen at the time as a fight of British good against German evil. It is not known how many Sampford Courtenay men took part in the war, but there are memorials to those who died, both in the church and chapel and on the wall of the church rooms. The church rooms' memorial, which was erected in 1919, reads:

*This tablet is dedicated by the parishioners of
Sampford Courtenay to perpetuate the memory of
those inhabitants of the parish who gave their lives
for their country in the War 1914–1918:
Edwin John Hawkins Pte 1st Somerset L.I.
24.10.1918 Escaudoevres.
William Henry Hill Pte 1/4th Devon Regt 7.11.1918
Baqubah Hospital.
Frederick Edward Horne Pte 1st Worcs. Regt
24.11.1917 Boulogne.
Samuel James Horne L/Cpl 1st Devon Regt
26.2.1919 Sampford Courtenay.
Wallace Edwin Lake Pte 12th London Regt 9.8.1918
Morlancourt.
Henry Phare HMS Indefatigable 31.5.1916 Jutland.*

Two of those who died fought in the Devonshire Regiment. The Devons took part in a total of 63 battles during the course of the war and lost nearly 6,000 men and officers, mostly on the terrible battlefields of northern France and Flanders. William Hill's battalion, however, was in action in Mesopotamia (modern-day Iraq), where conditions were as appalling as on the Western Front. Wallace Lake from Sampford Chapple was the 19-year-old son of William Lake, one of the college carpenters. Wallace died fighting with the 12th London Regiment (The Rangers) in the Battle of Morlancourt which took place on the 8 and 9 August 1918 on the Western Front. It was the beginning of the final '100 days' that led to the Armistice. Henry Phare, aged 21, was the son of John and Sarah Phare of Bank Cottage. HMS *Indefatigable*, aboard which Henry perished, was one of five ships manned at Devonport that was sunk by the enemy in the Battle of Jutland, with the loss of over 1,000 lives.

On a headstone in the churchyard, the death of a young former parishioner, who had lived at Halford, is recorded: 'Henry Vivian Drew, aged 19 years, was killed in action at Arras, France on 23 April 1917.' Other local young men known to have served in the First World War were Harold Manuell (son of William and Thirzena), Edwin Ash (Courtenay's

brother) and Herbert Piper (Len and Bert Piper's father). Herbert, who initially had trained as a baker in Exbourne, served as a baker during the war and, in this capacity, he would have kept up with the front lines. Revd Henry Burnaby served as an Army chaplain in France.

The school logbook and the Parish Council minute book of the period made various references to parish involvement in the war effort. Eggs were collected for military hospitals and, in 1917, voluntary national rationing (of food) was introduced. A 'Food Economy Committee' was established comprising local ladies, among them Mrs Manuell and Mrs Sloman. Although there were food shortages in the towns of items such as potatoes, butter and eggs, country areas probably fared better.

Devon farmers were ordered to plough up grassland to produce more crops; corn acreage in the county went up by 60 per cent in four years. In December 1915, Sampford Courtenay Parish Council wrote to the Devon War Agricultural Committee:

*No more men can be spared from the land as many
farmers are now left to themselves on the farm, while
others have only one man besides... there is some
grassland which would be better for being cultivated
and manured, but men are not available at present.*

In March 1917, following receipt of a circular on National Service, the council considered that most, if not all, the inhabitants of the parish were doing work of national importance.

During the war, Becky Horn worked in the Women's Land Army. After she had performed her morning duties as caretaker in the village school, she would help on local farms for two or three hours a day and was paid 3d. an hour. 'In nailed boots and leather leggings', she would 'bind corn behind the reaping machine, pull turnips, pick over or dig potatoes and pick apples.' She would often work with husband George for Farmer Lang at The Barton, who was left with two older men, Dick Holding and Harry Hill, throughout the war. Becky and George would drive bullocks and sheep to market in Okehampton. She recalled an occasion

Postcard from Edwin Hawkins to his sister Irene, 1918.

when they drove some sheep to a market at Copplestone, leaving Sampford Courtenay at 8.30a.m. as the factory hooter sounded at North Tawton and returning later that day by train from Bow Station.

Irene Sampson has unhappy memories of the First World War. Born in 1907, she was the youngest child of John and Hannah Hawkins of Solland and had three sisters and two brothers. Her elder brother Eddie (Edwin) was expected to take over the farm from his father at some stage; younger brother Clifford was destined for the Methodist ministry. Although his father appealed against it, Edwin, aged 20, was called up, just five months before the end of the war and, sadly, was killed two or three weeks before the Armistice. Irene remembers when the family heard the news of Eddie's death:

All the family had 'flu except for Father and Clifford. We were in the yard and had been thrashing and combing, tying up the reed and stacking it. The Church bells started to ring [to celebrate the Armistice] and I remember Father saying 'Too late for us!'

The school log on 11 November 1918 recorded the children attending the hoisting of the Union Jack in the village and the singing of patriotic songs.

During the First World War, horses were requisitioned from the farms for service on the Front. Olive, a bay mare who was used by the Hawkins family as a riding horse and to pull the trap, was taken from Solland. Her departure was recorded in John Hawkins' accounts book: '10.8.1914 Olive pony commandeered at Exbourne £40.' Olive, when pulling the trap, was accustomed to turning left at the Sampford Chapple crossroads to go down to the village and the Methodist chapel. When taken away by the soldiers, presumably to Sampford Courtenay Station, instead of going straight ahead, she went to turn down the lane as usual and had to be whipped on. This was reported to her owners by neighbours living at the Chapple Inn near the crossroads. The Hawkins girls cried when they heard what had happened. Olive, of course, like most of the other horses requisitioned for the war, never came back. Half a million horses used by the British Army during the conflict were killed. At the end of the war, many of the surviving animals were abandoned by the Armed Forces and starved as a result or were auctioned off to French butchers.

The Second World War, 1939–45

During the Second World War, the civilian population of Devon this time did not escape unscathed. Exeter and Plymouth were heavily bombed but Sampford Courtenay, sufficiently far away, was relatively safe. Only one parishioner is known to have been killed in this conflict – Stanley Beer, aged 20, of Sampford Station. Stanley served with the Devonshire Regiment and died in October 1940 during a bombing raid on the Essex coast where he was on guard duty. Those who lost relatives during the war included Canon and Mrs Squance, whose son John, aged 21, a flying officer in the RAF Volunteer Reserve, died in February 1945, and Sydney Coates, whose son was killed in Burma. Although some of the young men in farming-related, and therefore reserved, occupations avoided conscription, many in the parish did serve their country. Herbert Piper senr, who had served in the previous war, was this time enlisted as a builder. Amongst the many projects in which he was involved, was the building, at Hayling Island, Portsmouth, of the huge concrete caissons, which formed part of the Mulberry harbours used when the Allied troops landed in Normandy in 1944.

Two members of the parish with distinguished wartime careers were David Green and John Kilmartin. David Abbott Green was born at Brixham in 1919, but moved with his family to Lydcott Farm in the parish in 1926. His father, William, farmed Lydcott until 1946. At the time of writing his nephew Peter Green still farms Alfordon Manor just outside the parish. When David left Okehampton Grammar School, aged 16, farming was going through a difficult time and there was really only enough money in the farming operation for his elder brother Fleetwood. David worked briefly for an insurance company in Bristol, but in 1938, at the time of the Munich crisis, he joined the RAF Volunteer Reserve and learned to fly as a sergeant-pilot. He entered full-time service before the outbreak of war and was commissioned in 1940, gaining his first operational experience in No.44 Hampden Squadron. In No.207 Squadron, he at first flew Hampdens and then Manchesters and then went on to Lancasters. In 1942, he helped form No.457, an Australian Squadron. David Green somehow managed to be one of the few pilots to survive two whole operational tours, during which he was awarded a Distinguished Flying Cross and was also appointed a Companion of the

Private Stanley Beer of Sampford Station, 1940.

Main picture: *David Green,
Hastings, October 1939.*

Inset, below: *David Green,
sergeant-pilot, RAF Volunteer
Reserve, at Lydcott, 1938.*

Distinguished Services Order. Many thousands of those who flew on Bomber Command's missions lost their lives. It is said that David, when on some of his assignments, would circle his aircraft over Sampford Courtenay before leaving. Later in the war, he spent some time as a staff officer in Bomber Command HQ and was about to join the RAF's Tiger Force in the Far East when the nuclear bombs were dropped on Japan and the war ended. After the war, David decided to remain in the RAF, in which he enjoyed a very successful career that culminated in his appointment in 1967 as station commander of RAF Akrotiri in Cyprus. This led to his promotion to the rank of air commodore. He was awarded an OBE in 1958 and made a CBE in 1963. Following his retirement in 1971, he devoted his time to voluntary work in the West Country and he died in 1990.

John Ignatius Kilmartin, who was a fighter pilot during the war, spent the last years of his life, between 1989 and 1998, in Sampford Courtenay. He was born in Ireland and, after spending several years in Australia and the Far East doing a variety of jobs, he joined the RAF in 1936 and qualified as a pilot. Initially he was posted to No.43 Squadron and flew first Furies and then Hurricanes. By the summer of 1940, Flight Lieutenant Kilmartin, or 'Killy' as he was known, had already been credited with the destruction of ten enemy aircraft. In October 1940 he was awarded the DFC and subsequently an OBE. After the Battle of Britain, he served successively as commander of three other squadrons and was promoted to wing commander in 1942. He took part in the Normandy invasion of June 1944 and in 1945 flew Thunderbolts in Burma. The RAF Museum at Hendon has an oil-painting of Wing Commander Kilmartin in 1945 by Frank Wootton as well as a book of portraits of the 'Pilots of Fighter Command' by Captain Cuthbert Orde, which includes a rather splendid portrayal of

Flight Lieutenant John Kilmartin in front of Hurricane Mk 1 with No. 43 Squadron's 'Fighting Cock' insignia, 1940. [RAF Museum, Hendon – Ref No.X002-5530/006]

Kilmartin looking extremely dashing as a flight lieutenant. Not surprisingly, the portrait was used in an RAF recruitment poster in 1940. After the war he remained in the RAF until retirement in 1958, when he moved to Devon to run a large poultry farm in North Tawton. In 1989 he and his wife Paddy moved to Sampford Courtenay, to No.1 Shores' Cottages, now called Martinmas in his memory. John Kilmartin died in 1998 and, at his funeral service in Sampford Courtenay, the last post was played in tribute to his distinguished wartime career.

During the war, Sampford Courtenay, like the rest of the country, had to observe air-raid precautions and adhere to the blackout procedure. Windows were covered with oilcloth and car headlights were partially obscured with slatted covers so that just a glimmer of light shone through. Night vision on the roads, therefore, was extremely poor, but there was little traffic in the parish at this time to cause a major problem. Sampford Courtenay people were accustomed to the dark; electricity had not been installed on the outlying farms and there were no street lights. Many parishioners remember seeing and hearing British bombers. Len Piper, who was a young boy at the time, recalls: 'I remember the thousand bomber raids going over the South West to bomb Germany; the Lancasters and Halifaxes from airfields up country.' There were anti-aircraft searchlights in the parish, one near Bude in Honeychurch and one near Rowden Manor and occasionally they picked out German planes coming to bomb Exeter and Plymouth. Plymouth was the most heavily bombed city in England, size for size, and in 1940 and 1941, night after night, a red glow on the horizon between Belstone and Yes Tor could be seen from Sampford Chapple in the direction of the city. Even German aircraft going down in flames could sometimes be observed.

A bomb was actually dropped in the parish near Bude Farm, presumably jettisoned by an enemy plane before it returned home, creating a huge crater in the field. No one was hurt or any other damage done. As boys Les Beer and his friend Les Stanbury would stand on the railway bridge at Sampford Courtenay Station watching the Rowden searchlight sweeping round and lighting up the whole area. Bob Johnson and his friends derived similar amusement from the searchlight at Bude.

Later in the war, the Americans had aircraft at Winkleigh airfield and forces camped at North Tawton

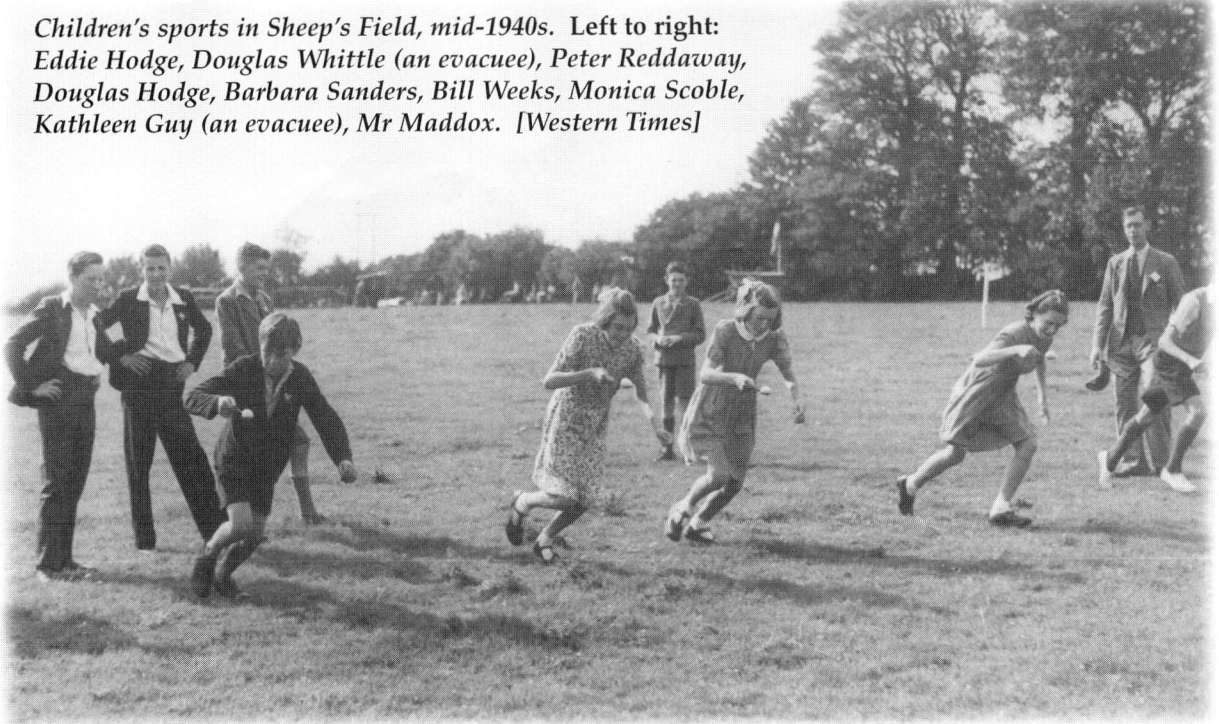

Children's sports in Sheep's Field, mid-1940s. Left to right: Eddie Hodge, Douglas Whittle (an evacuee), Peter Reddaway, Douglas Hodge, Barbara Sanders, Bill Weeks, Monica Scoble, Kathleen Guy (an evacuee), Mr Maddox. [Western Times]

Picnic in the hay field, Sampford Chapple, 1940s. The Robbins family left London during the war to live at Middletown – Mr Robbins is to the right of the ladder (with white shirt) and his daughter is on Bill Paddon's knee (right).

137

and on the moors south of Sampford Courtenay Station. Les Beer's sister Sylvia met and married one of the American soldiers stationed on Rowden Moor. German and Italian prisoners of war worked as farm labourers on Chapple Moor, which had been ploughed up for crop production. The Italians also picked withies to make baskets, which they sold locally. Although Joyce Hershey (née Stanley) was frightened to walk past them on her way to school, John Hodge remembers going to talk to them during school break times. He also recalls an incident when a British plane ran out of fuel and had to make an emergency landing on Chapple Moor. Fuel had to be fetched from Exeter and the plane took off again, providing much excitement for all the village youngsters.

There were a few Land Girls employed on the parish farms, including Doris Jennings, who previously had worked for the Post Office in Torquay and came to the area about halfway through the war. Initially, she was billeted at a hostel called Tenby House in Okehampton with two other girls, but then went to work for Hawkins Madge at Solland where she stayed for a couple of years. She remembers the time as hard work but enjoyable. Whilst at Solland, she met and later married Frank Guy from neighbouring Exbourne and did not return to Torquay. She has lived in Exbourne ever since.

Rather oddly, there were few references to the war in the Parish Council minutes. Use of the Sampford Courtenay fire-engine was granted to the Home Guard, but one wonders how effective the little engine would have been if a bomb had fallen on the village. The provision of temporary mortuary facilities in the event of civilian deaths was arranged by the council. Mr Coates

undertook to provide a room at The Barton for Sampford Courtenay and Mr Finch the Methodist chapel vestry for Sticklepath.

Several evacuees arrived in the parish during the course of the war, not only the London school with its teachers mentioned in Chapter Six, but various other families too. The London schoolchildren were billeted around the parish. One of these was Ronnie West, who was initially placed in North Tawton, but subsequently lodged with Charles and Doris Reddaway at Fir Cottage. According to their son John:

Ronnie was only a little tacker, 'bout the height of the table and he used to come up to the shoemaker's shop in North Tawton and want a 'tector put in his boots. He was a bit of a lad to deal with, a terrible temper and the people he was with in North Tawton got fed up and asked Mother to take him in. Mother would take in anybody.

Ronnie came from a large family who lived in the Elephant and Castle district of London. When it was time for him to return, Mrs Reddaway travelled up to the area to investigate – the conditions were so bad that she arranged for Ronnie to stay with her; he remained with the family until he married. Ronnie became a farm worker when he left school, first at Honeychurch, then Exbourne and later in another part of Devon.

Bob Johnson, also from London, was another evacuee who stayed in Sampford Courtenay; his story is told in Chapter Twelve.

Many anecdotes about the local Home Guard are reminiscent of the television programme 'Dad's Army'. In May 1940, the introduction of the Local

Eva Paddon with young Miss Robbins, 1940s.

Defence Volunteers was announced. Their responsibilities were observation and information, prevention of movement by enemy personnel landing from the air and to assist in patrolling and protecting vulnerable areas. In July that year, at Winston Churchill's suggestion, the LDV officially became the Home Guard. During 1940, the age range, with an official limit of 65, was not rigidly enforced but, in November 1941, conscription was introduced and, from January 1942, all male civilians aged between 18 and 51 were ordered to join the force. They were liable for prosecution if they failed to attend up to 48 hours of training or guard duties each month.

According to Philip Tilden of Rowden, who was one of the captains, there were 60 men in the Sampford Courtenay platoon, but others remember there being more like 30 or 40. Revd Burnaby was a captain too, Stan Sercombe from Yondhill was the sergeant and Roy Hawking from Glebe Farm, Honeychurch, the corporal. The unit had the use of an old Morris, which somebody had donated, as a staff car. The armoury, where a variety of rifles and Sten guns were kept, was in the cellar at the rectory. Phil Reddaway remembers there was a Lewis gun too. The force was a mixture of young and old, farmers and farm labourers, etc. Phil Reddaway was in the Home Guard for about six months before being called up, after which he served with the Army in the Middle East. The farmers included Bert and Harold Coates from The Barton, Walter Cleverdon from Cliston, Arthur Sleeman from Withybrook and Fleetwood Green from Lydcott. The older men included Charlie, Tom and Ern Reddaway and Bob Beer. Charlie Reddaway's son John, on his motorised cycle, was the dispatch rider. John recalls:

It was all rot really. Parson Burnaby and Philip Tilden would send messages to Major Murphy at Dunsland Court near Hatherleigh. I went there one Sunday night and found myself up the front of the house and there was a gang of them all sat up to dinner.

George Horn was also a member of the Home Guard. After the war he received a certificate, which was proudly displayed on the cottage wall. It read:

In the years in which our country was in mortal danger, George Horn, who served 4 years, 207 days, gave generously of his time and powers to make himself ready for her defence by force of arms and with his life if need be. George VI R.

Two lookout sites were established on high ground, one at Sampford Chapple and the other opposite where the Countryman is now. The Home Guard performed sentry duty at these positions during the early hours of the morning. It was feared that enemy parachutists would land under cover of darkness. The ladies' changing hut from the village swimming-pool

was moved to Sampford Chapple to provide some cover for the men on duty there, but those up on the moor were not so lucky. Bert Coates recalled:

I was assigned with Charlie Reddaway. We had to cycle up there [opposite the Countryman] one or two o'clock in the morning and stay till daybreak. We had to go whatever the weather, wet or dry... There was a wood-rick there, firewood in bundles, and we would sit on top. Then we would cycle home and do a day's work on the farm.

According to Bert Piper, junr (who was in the Home Guard before being called up in 1944, aged 18), Heber Harris disappeared one night when he was on sentry duty at Sampford Chapple. At last he was found – he had curled up under a hedge and fallen asleep.

Roadblocks of sandbags and barbed wire were set up on Appledore Hill and at the New Inn; these were manned every night. John Reddaway was on duty on Appledore Hill two nights a week and Revd Burnaby would drive him there. 'Revd Burnaby would say: "We'll go for a drive round Johnny if you like" and we used to drive round to see my father and Bert Coates who were on the same turn as us.'

Dennis Beer's Home Guard responsibility was to patrol the platform of the railway station. His only weapon was a long stick with 'a couple of great nuts on the end'. Brother Les asked him what he would do if the Germans came. He answered: 'Chuck the stick away and run, I reckon!'

Training sessions took place at the church rooms or on the village green, but the platoon participated in more serious exercises, including visits to the Army firing range on Dartmoor, described by Bert Coates as: 'up there with the big boys'. He recalled:

It was on the side of a hill and there were three or four sheets of galvanised for the target. This was in the winter as we couldn't go up there summer time as we had our farm work to do. There was always half a gale blowing there all the time; it was cold enough to cut your head off!

According to John Reddaway, an old chap from North Tawton called George Westlake would drive the men to the firing range on Sundays in the school bus. He remembers George commenting: 'If Gerry only know'd that he'd got to come now, Sunday dinner time, he'd get the ruddy lot of us; half the country's asleep!'

An exercise with comic results, which could well have been tragic, was one held in the disused quarry at Solland. Bob Johnson and Ron King from Great Cliston, then young boys, were bird's-nesting in the quarry when suddenly they heard cracking noises over their heads:

We had walked right into where the Home Guard were practising, pitching hand grenades. We skedaddled out

Fleetwood Green of Lydcott in Home Guard uniform, 1941.

of there, but even when we got back to Solland Farm, 300 to 400 yards away, we could still hear something striking the galvanised roofs of the outbuildings.

Inevitably, there were several scares, including an incident one night when a suspicious light was spotted on the footpath crossing the field from Wellsprings Lane to the village. The Home Guard were alerted, but it turned out to be a farmer checking his sheep and lighting his pipe. Another amusing incident, which was probably not very funny at the time, was an occasion when everyone thought the Germans really had invaded. In fact, it was only an exercise, but it is not clear if anyone in the village knew this at the time. Apparently, Courtenay Ash, the ARP warden, was telephoned at Ridgeway in the middle of the night by the Army who claimed that the Germans were invading. Effie, his wife, ran over the road in her nightie to wake up Blacksmith Horn, who was a member of the Home Guard. Len dashed out and knocked on Henry Sanders' door at one of the Alberries cottages, shouting: 'Hen...ry, the buggers be come!' He then ran down the village street, knocking everybody up. John Reddaway at Fir Cottage recalls:

I'll always remember. It was real. Len was quite serious. He said 'you've got to get Gus Cockerham up' (he lived at Cherrywell). I had to wake him up

and Sammy Northam, who lived at the council houses, Jim Stevens at Greenslade Cottage and Reg Harvey at the lodge at North Wyke. I had to wake them all up and I had not much in the way of lights on my bike. If someone had stepped out in the road that night, it would have been the end of me!

Everyone congregated by the roadblock near the New Inn and ended up sitting on the floor of the pub for the rest of the night. According to Phil Reddaway: 'The landlord opened up the bar and by the time daylight came, we were all blooming tight!'

Apart from all these excitements, life in the parish was fairly dull; many of the men were away and those who remained must have spent many boring hours on Home Guard duty. Many village activities had stopped and there would certainly have been concerns for relatives away on active service. At home there was much camaraderie as people united against a common foe. As J.B. Priestley said in one of his regular BBC broadcasts in June 1940:

I think the country man knows, without being told, that we hold our lives here, as we hold our farms, upon certain terms. One of those terms is that while wars still continue, while one nation is ready to hurl its armed men at another, you must if necessary stand up and fight for your own.

Chapter Ten

LEISURE

And all the village train, from labour free,
Led up their sports beneath the spreading tree;
While many a pastime circled in the shade,
The young contending as the old survey'd;
And many a gambol frolick'd o'er the ground,
And sleights of art and feats of strengths went round.
From 'The Deserted Village' by Oliver Goldsmith, 1770.

Until well into the twentieth century most social activities were provided within the parish and, even in the middle of the century, people did not venture far to meet prospective partners. Bert Coates remembered in the 1930s: 'North Tawton was about as far as you would go courting, because you had to cycle or walk.' Thus, over the years many Sampford Courtenay residents have intermarried and most of the old families are related to each other; according to John Hawkins: 'Kick one of us and we all limp.' Village 'socials' were well supported. Even up until the 1950s, as Len Piper remembers, 'It was a major event in those days if something was going on in the village.'

The Village Green

The village green over the centuries would have provided the venue for various leisure pursuits. In the nineteenth century, and, almost certainly before

this, 'fair' or 'revel' week was held at the beginning of July each year. It is not known where the fair (a sale of cattle and sheep) was held, but peripheral festivities such as sports and dancing, with visiting stalls and sideshows, probably took place on the green and continued for several days. Ann Palmer in her diary in 1832 (see Chapter Eleven), spoke of the 'follies and dissipations' of this season, suggesting that there was probably much consumption of ale and cider on such occasions. The revel outlived church ales and continued in Sampford Courtenay until the end of the nineteenth century.

Legislation during the nineteenth and twentieth centuries established village greens as 'land subject to a customary right of playing lawful sports or pastimes.' By the Commons Act of 1876, it became a criminal offence to damage a village green or to encroach upon it. Recent history suggests that this requirement was not always adhered to in Sampford

Church held given by Canon and Mrs Squance at the old rectory (Culverhayes), late 1950s.

141

Courtenay. Local residents appeared to use it for a variety of purposes unconnected with recreation. In the 1920s, one villager was keeping 'coops on the green for the use of geese, ducks or fowls.' In the 1930s this was proving a nuisance to the children who played there. Other problems included the dumping of refuse and the erection of a wireless pole. In 1949 the owner of the fowls was asked to remove them, but by the following year the green was in 'a bad state of overgrowth of weeds'. Arrangements were made to cut the grass twice a year, but there were further complaints about overgrowth and in 1954 the owner of the fowls, so unceremoniously removed, was invited to restock the green! By the 1960s another resident had been given approval to extend his garden onto the green. However, in 1967, a letter signed by 16 parents stressed the need for reclaiming the green as a playground for the 24 youngsters of the village. The chicken coops were again removed followed by the flower-bed and rose bushes so recently introduced.

Cutting the grass proved a continuing problem, although subsequent requests to plant vegetables on the green or graze it with goats were declined. It is now cut by contractors. A children's activity playground was provided in 1995. In 1995/6, with the assistance of the Sticklepath and Okehampton Conservation Group, the cobbled footpath at the top of the green was restored. Currently the village green provides a setting for sports and games at local events.

Church House and the Reading-Room

As detailed in Chapter Two, Church House (the church rooms) was used for social gatherings or 'church ales' from the beginning of the sixteenth century. It seems likely that these had ceased by the early-eighteenth century. The 'reading-room' was probably established in Church House soon after the village school vacated the premises in 1880. The first reference to it was in 1895, in a letter from Revd Little to the bursar of King's College. In January 1908 Revd Surtees wrote to the bursar:

The Reading Room give an 'invitation dance' which is quite a grand affair. The great idea, which differentiates it from other commonplace 'socials', is that we have jelly for refreshments.

The designation 'reading-room' seems to imply that the original intention would have been to provide a venue for villagers to have access to newspapers and books, the purchase of which would have been beyond the means of many. However, the reading-room in living memory (from the 1920s) was a young men's club. Phil Reddaway recalls the club in the 1930s: billiards, darts, dominoes and cards were

played and there was even a wireless set, which ran off an accumulator. When Phil joined, the subscription was 3d. per week. Bert Coates moved to The Barton as a young man in 1936 and immediately became involved with the reading-room; he was on the committee and, in later years, was chairman with Archie Watts as treasurer. The club was very successful in the 1930s with about 30 members. During the Second World War, many of the members were called up, but afterwards the reading-room became popular again for a short while. By the 1960s, due to declining numbers of young men in the village plus the attractions of television, membership fell to half a dozen or so and the club folded in the 1970s.

Church House was used for many social events until the early 1950s, when the Village Hall was established. Weekly whist drives, the annual hunt balls and New Year's Eve socials were very popular. However, presumably because of the connection with the church, the drinking of alcohol was not permitted and, when dances were held, drinks were consumed at Glebe House next door. In 1951 purchase of the old school building as a Village Hall seemed an ideal opportunity to acquire a premises which offered more freedom, particularly as far as the consumption of alcohol was concerned.

Church Teas, Suppers and Fêtes

During the later part of the nineteenth century, Church House possibly provided the venue for some of the many celebratory teas held by the church and chapel, although after 1880 they were mostly held at the new school. These teas appeared to come to an end shortly before the Second World War. After the war, at Revd Squance's suggestion, annual harvest suppers were held in Church House and these have continued to the present day. A harvest supper is also held each year at the Methodist chapel.

Harvest supper in the church rooms, 1981. Left to right, standing: *Doris Piper, Joyce Stacey, Anita Pope, Lawrie Quayle of Westward TV, Audrey Reddaway;* seated: *Kate Revell, Peter Reddaway, Len Piper.*
[Braetor Studio]

Above: *Hat-trimming competition, church fête at the old rectory, 1950s.* Left to right, standing: *Fred King, Ken Cleverdon, Jim Seaward, Bert Coates, John Reddaway, Joe Dore, Phil Reddaway, Ern Reddaway, Jack Seaward, Clifford Westlake, Will Reddaway, Ron King, George Sanders;* seated: *Walter Cleverdon, Roy Hawking, Bert Piper, Courtenay Ash ?, ?.*

Right: *Church fête at the old rectory (Culverhayes), 1958.*

In the nineteenth century, the rector organised 'tea treats' for the children and their parents at the rectory, but it was not until after the Second World War, during Canon Squance's incumbency, that church fêtes began. These are remembered by many parishioners. Fred Reynolds looked after 'skittling for a pig' *(see page 6)*, Jim Searle judged 'guess the weight of the sheep' and the Hatherleigh Silver Band played all afternoon. Arthur Squance introduced several innovations, such as 'guess the weight of the rector' and a hat-trimming competition for the men. When the rectory was sold by the Church in 1959, the fêtes continued in the rectory grounds for many years. They were held for a while at the Village Hall but at the time of writing take place in Church House.

Whitsuntide Club Days

The 1809 King's College survey recorded two friendly societies in the parish – one for men and one for women. The women's society (see Chapter Four), which was certainly in existence in 1788, held an annual dinner for members on Whit Mondays, and it is likely that the men's society held a similar function.

All the women members living within six miles of the society house were:

Required to attend precisely by eleven o'clock in the forenoon, in a clean and decent manner for the purpose of going to church and after divine service, to proceed to the society room, where a dinner shall be provided for all members, under the inspection of the stewards for the time being. Each member to pay 1s. after dinner.

The occasion sounds a rather sober affair. At some stage, one (or both of the friendly societies jointly) began holding 'club walks' on Whit Mondays. These were mentioned in the school logs from 1876 onwards, when the school closed for the occasion. Richard Pyke recalled these events, c.1880:

The members gathered outside the village inn and, after attending a church service, returned to it for the club dinner. For the rest of the day they stood about, looking rather bored, or perhaps finding a transient pleasure in watching such sports as the village school-master organised. It was regarded as essential that a brass band should be engaged for the day... We boys

143

Village outing, 1948.

Village outing to Dawlish, mid-1950s.

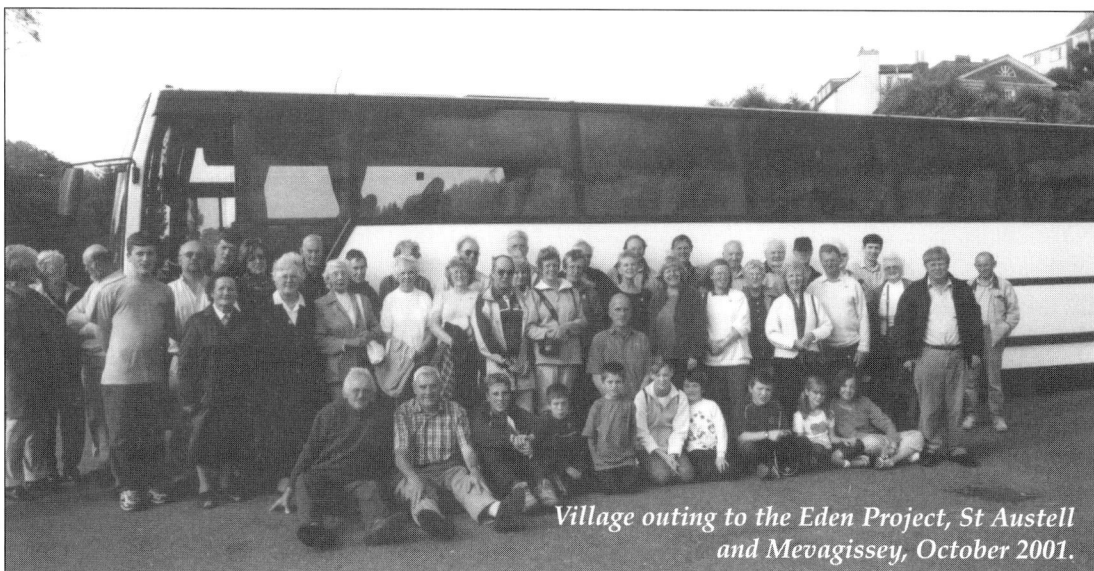

Village outing to the Eden Project, St Austell and Mevagissey, October 2001.

used to go out for a half a mile or so to a spot where we knew the musicians would form up and march into the village. It was a great thrill.

In 1912 the men's society was converted into 'Courtenay' branch of the Ancient Order of Foresters and, from then until 1934, an annual Foresters' day was held in the village on Whit Monday. It was one of the highlights of the year and everyone joined in. Phil Reddaway, when he left school in 1934, was the last person in Sampford Courtenay to join the Foresters. Each year the members would pay their subscriptions – so much towards the club and so much towards the annual dinner. On the day, the members would gather at the New Inn; Billy Parsons the tailor would come out of his cottage at the bottom of Rectory Hill, sit up on the mounting-block and call the roll. The band from North Tawton was in attendance. John Reddaway remembers the Foresters' banner on a pole. It always had a bunch of lilac tied to the top and was carried by an old chap who lived in one of the cottages on Hammett's Hill. The men would march up to the church for a service and back to the New Inn for the dinner. This was held in the large upstairs room; Phil remembers Jack Harris and Herbert Ash sitting at each end of the table and 'a drop of beer' being consumed. In the afternoon there would be a game of cricket for the men and sports for the children.

Village Outings

Early village outings to the seaside were organised by the school and the chapel. At first these were accomplished by horse and wagon to the station and then by rail, but by the 1930s charabancs were being used. The outings stopped during the war, but afterwards were started up again by Herbert Ash and continued until the late 1950s.

In 2001, and again in 2002, enthusiasm for a resurrection of the parish 'away-day' of the past was expressed and coach trips were organised by the Village Hall Committee. The first trip was to the Eden Project at St Austell and the second to St Ives. Both outings were well supported.

Nap Parties

The playing of 'nap' (napoleon – a card game) was very popular in the 1920s and probably earlier. Mary Cleverdon remembers her father Charles Bolt playing at Langmead in around 1920. Seven or eight local men, including Mr Southcombe and Orman Reynolds, the village schoolmaster, took part. There was a fair amount of drinking; play continued until the early hours, and sometimes until daylight. Wives, apparently, did not play; they were relegated to preparing the supper. John Reddaway remembers rabbit shoots or ferreting on Boxing Day and New Year's Day, followed by supper and a nap party.

The Swimming-pool

In the early 1930s one or two hot summers provoked some of the younger villagers to dam the stream east of Oxenpark to create a natural pool. According to Phil Reddaway, who was then a teenager, the water looked beautifully clear, but after one or two youngsters had jumped in and splashed about, the water soon turned red and muddy. (This part of the parish is on the red land.) Mrs Founds, who lived at Sampford Chapple, suggested the construction of a village swimming-pool. A site was chosen just south of Oxenpark, immediately east of the Weeks' large open barn. The pool was fed by the overflow stream from the village reservoir, which until this time just ran across the road. The site belonged to Farmer Lang at The Barton, who agreed to grant a 21-year lease to the village, rent-free.

At the time there was a recreation fund in the village, 'the purse strings of which were held by Rector Burnaby'. There was some dissension in the community about spending money from the fund on this project, but eventually the pool was built by William Ash & Sons, probably in 1934, at a cost of £80. It had a concrete basin, 6 feet deep at one end and 2 or 3 feet deep at the other, with a concrete path all the way round and high walls made of corrugated iron. There was a 'proper changing hut for the ladies and a little galvanised shed for the gents.' A large tree stump was used as a diving-board, and 'you had to be careful not to hit the side of the pool when you dived in from it.' The overflow water from the reservoir was filtered through stones and piped under the road. John Reddaway remembers the opening ceremony of Sampford Courtenay Lido, as it was known, by the Mayor of Okehampton. There was a small charge for entry.

The pool was popular for several years, although there were a few mishaps. Barbara Sanders fell in the deep end, aged five, and was rescued by Mrs Fewings from Sampford Chapple. Freddie Johns also fell in and nearly drowned but was rescued by Bert Piper. Unfortunately the water-supply posed some problems. During the hottest weather, the most suitable for swimming, the overflow tended to dry up. Also, at times there were cattle paddling about higher up the overflow stream which fed the pool and the water became rather muddy. According to Bert Coates: 'You wouldn't wash your boots in the water, let alone swim in it!' Silt would periodically have to be cleaned out and thrown over the perimeter fence; this eventually became high enough for people to stand on to look in. During the war the pool became less used and fell into disrepair. It was closed in the early 1940s and the ladies' changing hut, which had previously been the cricket pavilion, was moved to Sampford Chapple for use by the Home Guard. The pool was filled in, but evidence of its existence can still be seen.

The Village Hall

The village school closed at Easter 1947 and the following year the Local Education Committee offered the premises to the Parish Council for use as a community centre. The negotiations dragged on until March 1951 when the County Valuer agreed to sell the building for £600. However, the Parish Council would not undertake the purchase and it was decided that the way forward was for it to be bought by the villagers themselves. Not everyone agreed with the project and a parish meeting was called. Those present agreed to proceed and a Village Hall Committee was duly elected, with Arthur Squance as chairman, Walter Huntley from Honeychurch as secretary, Bert Coates as treasurer and 12 other members. It was decided that the members of the committee should find the purchase money amongst themselves. This was by means of interest-free loans for a period of five years, a husband and wife being treated as a single member of the committee. Eventually a dozen committee members advanced £33.6s.8d. each, to raise a total of £400. The loans were repaid in three instalments, the final one in October 1962, which was rather longer than the five-year period initially agreed. How the rest of the money was raised is not clear from the records. Other residents were appointed to collect subscriptions from the rest of the parish towards the purchase of the building and of necessary items. Also a loan from the National Council of Social Service was taken up in November 1952 (repaid by 1957). Fund-raising events helped towards the cost of alterations and repairs. In December 1951 tables and chairs were acquired (these are still in use at the time of writing) and, the following summer, electric lighting was installed, although heating was provided by paraffin stoves. On 10 December 1952 the conveyance of the building from Devon County Council to the trustees of the Village Hall (Arthur Squance, George Sanders,

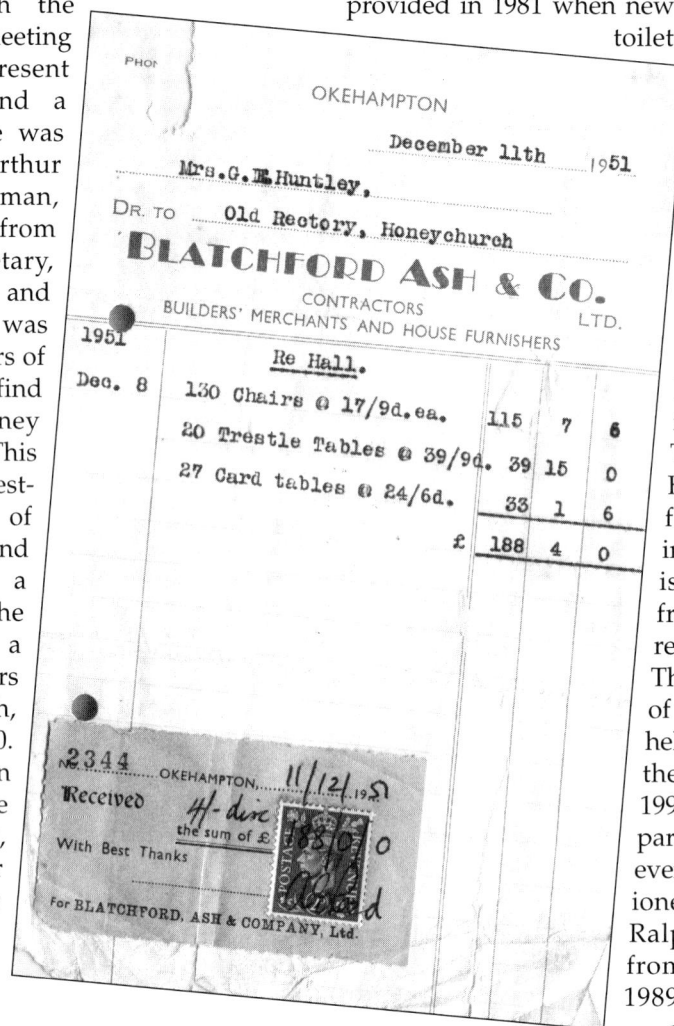

Purchase of chairs and tables for the Village Hall, 1951 – these are still in use in 2003.

Walter Huntley and Bert Coates) finally took place. In September 1953 the property was vested in the Official Trustee of Charity Lands.

The building was further updated over the years. Devon County Council installed a septic tank at the premises in 1949. A kitchen extension was added in 1953 at a cost of £106, water being provided from a rainwater tank on the roof. This also supplied a flush toilet installed in 1958. Mains water was not connected until 1960. The oil stoves were replaced by electric heaters in 1966/7. Mains drainage was provided in 1981 when new ladies' and gentlemen's toilets were built and the kitchen renovated. Money was raised for the 1981 works in the form of grants, and numerous donations and interest-free loans from parishioners. Becky Horn officiated at the opening ceremony.

Since the 1950s the hall has been the venue for many social events. The annual Eggesford Hunt ball was held there from 1951 until 1992, in the early years organised by Stan Staddon from Cliston and more recently by Ralph Squire. The Okehampton branch of the Young Farmers' Club held their annual party in the hall from 1978 until 1996. Children's Christmas parties, followed by social evenings for adult parishioners, were organised by Ralph and Renee Squire from 1972–1985 and 1989–1994. Children's pantomimes, scripted by Marion Pratt of Higher Town, were held in 1986, 1987 and 1988. The theme was always a combination of two pantomimes – Cinderella and the Nine Dwarfs, Babes in the Wood meet Robin Hood, and Aladdin and the Forty Thieves. Each production was very much a community effort, with parents providing the costumes and, although some of the older parts were played by children from North Tawton, all other parts were played by Sampford Courtenay children, including even the very young in supporting roles and contributing to dance routines. A local newspaper report of the 1987 pantomime recorded: 'It was two good evenings of entertainment, greatly enjoyed by

Christmas party at the Village Hall, late 1950s.

Becky Horn, aged 93, opening the extension at the Village Hall, 1981. Left to right, back row: Courtenay Ash, Arthur Sleeman, Roy Hawking, Renee Squire, John Watson, Ralph Squire, Len Piper; front row: Becky Horn, Marguerite Pye, Pat Watson, Anita Pope, Doris Piper, Effie Ash, Bill Goundry.

Above: *The Eggesford Hunt at the New Inn, 1986.*

Left: *Dog show at Culverhayes, May 2000.*

all who went along and a fine example of what can be achieved in a small village.'

It has always been a struggle to raise the necessary money to adequately maintain and update the building. This has only been possible due to the hard work and ingenuity of the many parishioners who have supported the hall through the years. Many activities have been organised, including whist drives, jumble sales, skittles evenings, film shows, dance classes, 50/50 auctions, sponsored walks and even sponsored turkey plucks! Surplus funds raised have been used for different improvement projects. The hall is also hired out for private functions. In the 1980s ideas for a swimming-pool or tennis-court in the grounds were put forward but rejected as the space was inadequate. However, the interior of the hall was marked out for badminton, which was played for about six months in 1985, although some problems were encountered with the ceiling heaters.

Unfortunately, by the late 1980s, there was a lack of support for the majority of functions and new ideas, such as old-tyme dancing and aerobics classes,

were short-lived. The possible sale of the hall was discussed. However, the hiring out of the premises to Blyth and Exbourne Schools over the next few years helped considerably towards finances. Also, monthly bingo evenings, organised by Les Beer from 1991, proved popular and these continue at the time of writing. In 1994 Exbourne School vacated the building and, between April 1996 and October 2000, the Village Hall Management Committee held no meetings, the hall running at a loss each year. In October 2000 a parish meeting was called to discuss the way forward. It was agreed that keeping the hall was worthwhile and a new committee was elected, mostly comprising the members of the Millennium Working Party (see below). The resurrection of former events, such as 50/50 auctions, car-boot sales, barn dances, skittles and whist and the introduction of new ideas such as quiz nights, dog shows and jazz evenings has proved successful and the hall made a substantial profit in 2001 and 2002. Funds are now healthy in 2003, but considerable expenditure is needed on the premises. Some projects have already been carried out by a small group of hard-working committee members and it is hoped that grant assistance will be obtained to pay for major structural work in the near future.

The Cricket Club

The date of the formation of the first cricket club is unknown, although Revd Little, in a letter to the bursar of King's College in 1896, mentioned 'going off to play in a cricket match'. Futhermore Revd Fulford Williams, in 1957, recalled 'a village cricket match half a century ago'. There was certainly a club in the 1920s and the pitch was in the field, belonging to Jack Harris of South Town, where Cricket Farm is now located. In about 1928/9 Fred Taylor took over South Town and the field ceased to be used. The club played a couple of seasons in other places but then folded.

The second club was formed in 1966/7 with Courtenay Ash in the chair. The club at nearby Exbourne had closed down and many of the players transferred to Sampford Courtenay. The first captain was Pat Cockwill followed by Alan Theedom. Matches were played on Saturday and Sunday afternoons and Wednesday evenings, from mid-May until early September; the pitch was initially in a field belonging to John Grey, then in The Barton field (Dadgel) near the Village Hall, and lastly in a field belonging to Tim Townsend Green at Southey. John and Victor Hodge cut and rolled the field, players' wives made the teas and, at the end of the season, there was an annual dinner, held in later years at the Pretoria in Okehampton. In the 1970s the pitch was proving a lot of work to maintain; the team was composed of working men who found the commitment of three days a week too much and in 1974 the club again folded. In 1995 there was a suggestion of re-forming the club, but nothing materialised.

SAMPFORD COURTENAY CRICKET CLUB

President - N. C. ADAMS, Esq.

FIXTURES 1971

Chairman - C. S. Ash, Esq.

Hon. Secretary - Mrs D. M. Piper
Allberries, Sampford Courtenay
Tel. North Tawton 285

Hon. Match Secretary - D. Weeks, Esq.
Post Office, Exbourne, Nr. Okehampton
Tel. Exbourne 225

Hon. Treasurer - N. A. Bloxham, Esq.
Lower Trecott, Sampford Courtenay
Tel. North Tawton 269

Captain - A. Theedom, Esq.

Vice - Captain - C. Dennis, Esq.

Vice-Presidents

Mrs C. Ash	Mrs K. M. Bloxham
Miss Ewen	Mrs J. Reddaway
Rev. D. Bickerton	

Messrs

G. T. Caswell	W. G. Clark
A. E. Coates	R. Hawkin
L. W. Horn	H. Gibson
W. Paddon	G. Parsonson
H. Piper	C. D. Reddaway
C. Talbot	J. I. Reddaway
W. Tate	T. Reddaway
F. Scoble	A. Ward
L. W. Piper	

Cricket club fixtures, 1971.

		Opponent	Gd	R'lt			Opponent	Gd	R'lt
May	15 St	Beaford	A			10 St	Goodleigh	H	
	22 St					14 W	Lydford	A	
	26 W	North Tawton	H			17 St	Beaford	H	
	29 St	Torrington	H			21 W	Lydford	H	
June	2 W	Bridestowe	A			24 St	St Germans	H	
	5 St	Brixham 2nds	H			25 Sn	Torrington	A	
	6 Sn	Moretonhampstead	A			28 W	Hatherleigh	H	
	9 W	Hatherleigh	A			31 St	Lewdown	A	
	12 St	Raleigh (Exmouth)	H		Aug.	1 Sn	Whipton Sun XI	A	
	13 Sn	Sandford 2nds	A			7 St	Lydford	A	
	16 W					8 Sn	Moretonhampstead	H	
	19 St	Whipton 2nds	H			14 St	Single Wicket Comp		
	20 Sn	Cheriton Fitzpaine	H			15 Sn	St Germans	A	
	23 W	Bridestowe	A			21 St	P'th Nondescripts	H	
	26 St	Raleigh (Exmouth)	A			22 Sn	Incorrigibles	A	
	30 W					28 St	Lewdown	H	
July	3 St	North Cornwall	A			29 Sn	Okehampton	H	
	4 Sn	Incorrigibles	H		Sept	5 Sn	Okehampton	A	
	7 W	North Tawton	A		TIMES		Saturdays and Sundays 2 30 p.m.		
							Wednesday Evenings 6.30 p.m.		

Cricket Club, c.1920. Left to right, back row: Cecil Ash, Jim Seaward, Bert Horn, Courtenay Ash, Gus Cockerham, Ern Reddaway; front row: Reg Phare, Jack Reddaway, Revd Henry Burnaby, Edwin Ash, Ern Tucker.

Cricket Club dinner at the Pretoria, in Okehampton, 1972. [Braetor Studio]

The Football Club

Little is known of the football club which played in the parish in the early 1920s. Apparently matches took place on Southey Down, but by the late 1920s the club was no longer in existence.

The Amateur Dramatics Society

In the late 1920s Agnes Lethem, the headmistress of the village school, ran an amateur dramatics society – productions were held in the reading-room. Irene Sampson remembers taking part in *Eliza Comes to Stay*. Other members included John Snell of Middletown, Vera Knight, the daughter of Will Knight who ran the station slaughterhouse, and Marjorie Kelland, the assistant schoolteacher. It seems the group folded when Miss Lethem left Sampford Courtenay in 1932.

Pony Races

Some of the older inhabitants of Sampford Courtenay parish remember the pony races that were held on Southey Down during the mid-1920s. These were documented in the school logs, and indeed school was sometimes closed early to allow the children to attend. It appears that the jockeys were adults and the races were taken quite seriously with betting on the likely winners. Henry Cleverdon from Cliston and Henry Reddaway from the Chapple Inn both entered ponies and the latter also ran a beer tent. Henry Reddaway's grandson Phil remembers one amusing occasion when, for a laugh, a farm worker at Yondhill rode one of the farm cart-horses in a race. The horse, unused to such events, shied at all the red flags but nevertheless somehow managed to come in third!

Football club, 1920s.

Greyhound Races

For a short time, just before and during the Second World War, Billy Hearn, who lived in one of the council-houses at Sampford Station, organised greyhound races twice a year in a field near his house. The hare was pulled along on a wire, operated manually. At this time many local residents kept greyhounds for rabbiting, but any breed of dog could take part.

The Sewing Club

During the 1950s and '60s a sewing club was organised by Pearl King, who lived in Sampford Chapple and was a teacher at Okehampton Grammar School. Meetings were held in the upper room of Church House and instruction was given in various handicraft skills, such as making lampshades.

The Brownies

For a number of years there was a Brownie pack in Sampford Courtenay. Marguerite Pye had been involved with the organisation in Kent, before moving to the village, and in the 1970s became a Brownie leader in Hatherleigh. Anita Pope suggested starting a pack in Sampford Courtenay and, early in 1978, Marguerite agreed to take on the project. At the time there were seven girls of the right age plus four more who would be old enough to join within a few months. The highest number of members in the pack at any one time was 16. Marguerite trained Valerie Letheren (née Squire) as her assistant and Valerie took over from Marguerite in 1986. However, by 1988 the number of girls had reduced to five, and, although North Tawton had a waiting-list, the Sampford Courtenay pack was forced to close.

The Social Club

A social club for the over sixties was started in 1975 by Doris Goundry. Initially there were about 30 members and monthly get-togethers were held in Church House. In recent years the club has been run by Marguerite Pye and afternoon meetings are now held at Middletown. In 2003 there are about a dozen members who meet over a cup of tea and sometimes play beetle or scrabble.

The Flower Club

The Flower Club was founded in 1985 by Vera Dyer and Betty Wilkins, who shared a common interest in flower arranging. At the beginning, there were 12 members, but at the time of writing the club (run by Rosemary Lowe, assisted by Joan Cooper and Joan Maunder) has grown to 38 members who come from both within and outside the parish. In 1988 the club became affiliated to NAFAS (the National Association of Flower Arranging Societies) which has enabled members to become more involved in area festivals and exhibitions at such venues as Exeter Cathedral, Buckfast Abbey and Castle Drogo. Monthly meetings are held in Church House. The annual programme comprises demonstrations of the many varying styles of flower arranging (including some by area demonstrators), workshops, talks on gardens, slide and video shows and visits to gardens and flower festivals. Floral arrangements for weddings and receptions are occasionally undertaken by members of the club. A major event organised by the club in recent years was decorating St Andrew's Church in 1999 as part of the Tudor festival (see pages 154 and 156). Care was taken to choose herbs and flowers that would have been in existence in the sixteenth century and the church looked and smelt magnificent, with

Brownie bazaar at Middletown Farm in aid of Year of the Child, September 1979. Left to right, back row: Edna Coates, Margaret Cartwright, Anita Pope, Marguerite Pye; front row: Janet Dunn, Elizabeth Townsend Green, Fleur Horton, Linda Lippiatt, Caroline Pope, Hazel Horton. [Braetor Studio]

rosemary and thyme in abundance and foxgloves and gilly flowers (pinks) used in profusion everywhere. Also 100 'tuzzy muzzies' were made for sale to visitors to the festival. These were Tudor posies of flowers and sweet-smelling herbs which would have been used by ladies of the period to combat the unpleasant odours in the streets.

The Art Group

The Art Group was started in the early 1980s by Dulcie Corner who was then living at Culverhayes residential home. At first weekly afternoon meetings were held in the upper room of Church House, but in recent years they have been held in the chapel Sunday school. Summer painting trips to venues such as Castle Drogo or Rosemoor Gardens are occasionally organised. After Dulcie moved out of the parish, Lin Bourne ran the group for about ten years. Since 2002 Kaye Hodge has been the organiser.

The Women's Institute

There has never been a branch of the Women's Institute in the parish but a combined group, representing Exbourne, Jacobstowe and Sampford Courtenay, holds regular meetings in Exbourne Village Hall.

Young Farmers' Club

The Young Farmers' Club also did not have a branch in the parish, but the North Tawton branch (now closed) was well attended by young people from Sampford Courtenay. It played an important role, particularly between the world wars, providing both social and instructional activities. There were classes for such skills as butter-making and stock judging. Many Sampford Courtenay couples met their prospective partners at Young Farmers' events.

National Celebrations

In 1897 Charles Grant, the bursar of King's College, wrote to Revd Little suggesting the possibility of a local celebration to mark Queen Victoria's diamond jubilee, which he thought would be popular 'if eating and drinking can be safely indulged in without danger of excess.' The college donated jubilee mugs for the children. One of Irene Sampson's earliest memories is going as a small child to village celebrations on the occasion of George V's coronation in June 1911. She remembers a long table in the square and being given a coronation mug. In 1935, to celebrate George V's silver jubilee, a public tea plus a sports event were held. There was an enormous bonfire and a tree (now gone) was planted in front of Higher Town. A commemorative walnut tree was planted in Honeychurch churchyard. The coronation of Elizabeth II in 1953 was celebrated in a similar fashion with another large bonfire. Bob Johnson remembers 'draying' all the faggots of wood for the bonfire with Ron West. Sports were held in the Barton field to the north of Weirford Lane and included energetic games such as jousting from a wheelbarrow, which, if the manoeuvre was not managed successfully, resulted in a bucket of water cascading over the heads of the occupant and the pusher of the wheelbarrow. Another game was trying to dislodge someone who was rather precariously balanced on a horizontal pole on trestles.

Above: *Bill Weeks of Hillside, Honeychurch, with father Richard and Revd Burnaby assisting, planting the commemorative tree outside Higher Town, 1935.*

Right: *George V's silver jubilee bonfire, 1935. Left to right: Samuel Northam, Courtenay Ash, Cecil Ash, ?, George Sanders, Ern Reddaway, ?, Revd Burnaby, Bill Paddon, Bill King.*

Opposite page: *Coronation sports, 1953. Tom Reddaway is trying to dislodge son-in-law Phil Reddaway from the pole. Arthur Squire is holding the pole.* [Red Lion Studios]

❧ Tudor Fête, June 1999 ❧

Left: *Dancers in the village square.*

Below: *Mummer's play in the village square.*

Left and below: *Parishioners in period costume.*

Prayer Book Rebellion display, St Andrew's Church, 1999. **Left to right:** *The Dean of Salisbury, Revd Mark Butchers, David Knights, Bob Dean, Anthony Morris, Don Miles.*

Right: *Mary Cleverdon presenting commemorative medals at the golden jubilee celebrations, June 2002.*

Golden jubilee day, 3 June 2002.

The Queen's silver jubilee in June 1977 was a whole-day affair. In the morning there was a church service and a presentation of mugs to the children. In the afternoon there were sports and an exhibition of parishioners' handicrafts. A bonfire, barbecue and fireworks were arranged for the evening and the celebrations culminated with a social in the Village Hall that commenced at 11p.m. Due to bad weather the fireworks were postponed to Bonfire Night, when a commemorative chestnut tree was planted on the village green. In 1981 there was a street party to celebrate the wedding of Prince Charles and Princess Diana.

The next major event was a Tudor fête held on 12 June 1999 to commemorate the 450th anniversary of the Prayer Book Rebellion. The event was part of a project planned and organised by a small committee comprising Revd Mark Butchers, Bob Dean, David Knights, Don Miles and Anthony Morris. The other part of the project was the design and construction of a mounted display in the church, giving details of the rebellion. This was funded by donations from various bodies and individuals. An accompanying booklet was compiled by Don Miles. On fête day, with advice from a local Tudor group, many members of the parish dressed in Tudor costume. There were old-fashioned stalls, Tudor dancing and an open-air mummer's play in the square and demonstrations of archery and combat on the village green. The day was a great success.

In 1997 a parish meeting was held to consider projects to celebrate the arrival of the new millennium. By the beginning of 2000 many of these had been implemented, such as the production of a new parish trail leaflet, reinstatement of the village green cobbled path and the creation of the Prayer Book Rebellion display. Early in 2000 a Millennium Celebration Working Party, under the auspices of the Parish Council, was set up. The group's objectives were to organise events and raise money to fund the establishment of permanent memorials. Fund-raising events began in March and a Millennium Day was organised for 27 May, when activities included a treasure hunt, sports and games, etc., in the daytime and a barn dance and supper in the evening. Money raised over the year was used to fund several memorials: a granite commemoration stone inscribed 'Sampford Courtenay 2000' in the village square, a Prayer Book Rebellion plaque on Church House and the restoration of Honeychurch Well. A time capsule was subsequently buried behind the stone. Another project supported by the fund has been the production of this, *The Book of Sampford Courtenay with Honeychurch*. The Millennium Working Party has now been incorporated within the Village Hall Committee.

The most recent event celebrated in the parish was the Queen's golden jubilee in 2002. Various festivities were organised for 3 June and included a lunch in the village square, a puppet show and games for the children, a treasure hunt with buried treasure, a tug-of-war and wellie throwing for all ages, and a 'Best Golden Jubilee Hat' competition. The children received jubilee medals and prizes for best handicrafts with a jubilee theme. The day ended with a barn dance and barbecue at the Village Hall. The event was extremely well supported and enjoyed by many members of the parish.

Flower and Produce Show

The annual flower and produce show was started during the Second World War by William and Bessie Hawking of Glebe Farm, Honeychurch. Its initial purpose was to raise money for the Red Cross in connection with the war effort. Their son Roy soon became the treasurer and Walter Cleverdon the secretary. At first the show was held in early September in Church House, but in the early 1950s it was moved to the Village Hall. There were classes for fruit, vegetables and home-made produce; the latter included bottled fruit. There were only two children's classes – a bunch of wild flowers and ten wild blackberries. Until 1972 there were several farmers' classes – turnips, swedes, mangolds and flatpolls (a type of cabbage used for animal feed). During these early years many people in the parish grew their own vegetables, more so than today. Ralph Squire, in his youth, remembers going with his father William from Slade Farm in Honeychurch with a tractor and trailer, which was necessary for all the family's entries in the vegetable and farmers' classes.

In 1973 homecraft was introduced, which comprised knitted, crocheted and machine-made articles and 'something new for something old'. Over the years the classes have been varied to provide additional interest; there are now more classes in the children's and homecraft sections.

Schedule of Local

FLOWER and VEGETABLE SHOW

to be held on

Saturday, September 2nd, 1967

Confined to the parishes of

Sampford Courtenay and Honeychurch

President : F. J. COATES, Esq.

RULES

1. Entry Fees 6d. for Each Entry in each class.
2. Entries in by 7 p.m. on Saturday, August 26th.
3. All Exhibits must be brought to the Village Hall by 12-30 p.m. on Saturday, September 2nd.
4. All Exhibits must be grown by the Exhibitor, and all Vegetables must be washed and trimmed.
5. Exhibitors wishing to take away Exhibits must do so between 6-30 and 7 p.m. None to be removed before 6-30 p.m. Remainder will be auctioned.
6. Entries to be sent to Mr. H. Piper, Mr. R. Beer, Mr. R. Hawking, Mr. W. H. Cleverdon (Hon. Secretary).

Schedule for the flower and vegetable show, 1967.

Left: *Flower and vegetable show, 1950s.* [*Western Times*]

Below: *Flower and vegetable show, 1954.* Left to right: *Walter Cleverdon, Bob Johnson, ?, William Squire, Mr Kingdom, Len Piper, Valerie Hawking, Bert Piper senr, Roy Hawking, Bill King, Hugh Piper, Henry Cleverdon.* [*Western Times*]

Left: *Flower and vegetable show, 1953.* Left to right: *Will King, Fred Coates, Hugh Piper, Roy Hawking, Len Piper, Courtenay Ash, Becky Horn, Bert Piper, Mr Kingdom, Valerie Hawking, Len Horn, Bill Cockwill, Walter Cleverdon and young Vera Hawking (centre front).* [*Western Times*]

Right: *Flower and produce show, 2002. Christine Marsh, Mayor of Okehampton and president of the show, with cup winner Sam Robertson.*

In recent years the show has moved to an earlier date in mid-August. Trophies, some donated by past supporters of the show, are awarded to competitors achieving the highest number of points in each section.

The event in 2002 offered 108 classes, including 19 for children and 19 in the craft section. Sam Robertson, who lives in the village, emerged yet again as the most successful exhibitor, with over two-thirds of his 45 entries carrying off prizes. Sam has been the highest overall points scorer for many years and the high standard of his entries continues to thwart his challengers. The show is always well supported by exhibitors and visitors.

Britain in Bloom

Sampford Courtenay's success in the Britain in Bloom competitions over a period of 20 years was an outstanding example of community spirit and hard work and must be regarded as one of the village's greatest achievements. The parish first considered taking part in the competition early in 1970, when entry details were received by the Parish Council from the West Country Tourist Board. The council chairman at the time, Roy Hawking, was a keen

Carpenter's Barn, Britain in Bloom, 1977.

gardener; he called a parish meeting, at which general interest in the project was expressed, and lodged the first entry form. In April a special committee was set up with Roy as secretary and David Bickerton as chairman. Other members of the committee included Courtenay Ash, Harold Gibson, Will King, Charles Reddaway and Tom Reddaway, and (from 1973) Ralph Squire. In May it was also decided to enter the Council for the Protection of Rural England's 'Best Kept Village' competition. The plan was that each household in the village would make an attractive display in the small front gardens, supplemented with tubs, troughs and hanging baskets. The area within the project extended from Langdale in the north to the council-houses and Cherrywell Cross in the south and initially from Moorview, Sampford Chapple, in the west to the village sign on Green Hill in the east. Sampford Chapple was not included in later years. The area also encompassed the properties up to and including the Village Hall.

During the first year, the central fund was very small and was helped by various events to raise money. Considerable expense still fell on the householders but they all entered into the project with enthusiasm and a fine display resulted. There was little central organisation except for the purchase in bulk of bedding plants which, in this and subsequent years, were acquired on the Friday before the Whitsun Bank Holiday weekend. These were laid out in Church House for collection and included geraniums, fuchsias, begonias, busy lizzies, petunias, pansies, salvias, dahlias, lobelia, alyssum, ageratums, asters, verbena, phlox, french marigolds, antirrhinums, nicotianas, etc. Planting was always carried out after the 'Franklin' nights of May had passed, the last date when frosts could be expected locally. Judging usually took place in July and that first year, 1970, Sampford Courtenay was awarded the WCTB's Abbiss Certificate of Exceptional Merit for the Britain in Bloom competition and was runner-up in the CPRE's Best Kept Village contest. This success encouraged the village to enter again in 1971 when it won the Ayre Cup for villages with a population of under 2,000. Then followed a series of awards each year as follows:

1972   *Abbiss Certificate of Exceptional Merit.*
1973   *The Gordon Ford Trophy.*
1973   *Runner-up in the Best Kept Village competition (under 500 population class).*
1974   *Past Winners' Trophy.*
1974   *Winner of the Best Kept Village competition (under 500 population class).*
1975 & 1976   *Silver Salver.*
1977, 1978 & 1979   *Cox Trophy.*
1980, 1981 & 1982   *Abbiss Certificate of Exceptional Merit.*
1983   *Silver Salver.*

Left: *Charles Reddaway outside Fir Cottage, 1978.*

Below: *Britain in Bloom – Sampford Courtenay winners of the 1984 national competition. Left to right: (Judge), Doris Piper, Anita Pope, Courtenay Ash, Shirley Reddaway, Roy Hawking with rosebowl, Jean Hodge, Sheila Cartwright, David Bickerton, Len Piper, (Judge).*

Below: *Celebrating the village's success in the European Entente Florale competition, 1985. Left to right up the steps: John Watson, Trevor Moss, Norman Pye, Jean Hodge, Marguerite Pye, Pat Watson, Marion Pratt, Vera Dyer, Effie Ash, Courtenay Ash, Tommie Tucker, Renee Squire, Stan Dyer, Roy Hawking, Betty Robertson, Ralph Squire, Teresa Squire; in front of window, standing: Pam Clayton, Denise Stimson, Jenny Knott, Rosemary Spiers, Don Miles, Ann Miles; seated: Marion Sercombe with Katie Pratt and Tweed the dog, Vera Wilson, Doris Piper, Margaret Cartwright.*

Courtenay Ash, Renee and Ralph Squire with the Entente Florale trophy, 1985.

Left: *Sampford Courtenay village sign, Entente Florale winners, 1985.*

Right: *European Entente Florale plaque and cup, 1985. Left to right: Courtenay Ash, Renee and Ralph Squire, Mrs Preece, Roy Hawking.*

At the presentation of the Cox Cup for small villages in the late 1970s, Mr Preece, the secretary of the Tourist Board's Blooms Committee, commented:

This very small village puts up year after year tremendous results and it is entirely the work of the villagers themselves. This is par excellence what Britain in Bloom is about, an achievement by all concerned in a community effort.

It was important to add something extra year by year and to make displays on the roadside verges and at communal buildings, such as Church House and the Village Hall. Fund-raising events continued to help provide the £200 to £300 needed for plants each year. Those unable to take part were willing for committee members to plant tubs, etc., outside their cottages. Ralph and Renee Squire and Roy Hawking would

travel from Honeychurch to Sampford Courtenay every summer evening to water many of the tubs and baskets. The Brownie pack looked after the Village Hall tubs and Sam Robertson those outside the Methodist chapel.

The year 1984 was special; the village square and the New Inn were really outstanding and all the other displays were particularly good. By then, there was a Britain in Bloom competition for villages with a population under 500, which suited Sampford Courtenay very well. In July the village won a rosebowl and the Sutton Seeds Cup for the South West area and was then entered for the All England and the Great Britain competitions organised by the 'Keep Britain Tidy Group'. This was the first year that there was a category for small villages in the national competitions. Judging took place throughout the country in early September and the results were announced at Vintners Hall in London on 4 October. Six people from Sampford Courtenay attended and were delighted to receive crystal rosebowls as winners of both competitions, as well as 25 rose bushes for the tidiest village. The judges commented:

Every opportunity has been taken to brighten up this naturally attractive village, which was a blaze of colour from end to end. Every nook and cranny, doorway and window, overflowed with flowers. For visitors an outstanding spectacle.

Winning the 1984 awards had not been achieved without some problems. At the end of that summer, there was a drought and a resultant hose-pipe ban. Ralph Squire recalls how the local people managed to keep all their treasured flowers well watered. He would take his tractor and link box to Frankland Ford to collect churns of water and villagers would fill an assortment of buckets and bowls from the village stream. A bucket was permanently left under the outlet pipe outside Middletown; anyone passing would pull out the full bucket and substitute an empty one. There were at least 400 flower containers of one sort or another to water so it was a mammoth task. A story is also told of villagers shovelling up sheep droppings from the main street the day before judging was taking place after a flock of sheep was unexpectedly driven through. The flower-beds on the crossroads, so carefully tended by Tom Reddaway, were, on more than one occasion, trampled by cattle or sheep being moved by local farmers.

At the end of that year several householders felt that they could not undertake another season of constant watering and it was therefore with some concern that they heard that Sampford Courtenay had been nominated to represent Great Britain in the 1985 European Competition, the 'Entente Florale'. On this occasion funds were available from West Devon Borough Council, Okehampton Chamber of Trade and the Parish Council. A note to the villagers from David Bickerton read:

Now we have to make an even greater effort to represent Great Britain... so please everybody do your very best so that we may make a worthy entry. Even more tubs, troughs and especially window boxes and hanging baskets will make a lovely show... This is an important and exciting year... Let us make a great effort so that the village will be a joy to visit.

The local press likened the event to the participation by Sampford Courtenay four centuries earlier in the Prayer Book Rebellion and dubbed it the 'battle of flowers'. This time the village was lined up against the picture-postcard villages of Austria, Switzerland, France, Belgium, Ireland and Luxembourg.

In accordance with the rules, Sampford Courtenay was ineligible to enter the small-village section in the 1985 Britain in Bloom competition, but even so, in July it was awarded the Salver for villages with a population of under 750 to boost its hope of a European honour later that year. The *Western Morning News* in July described the floral display in the village:

In every nook and cranny, crevice and cleft, there is a pot of flowers of some sort or another. There are troughs and tubs, baskets and barrels – and even milk churns, coal scuttles, a wheelbarrow, old iron cooking pots and teapots have been pressed into service as utensils in which to grow flowers. The flower baskets of deep blue lobelia and multi-coloured begonias and petunias hang everywhere... The barrels and tubs adorn the frontages of the cottages and houses – blazing beds of begonias and nemesias, the blood-red scarlet of salvias and the sunset orange of nasturtiums and marigolds. The troughs cling precariously to window sills – great streaks of colour whether it be provided by the soft blues of ageratum or snow flurries of alyssum.

Everybody had made a tremendous effort. The European judges visited the village in July, but Sampford Courtenay had to wait until September for the results. A party of six people went to Berne in Switzerland for the announcement – Courtenay Ash, Roy Hawking, Don Miles, Ralph and Renee Squire and Roy Hawking's son-in-law Philip Collins. They were delighted to hear that they had won the Entente Florale small village trophy (given by the International Horticultural Producers), beating runners-up Kaiserstuhl in Switzerland. The triumphant party, bearing the great silver cup and bronze plaque, were hailed like FA Cup winners at a welcoming reception and procession in the village. Congratulations poured in from every direction, including those of Her Majesty the Queen. West Devon Borough Council erected new road signs on the approaches to the village marking the achievement. Many visitors came to see the flowers.

Following David Bickerton's retirement as rector in 1985, Marion Pratt became chairman of the Britain in Bloom Committee. In 1986 Sampford Courtenay won the Abbiss Trophy, the only award to have eluded the village in the previous 17 years, and again won the All England and Great Britain trophies, presented at Vintners Hall by HRH Princess Anne. In 1987 the village won the Premier Award and Past Winners' Trophy, in 1988 the Silver Salver with Merit, in 1989 the Sutton Seeds Cup and in 1990 the Abbiss Certificate of Exceptional Merit. In later years it became more difficult to win the competition as the deciding factor appeared to be to demonstrate significant additional effort compared to previous years. The village felt that further improvement was not achievable and the last year Sampford Courtenay entered the competition was 1993.

Sampford Courtenay footpath day, September 1998. [Crediton Country Courier]

Footpaths

Some of the parish roads were not tarred in the 1930s; four were eventually downgraded to unclassified roads or green lanes. Various footpath surveys have been carried out over the years and in 1971 the Parish Council submitted a list of 25 possible paths. Following discussion on suitability, proof of usage, etc., these were whittled down by the County Council to the 11 currently in existence. In 1992 the Parish Paths Partnership, a Countryside Commission initiative, was introduced. This scheme provides grant money to parishes to improve and maintain their local footpaths. Sampford Courtenay joined the scheme and much has been done in recent years to improve the paths. A parish trail leaflet gives details of a circular walk, starting from the village, which includes a visit to Honeychurch.

Proposed Golf and Country Club

In 1989 Fairway International Ltd, based in Bideford, submitted a proposal to West Devon Borough Council to build a large £22 million tourist complex in the parish. The complex, to be sited on about 350 acres at Hatherton and Ventown Farms, would include a luxury hotel, an associated holiday village, two golf courses, restaurants, a swimming-pool and all-weather tennis-courts. In November a public meeting was called in the parish, which identified that the majority of residents were against the proposal. The meeting provoked a display of 'true rebellion spirit' from many present and there were several angry exchanges. Local concerns included effect on the environment, congestion on the roads and failure of the project leading to redesignation of the site for housing. A local action group was formed to oppose the plans and a petition circulated. Both the Parish Council and County Council opposed the development but the Borough Council decided to grant outline planning permission. The matter was referred to the Secretary of State who called a public enquiry in May 1991 and in December conditional approval was granted. The application has since been twice renewed but as yet the development has not gone ahead.

Chapter Eleven

SOME PARISH PERSONALITIES

Ann Palmer, 1806–34

Full many a gem of purest ray serene
The dark unfathom'd caves of ocean bear:
Full many a flower is born to blush unseen,
And waste its sweetness on the desert air.
From 'Elegy written in a Country Churchyard'
by Thomas Gray, 1751.

Ann Palmer did not achieve national fame; she was a simple Sampford Courtenay village girl who had a very short life, but her diaries were considered of such merit by the rector, George Richards, that, a few years after her death, he arranged for extracts from them to be published in a small book. Revd Richards' opinion of the spiritual state of his parish is documented in Chapter Two. In a memoir which introduced Ann's book, he described her as 'a Christian in humble life' and his aim was 'to prove that true religion can rise, flourish and evidence its growth, in the most uncongenial soil and under circumstances apparently the most unpropitious', with the hope that others in his flock 'might be stimulated by such an home example'. The details of Ann's life which follow have been taken from Richards' memoir.

Ann was born in 1806. Her father John, a tailor, lived in the village, probably at Higher Mount Ivy, and her mother in the same dwelling kept a small miscellaneous shop, 'which was furnished with almost every common article of food and apparel which were usually enquired for by those who were in low stations of life.' Ann derived 'few advantages from the situation in which providence had cast her lot'; she had little formal education, just a few years at the village school, and rarely travelled out of the parish. From childhood she had an eager desire for reading, but her access to books was extremely limited. However, she read a portion of the Bible every day and was able to repeat its text with surprising accuracy. She regularly attended the Sunday services at St Andrew's Church and instructed the children at the church Sunday school. Soon after her birth, Ann began to suffer from a hereditary disease which disfigured her person, causing 'many painful wounds over different parts of her body'. Although she had many periods of comparative health and was able 'to attend to the concerns of her little

shop', as she grew older, so the disorder advanced. Richards felt that, undoubtedly 'the state of her body contributed to the cultivation of her mind and... influenced her to renounce the vanities of an alluring world.'

Ann commenced writing the diaries in 1827. Unfortunately for the reader today, Richards omitted topics 'peculiarly local and domestic' from his book and his extracts were mostly of a spiritual nature:

> *1.4.1827 Though the waves of temptation may beat around me, yet if I can but lean on Thee as the anchor of my soul, I shall be safe.*
> *30.4.1827 Oh what a delightful season is this! The face of nature wears a smile, while the rosy-footed Spring steps forth with all her beauteous train; the music of the feathered songsters, the verdure of the fields and the balmy breath of flowers awaken in my breast the most pleasing sensations.*
> *1.12.1830 Oh how deep, how piercing is the anguish that now overwhelms me... my mother, my beloved mother, is no more. But yet other sorrows press heavily upon me.*

Ann's mother, a widow by this time, had died in embarrassed circumstances and, so great were the financial difficulties which immediately followed, that Ann was doubtful whether she could continue her shop. Ann also had to cope with the deaths of an aged aunt, who lived with her, and of a younger sister Eliza, aged 15, 'born deaf and dumb and an idiot'. However, with the help of friends, Ann was able to retain the shop.

An entry in her diary in June 1832 mentioned a dreadful fire which had broken out at North Tawton, 'which raged with such fury, that in a few hours 35 dwellings were destroyed' leaving the inhabitants without roofs over their heads. A subsequent entry a few days later recounted a collection in Sampford Courtenay Church 'for the poor sufferers at North Tawton'. On the same day Ann referred to the temptations of the coming revel week:

> *1.7.1832 May God's presence be with me during the ensuing week and prevent my being ensnared by the follies and dissipations which unfortunately abound at this season.*

Over the next few months, illness kept Ann from church and, on many occasions, from teaching at the Sunday school. In April 1833, a young friend died at the age of 17 of the same complaint from which Ann herself was suffering. The following lines, inscribed on her tombstone in Sampford Courtenay churchyard, were composed by Ann Palmer:

'Tis friendship brings this tribute to the tomb
Of her, in life and death so fondly lov'd;
Whose early flight cries with a warning voice,
'In youth and health prepare to meet your God'.

A rather morbid admonition, which is probably not to modern taste! Another of Ann's young friends died later that year. An examination of the Sampford Courtenay burials register reveals many cases of young people dying in their teens and twenties during the nineteenth century. On her friend's death, Ann remarked:

What is our life? It is only a vapour that appeareth for a little time and then vanishes away... I have a sweet hope, that though thou shouldst call me suddenly away from this world, it would only be a sudden call to glory.

Ann's last diary entry quoted in the book was on 4 January 1834. In June that year, 'she was seized by a violent attack of erysipelas, which brought her to the very confines of the grave.' She partially recovered but 'an internal disorder of a most painful and irritating description' led to her death in November. The regard in which Ann was held by the parish:

Was strikingly demonstrated by the numerous and respectable train of sincere mourners who, on the day of her funeral, crowded the churchyard to witness the interment of one who, on account of the various qualities which distinguished her, had long been considered as the ornament of her native village.

Opening the Methodist chapel Sunday school, 1933. Left to right, back row: Courtenay Ash, Revd Leaver (partly hidden), William Hawking (partly hidden), John E. Hawkins, Revd Westlake, Revd Richard Pyke, Revd Powell, Robert Hawkins, Jim Searle; fourth row: (Man with back to camera not known), Ivy Reddaway, Myrtle Hawking, Daisy Lake, Annie Hawkins, Mrs Searle, Eleanor Manning (in front of window); third row: Bert Piper, Ivy Lake, Harry Lake, John Reddaway, Pearl Lake, May Lake; second row: Christine Glanville, ?, Phyllis Joslin (with light-coloured hat and coat), Nova Lake, Audrey Reddaway, Clarice Lake, Joan Reddaway; front row: Rodney Ash, Kathleen Glanville, ?, Len Piper (with hand to mouth), Desmond and Horace Hawkins (hand in hand).

Richard Pyke, 1873–1965

Richard Pyke was one of Sampford Courtenay's noblest sons. It is remarkable that, despite his humble origins, he progressed to be President of the Methodist Conference (the highest honour in the Methodist Church), the Governor of Shebbear College in Devon and a prolific writer. He was born in 1873, the son of Samuel Pyke, a farm labourer at West Trecott. The family initially lived at Trecott Cottage, but at some stage moved to one of the village cottages. Pyke went to the village school from 1877 until 1885, when he was able to leave having passed Standard IV. His early life in Sampford Courtenay is well chronicled in his autobiography *Men and Memories*, written in 1948. He had a happy childhood:

No boy at Eton or Harrow could be happier. With a pair of good hob-nail boots, corduroy trousers and the best of fathers and mothers, each day brought its glee. It is not elaborate planning or costly toys that give a child pleasure. Freedom, fresh air and good food are more than these... within a village there are all the conditions and requirements of abounding happiness.

Initially, Richard Pyke became a farm labourer like his father. It is possible that he worked at first at Beerhill for the Hawkins family with whom he was great friends, but by 1891 he was working at Frankland Farm for two spinster ladies, Miss Elizabeth and Miss Jane Dayment, who were then in their sixties. He lived in and probably shared a room with their old servant James Badcock. He would have worked hard, but there were compensations:

Summer was a prolonged delight. Is there any scent in the world so delicious as that of a hay-field?... Autumn bestowed a rich satisfaction: we reaped then the fruits of our toil.

However, leisure time was very infrequent; holidays were practically unknown. Christmas Day, Boxing Day and Good Friday liberated the worker when he had fed the cattle and milked the cows. Otherwise work went on from seven in the morning to five at night for six days a week. It is admirable how Richard Pyke became so literate and, no doubt, eloquent, as 'there were few books or newspapers. No-one read as people read today. There were no lending libraries and no cheap novels.' His own home contained few books; besides the family Bible, there was the *Pilgrim's Progress* and one or two other religious volumes.

Pyke's family were regular worshippers at Sampford Courtenay's Methodist chapel, which was an important influence in his early life. Whenever a young man in the Methodist community showed any kind of promise, he was encouraged to direct his mind to preaching. On Mondays, Pyke invariably could remember the Sunday sermons word for word,

and, impressed by this, a local preacher suggested that he take some part in an evening service at North Tawton. Pyke was aged 16 and his guide and friend was Robert Hawkins. He carefully chose his text and, after the service, it was judged that he was competent to go it alone, and so began a ministry which was to last for many, many years. From this time he began reading; an early purchase was *Paradise Lost*, for which he paid 1s.6d., a vast sum considering the weekly wage of a farm worker then was only 12s. At 19 years of age Pyke found himself, with 15 others, facing a group of examiners as a candidate for the ministry. He was successful and was admitted as a student to Shebbear College in North Devon. Richard Pyke's days in the fields had come to an end.

Shebbear was where the Bible Christian movement first began in 1815. The college, called at first the Bible Christian Proprietary Boarding School, was established in 1832, acquiring the name Shebbear College in 1852. Introduced fairly early in its history was a system by which candidates for the Bible Christian ministry spent a short period of training at the college. Pyke attended there for a year and entered the ministry on the Shebbear Circuit in 1894. He moved to Barnstaple in 1896 and Plymouth in 1899. In 1900, he married Mary Dyer and they had two sons and three daughters. By 1907, when the Bible Christians joined with other Methodist movements to become the United Methodist Church, he was ministering in London and, in the larger Church, his reputation was growing. By 1913 he had returned to the West Country and in 1915 he was appointed Governor of Shebbear College. From then until the second half of the twentieth century, Pyke was continuously involved in one capacity or another in the government of the college. When he took over, the number of pupils had fallen and funds were short. Fees had fallen too low to meet costs, but any increase would have reduced numbers further. In 1917 Pyke negotiated with the Board of Education for the payment of grant and by 1920 the Board of Governors consisted of both members appointed by the United Methodist Conference and by the Devon Local Education Authority. In the seven years he was governor, Richard Pyke did much to improve and update the school.

By 1922, he was glad to 'shed the cares of one little kingdom' and return to the Methodist circuit. He exchanged locations with John Ford Reed, who came from Bristol South. In 1927 he was appointed President of the United Methodist Conference and moved back to Plymouth. He played a leading role in the complicated negotiations which led to the wider union in 1932 of the United Methodist Church with the Primitive Methodists and the Weslyans to form the Methodist Church of Great Britain. In 1939 he was elected president of the enlarged conference, one of the few men to hold such office who were primarily circuit ministers. In 1942 he became bursar of both Shebbear and Edgehill Colleges. Edgehill Girls' College, outside Bideford, had been purchased by the Methodist Conference in 1883. In 1949 Pyke retired to Bristol, but continued as secretary of the governors. Over the years he wrote more than a dozen religious books.

In January 1965, Richard Pyke laid the foundation-stone for Pyke House (a new dormitory block at Shebbear) – the last public function he carried out. He died in September 1965 at the age of 91, at the time the senior surviving president of the Methodist Conference. His funeral was held at Lake Chapel close to Shebbear College and the school, as a final tribute, formed a guard of honour. His obituary in the 'Old Shebbearians' Association' magazine, written by a Shebbear 'old boy', described him as:

A man of outstanding ability and of formidable personality... his gentleness and affection were... hidden behind a shell that could be cool and hard, as well as glint like steel... He spoke with disciplined passion and wrote tirelessly in books and newspapers. [He] was a man of educated and unerring taste in letters, art and music, as well as in morals and religion... [He] fought like a tiger for what he considered right... Governor Pyke was one of the biggest characters I have met in my life.*

Philip Tilden, 1887–1956

The architect Philip Tilden was one of Sampford Courtenay's most illustrious personalities. He and his wife Caroline bought Lower Rowden, together with the White House, from King's College in 1920. It would seem that the Tildens soon acquired Higher Rowden as well, although it was sold at the auction to someone else. The King's College sale catalogue described Lower Rowden as requiring a new gable-end on the east to convert it into a convenient roomy cottage. Tilden did much more than this. He was already a well-known architect, specialising in the restoration of country houses, and he transformed the modest farmhouse into a much grander building. A considerable amount of high-quality sixteenth- and seventeenth-century material was introduced into the house both from local sources and from other houses that Tilden was working on at the time. Rumour has it that certain 'artefacts' from Great Cliston found their way to Rowden, which now boasts the epithet 'Manor', although it never was such. The Tildens bought further property in the parish, at Falcadon and The Lake, in 1921.

Philip Tilden was born in 1887 in South Kensington, the only son of Sir William Tilden. He was educated at Bedales and Rugby and trained as an architect at the Architectural Association. He married Caroline Brodin in 1914. He had a flair for draughtsmanship and soon became one of the most fashionable architects and designers of his day, being patronised by such well-known figures as the Prince of Wales, Winston Churchill, David Lloyd George and Gordon Selfridge. He was best known for his sensitive and sympathetic work on old houses; his projects included Allington Castle for Sir Martin Conway in 1918, Churt for Lloyd George in 1920 and Chartwell for Churchill in 1923. In later years, he worked on properties in the South West, including Antony for Sir John Carew-Pole. In the 1950s he remodelled Broadhembury for Sir Cedric Drewe, re-thatching and restoring many of the old houses. In Sampford Courtenay, apparently, he designed Hazelwood for Thomas Lang.

The Tildens owned Rowden Manor until 1945, with Caroline running the farm. In his autobiography *True Remembrances: the Memoirs of an Architect*, published in 1954, Tilden recalled:

I could never lead a continuous existence in Devonshire owing to my overlapping work, for no sooner was one thing begun than the embryonic stage began with some other... I should find myself for days and even weeks together in London.

Philip Tilden's work has been described as 'lush and luxurious', with a tendency to over-elaborate. His literary style certainly displayed this inclination, as can be seen in his description of both the Rowdens and Sampford Courtenay:

Rowden Manor, 2002.

For nearly 30 years this originally derelict oasis was our home, gradually changing from an unloved and untended, overgrown and bewildering farm into something far more bewildering, but bewildering in its orderly disorder... At our first coming we fought with rats, then we fought with rabbits, and always with the vagaries of Devonshire weather. We dug in the unmeaning heaps that lay round the old house, and with fingers wringing wet and aching from the cold, pulled out the slimy granite. From ruined barns, where the percolating rain had eaten at the very heart of the old oak, we rescued and reclaimed.

There were... three interlocked farms, each possessing its own house... Close beside the road was the first farmhouse [The White House], *the first that we slept in ourselves and in which we had our battle with the rats. It had been gaunt and eyebrowless when we came, the soaking rains of many winters having streamed from the roofs down the dun cob of the thick rough walls. But I protected it by a cornice... and washed the walls with gentle yellow, dug from our own pockets of yellow clay. Through the great gates, and lying well back from the road, tied to ranges of buildings and barns, was the second house* [Higher Rowden]. *It was of old foundation and its streamline roof of thatch tilted and waved... On the edge of the hill, overlooking the valley of the stream that joins the Taw in our own ground, lay our house* [Rowden Manor]. *A violent swerve in the road served to enhance the importance of its position, for as one topped the hill... the road seemed to lead straight to the house and no farther... But before the house the road sweeps, skirting the curved high wall topped with thatch and dipping suddenly, plunges headlong down into the valley. Within, the rooms were low and long, their ceiling beams like the keels and ribs of old ships... From the leaded windows, set in their oaken frames, we could gaze across... to the outline of the Dartmoor hills.*

A battle was fought nearby at the time of the Prayer Book Rebellion, when they crucified the vicar on the church door [quite untrue], *and the inhabitants of the white and thatched village street with its cliff-like church tower still have all the inclinations to take the law into their own hands again* [an intriguing observation of Sampford Courtenay villagers!].

During the Second World War, Tilden found himself 'in command of a Home Guard unit of 60 Devon farmers' at Sampford Courtenay. By night he 'patrolled roads and railways' and by day 'travelled all over the county lecturing to Women's Institutes'. He also helped to look after the ruins of Exeter and Plymouth. In 1945 the Tildens sold Rowden and moved to Wortham Manor, a fifteenth-century manor house at Lifton which Philip Tilden restored. In 1950 they bought Dunsland House at Bradford near Holsworthy where Tilden carried out extensive restoration work. Dunsland was acquired by the

National Trust in 1954, but was tragically burnt down in 1967. Philip Tilden died at Shute near Axminster in 1956.

Some parishioners remember 'Lady' Tilden running the farm at Rowden which, at the time, was in a poor state and overgrown with trees, etc. No arable crops were grown; the main source of income from the farming operation for many years appeared to be from sawn logs and timber. Many of the local men would go there to shoot woodpigeon, snipe and rabbits. In the 1930s Lilian Loosemore, then aged 15, and her invalid sister were invited to stay for a week at Rowden by 'Lady' Tilden. Lilian remembers being collected in a chauffeur-driven car, but the girls did not appear to enjoy the holiday very much. Others recall Philip Tilden as a handsome man, but, not surprisingly, as 'a bit of a curiosity'.

Henry Mayo Bateman, 1887–1970

H.M. Bateman self-portrait.

Another Sampford Courtenay resident to achieve national fame was cartoonist H.M. Bateman, who lived in Brook Cottage, near the New Inn, in the 1950s and early 1960s. He was born in Australia in 1887, but his family returned to England in 1888. He was educated in the South East, at Forest Hill House, and studied drawing and painting at Westminster and New Cross Art Schools. By the time he was 14, he had decided upon his future – he would draw for publication. In the early-twentieth century, before the introduction of radio and television, the public looked for entertainment in the printed page. Black and white artists, or caricaturists, recorded the contemporary scene. Bateman has been described as a social philosopher but perhaps he was more of a moralist spelling out warnings to those who did not conform to the rules of accepted society. By the time he was 16, he was selling some of his efforts to penny comics of the day and at 17 sold his first cartoons to *The Tatler* at a guinea a time. In early life, he was on the point of dropping humorous art altogether in favour of classic painting, and the conflict in his mind led to a breakdown when he was 20. He decided, however, not to become a serious artist because his magazine work was proving so successful. By 1909 there was hardly a newspaper published in London, that contained a humorous section, to which he did not contribute. His first collection of cartoons, called *Burlesques*, was published in 1916. Nine further collections of his cartoons appeared during the next 18 years.

In 1910 his series 'Social Terrors' began to appear in *The London Opinion* and another series 'Suburbia' in *The Sketch*. A brief spell in the Army in 1914, at the age of 27, ended within months when he was sent home with rheumatic fever. Bateman's drawings first appeared in *Punch* in 1916 and his relationship with this magazine was to continue through the next two decades. In 1922 he drew 'The Guardsman who dropped it', the single most popular cartoon he produced, earning him what was in those days a small fortune – 200 guineas. In 1926 Bateman married Brenda Collins, who was 16 years his junior, and they had two daughters. Most of Bateman's cartoons in the 1920s appeared in *Punch* and *The Tatler*; the majority of the 'Man who...' cartoons described some terrible social misdemeanour, for example, 'The Man who bid half a guinea at Tattersalls'. By the 1920s Bateman was a household name and by the 1930s he was the highest-paid humorous artist in the country.

From the 1930s until his death, H.M. Bateman concentrated more on serious painting. His last cartoon for *Punch* was in 1934 and for *The Tatler* in 1936. He was by then only in his late forties, but he managed to live the rest of his long life almost entirely on his past earnings and royalties. However, Bateman became unnecessarily parsimonious and intolerant and intolerable at home. He had a long-standing battle with the Inland Revenue, dating from an early brush with a condescending official, that continued throughout his life. A story, written by him following his move to Sampford Courtenay in 1953, described the sole survivor of an immense catastrophe, who each morning scans the countryside for another human being. At last he sees another man and rushes to meet him. Eventually, he realises what the man is saying: 'I am H.M. Inspector of Taxes. You do not appear to have rendered a return of income for the past twelve months. I shall require it within ten days.'

In the 1940s Bateman became unhappy and depressed and very difficult to live with. Eventually, in 1946, his wife left him. When he moved alone to his tiny thatched cottage in Sampford Courtenay, he became much more peaceful. His life was quiet and contemplative and he spent much of his time walking over the moor with his little dog. He painted and wrote, including a book on fly-fishing published in 1960. He was a keen fisherman, often going with a friend to the East or West Okement. In the early 1960s Bateman sold Brook Cottage and moved to rooms at West Trecott. Following occasional bouts of asthmatic bronchitis, the damp winter weather in Devon forced him on trips abroad during the winter months. There were a couple of visits to France and then to Malta, but Bateman soon moved across to Gozo, Malta's smaller neighbour. It was on Gozo that he died early in 1970; he did not return from one of his daily walks and was found lying peacefully by the side of the road, where he had stopped to rest in the morning sunshine. Bateman's funeral was held at the English church on Malta.

During his time in Sampford Courtenay, Bateman did some sketches and watercolours of village properties for local residents. At the end of his autobiography, written in 1937, he remarked:

I confess, like most people, I am not entirely satisfied... I would like to have painted a quite serious picture, one that did not depend upon any sort of comic situation to make its appeal... The picture I have in mind is quite a simple one. A landscape perhaps, with just the way light falls on a house or a tree... so long as it expresses the beauty of earth and sky and water.

One wonders if he subsequently achieved this wish.

Above: *H.M. Bateman.*

Right: *Brook Cottage, H.M. Bateman's home in Sampford Courtenay.*

The Cooper family, with Becky pictured first left, in the back row.

Rebecca Horn, 1888–1982

Rebecca Horn, or Becky as she was known, was regarded as one of Sampford Courtenay's best-known and well-loved 'characters'. She was a strong-willed person but had a tremendous sense of humour with a kind and generous disposition. She was a loyal friend both to those close to her and to the parish.

In 1881 Becky's mother, Rebecca Brook, lived in a cottage (now gone) at Chichacott Cross, just outside the Sampford Courtenay parish boundary. She was then aged 30 and still unmarried but with four children at home (three boys and one girl) aged from six months to 11 years. How Rebecca Brook supported herself and her children was not recorded but it is known that for many years she worked in the local woollen trade. At some point during the next year or two she married John Cooper (who in 1881 was aged 40 and a farm labourer at Wood Farm in Sampford Courtenay). The couple lived at first in Okehampton parish and by 1888 had had four daughters. Rebecca junr was the youngest at this stage, born in April 1888. Becky was an ailing baby, but she was to outlive all her siblings, including two younger sisters born in 1890 and 1893. Three children born to the Coopers did not survive infancy. How Mrs Cooper coped with the births of nine children (including two sets of twins) and the deaths of three of them between 1883 and 1893, is hard to

Becky Horn, 1970.

imagine. In 1889 John Cooper went to work for William Lang at Withybrook Farm and the family took up residence in a four-roomed cottage nearby.

Most of the Cooper children did not receive a full education. On the family's arrival in Sampford Courtenay parish in April 1889, Albert and Florence (two of Rebecca's older children) were admitted to the village school. The log recorded: 'The boy nearly nine unable to say his letters.' In September 1891, Edith registered: 'Eight years old, only knows her letters and none of her figures.' The Coopers' five other daughters all started school well after the age of five; Becky herself was just over nine years old when she first attended school in May 1897. She left in December 1901, after just four and a half years' elementary education. Little is known of Becky's years at school. She and her siblings would have had to walk the two and a half miles from Withybrook Cottage to the village. In 1899 Becky received an honourable mention for her knowledge of religious instruction; she was a staunch Methodist. The older girls would no doubt have had to help in the home. Becky remembered:

Mother never gave us any toys; we were never allowed to play, we used to have to go out to pick up sticks for the fire. Mother made all the clothes for the family at home. She would cut up one thing and make another.

In 1898, when Becky was ten years old, the family moved to a small cottage on Hammett's Hill. William Lang had moved from Withybrook to take over The

Becky Horn, 1911.

Barton from Tom Sloman and John Cooper went with him. The Coopers' new home was one of four farm-workers' cottages belonging to The Barton. In 1902, aged 13, Becky went to work for Joyce Horn's grandmother Johanna Ward at Higher Town. Mrs Ward was a widow and lived with her son John, who was the King's College steward. Becky lived in at Higher Town for about four years, earning 2s. a week. She did farm work, including milking the Wards' two cows by hand and making butter and cream. In 1906 Johanna Ward died, John Ward married and Becky was not needed. She then went to work as a servant maid to a gentleman in Okehampton called Mr Dunn. Around this time she met George Horn, a farm worker in the Okehampton area, and they began 'walking out'.

In 1908 John Cooper retired; he was by then in his late sixties, and he had to give up the tied cottage. George suggested that he and Becky should get married and try for the cottage. Back in the village, Becky would be able to look after her parents. Apparently the parish would pay her half a crown a week to do this. Becky had known Farmer Lang since childhood and thus did all the negotiating for the cottage and getting George a job at The Barton. Becky and George were married in March 1908, just before Becky was 20 and George not quite 21. Becky remembered: 'Father couldn't read nor write, Mother couldn't read nor write and we weren't old enough to sign our papers. So Farmer Lang had to sign them.'

The couple set up home in the Hammett's Hill cottage, the right-hand one of the pair. They were to live there for the rest of their lives, subsequently buying the property and the cottage next door.

After they had been married for about a year, a caretaker was needed at the village school. Becky applied for and got the job, for which she was paid 2s.6d. a week. She had to go up to the school each morning to light the three fires, which were slow combustion stoves which ran on coke and needed a good hour to generate any heat. Accordingly, Becky had to 'have lighted them and be out the door by 8 o'clock.' She also had to clean the classrooms; the children with their muddy boots (the parish roads were unsurfaced at this time) made quite a mess on the floors. Becky recalled walking up to the school on snowy winter mornings when she would walk in the postman's footprints. 'There were no wellington boots or mackintoshes in those days. You just got wet.'

George, who Becky described as delicate, did not serve in the First World War, but continued at The Barton. Becky joined the Women's Land Army and helped out at The Barton and other farms in the parish (see Chapter Nine). George tilled the garden at Hammett's Hill and for many years the couple kept a pig. A local man called Harris would come to kill the pig and Becky would salt half of it and sell the other half. The money earned would then be used to buy the next animal. They would raise two pigs a year. Farmer Lang would let them have the occasional swede or two from the field. Becky also took in lodgers, including temporary farm labourers during both world wars. In the 1930s, The Barton's other farm workers were Jack Wooldridge, next door to the Horns, and Sam Phare, opposite in one of the Shores' Cottages. Len and Bert Piper were then young boys living just up the road at Greenbank Cottage and they remember the three workmen setting off for The Barton each morning at seven o'clock: 'You could set your clocks by them.'

Becky's father died in 1920 at the age of 79, but Mrs Cooper lived on her own (at Old Rectory Cottage) for many more years. During the last three years of her life she lived back with Becky at Hammett's Hill and died in 1940 at the age of 88. John Reddaway remembers Mrs Cooper:

She was a little white-haired old lady. When we were boys, we used to make pea-shooters out of elder sticks, taking out the pith from the middle. Unfortunately, you could never quite get that bit of spring you needed and I used to joke to Mrs Cooper 'Can I have a spring out of your stays Mrs Cooper' and she would come out with one.

Becky helped out in the house at The Barton, in later years occupied by William Lang's son Thomas and his wife Rhoda. When the Langs retired from farming in 1936 and moved to Hazelwood at Beacon Cross, Becky continued to 'do' for them. Even when they subsequently moved to Exeter, she would travel to them by bus. Becky had various other jobs around the village; she worked for the Ash family at Glebe House, doing their laundry in a huge copper in the outhouse, she was the caretaker at the Methodist chapel and Sunday school for 30 years and, apparently, even assisted with the annual spring clean of the church at Honeychurch.

When the Coates family took over The Barton from the Langs, they brought their workman with them and George was not needed. He stayed on for about six months and then went to work for Hawkins Madge at Solland. Len Piper remembers him going to work:

Every morning, whether it was the middle of summer or winter, he would walk up through the village past the forge, pushing his bike. He never had a coat on; he used to fold it up neatly and put it on the handlebars and stride up the hill in his shirt sleeves.

Margaret Weeks, Farmer Madge's daughter, remembers George and his bicycle; apparently, no one ever actually saw him riding it. He did manual work at Solland – such as gardening, hedging and ditching – and Becky did some work in the house for Mrs Madge. George stayed at Solland until the Madges moved to Exbourne in 1946. Becky continued to do some cleaning work for them there. George then did part-time gardening and odd jobs for Frank and Doris Guy of Exbourne, firstly at their smallholding at Tor View and later at their garage on the crossroads.

Becky and George did not have any children. Dear old George was very quiet and rather slow. He needed organising, which Becky was well able to do, but he helped his wife with her duties at the school.

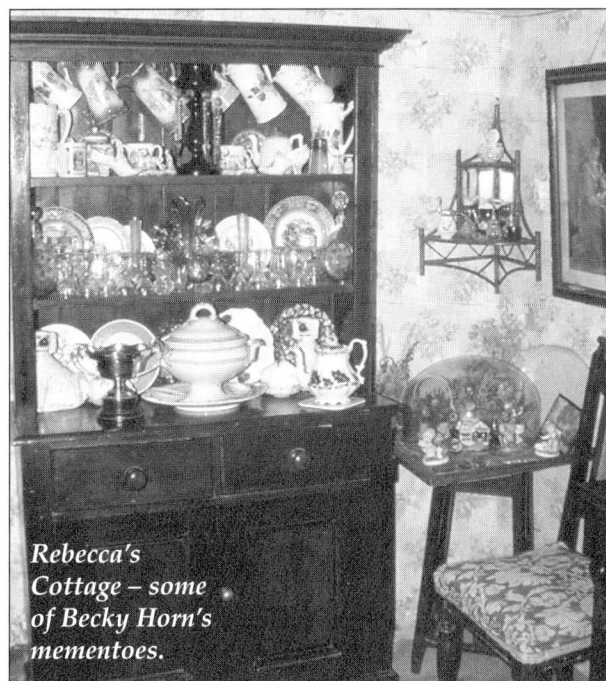

Rebecca's Cottage – some of Becky Horn's mementoes.

Freddie Johns remembers Becky making the children's costumes for school concerts: 'She was always sewing.' She continued to look after the school building when it became the Village Hall in 1951 and she was in charge at all the functions and would invariably commandeer the washing-up of the teacups, etc. Becky and George celebrated their golden wedding anniversary in 1958 with a grand party in the hall, 'the most fabulous day of my life' Becky later recalled. In 1961 George died and in 1964 Becky gave up her position as caretaker of the Village Hall. However, she did not forget the hall; when money was needed some years later to provide new kitchen and toilet facilities in the building, she gave very generously and she was asked to officiate at the opening ceremony in 1981.

Becky continued to look after the Ash family, but in reality they were taking care of her. She always enjoyed good health, which she attributed to working hard and not having anything, such as children, to worry about. She said: 'Although we were poor we were happy and had some good old days. We never wished for what we hadn't got.' Becky died in March 1982, about a month before her 94th birthday. Entering her cottage, afterwards called Rebecca's Cottage in her memory, was like stepping into the nineteenth century. She was a great hoarder and accumulated many interesting curiosities including clocks, stuffed animals and numerous other ornaments. Each piece of china, etc., held memories for her. Two of her clocks came from Withybrook Farm. She donated another to the Village Hall; it now holds pride of place near where the school bell used to hang and has recently been cleaned and restored. Many villagers recall the sale of the contents of Becky's cottage held in the village after her death. Her life is commemorated in the Village Hall by a brass plaque: 'In gratitude and loving memory of Rebecca Horn 1888–1982' and two photographs, one a school picture, preserved by Becky, taken at around the turn of the last century, in which she occupies a fairly central position, and the other of her proudly opening the Village Hall extension some 80 years later (see pages 7 and 147).

Faces of Sampford Courtenay

Above: *The Hawkins family, 1942. Left to right: Muriel, Clifford, Irene, John E. and Eleanor.*

Above: *Bill Paddon with Robbins children from Middletown, c.1940.*

Top left: *Gathering stooks of corn at The Barton, c.1940. Ivy Reddaway is pictured in the centre.*

Left: *The Hawkins family and friends, c.1919. Left to right, back row: Eleanor, Ralph Finch (from Sticklepath) ?, ?; front row: Kathleen, Irene, Muriel.*

Emma and Charles Reddaway, 1930s.

Above: *Jessie and William Charles Horn, c.1895. William farmed Ball then Webber Hill.*

Left: *Bert and Ivy Coates of The Barton, c.1950.*

Above: *Alice Johns and Mary Bolt outside the New Inn, mid-1930s.*

Right: *The Bolts, c.1916/17. Left to right: Charles, Sydney, Tom and William.*

Left: *Church fête at the old rectory (Culverhayes) in 1957. Left to right: Shirley Reddaway, Mary Mayo, Joan Reddaway, Ivy Reddaway, ?.*

Myrtle Williams making butter at Lydcott, 1920s.

Right: *Christening of twins Richard and Wilfred Weeks at Honeychurch, 1955; grandmothers Clara Weeks (left) and Edith Gimblett with Canon Squance.*

Right: *Presentation of seat to Tom Reddaway (wearing hat) of Rose Cottage, 1968, in gratitude for his care of the flower-beds on Sampford Courtenay crossroads. Left to right, back row: Ern Reddaway, Charles Reddaway; middle row: Katherine Adams, Pauline Reddaway, Joyce Horn, Lilian Piper, Audrey Reddaway, Mrs Parrett; front row: Beatrice Reddaway, Tom Reddaway, Norman Adams, Edith Kitt, Jane Fellows.* [Braetor Studio]

Left: *Fancy-dress party at the Village Hall, 1984/5. Left to right: Doris Piper, Jean Hodge, Sean Pope, Pat Squire.*

Fête at the Village Hall, 1981.

Chapter Twelve

IN CONCLUSION –
SOME MEMORIES OF PARISH LIFE

A time there was, ere England's griefs began,
When every rood of ground maintain'd its man;
For him light labour spread her wholesome store,
Just gave what life required, but gave no more:
His best companions, innocence and health;
And his best riches, ignorance of wealth.
From 'The Deserted Village' by Oliver Goldsmith, 1770.

Life in the parish was often hard, particularly prior to the twentieth century, but there are many memories of happy times and amusing experiences, of which these are but a few:

Irene Sampson (née Hawkins)

Irene Hawkins was born at Solland in 1907 and lived there until her marriage, in 1935, to Herbert Sampson of North Tawton, where the couple still live in 2003.

The first thing I remember is Mother wearing a black arm band when I was three. She said the King had died. When I was born, my brother Clifford was three, and he said 'I've got a little brother' and Mother said 'It's not a little brother, it's a girly' and I was called Girly thereafter. I am sure that nobody had a happier home life than I had. Mother was everything to me; she was wonderful. Father was very good, but he was strict. One wall of the dining-room had oak panelling with a small ledge at the top. Father kept a cane there and if we misbehaved, his hand went over his shoulder to the cane. The cane would come down and be banged on

Irene Hawkins, c.1921.

the table, but he never once touched us with it.

We had huge open hearths at Solland. The fire was laid on a cast-iron grating, supported on bricks, and there was a large moulded cast-iron fire back. Father used to bring in what we called the back log and rest it against the fire back and build the fire in front of that. We got all the wood for the fire from Solland Quarry. We used ash and elm; Father wouldn't use oak – it was too good for burning. Also hedge parings, cut by hand, were burned. The fire was going all day in the dining-room. In the kitchen was another enormous fireplace; over the fire there was a large kettle, with a 'hand-maid' as we called it to tilt the kettle, and also a crock of water, which was used for washing the dishes. On washday Lizzie the maid would bring in the copper to hang on the chimney crook. Monday was washday and it would last all through the day. All the water came from the pump-house, pumped up from the well. We used brush-wood in the kitchen bread oven as it burned fiercely. You started with brushwood and then thicker wood until it got really hot and turned to charcoal. Mother took out the red-hot charcoal with a long

scoop. You couldn't control the temperature of the oven, but Mother knew exactly what to do. She would bake a sponge before the bread and also made yeast and saffron cake. We had an American range, which burned wood and some coal, for most of the cooking. However, Mother would cook breakfast over the open fire in a very large frying pan. How she did it I do not know. We had two men and the maid living in as well as the family. [Irene was one of six children.] We had all our meals in the dining-room; we all sat at the same long table, with the servants at the bottom, 'below the salt'. However, the servants did not join in the conversation unless they were spoken to.

There was a dairy with slate slabs, and netting and shutters over the windows. It was very cool, just like a refrigerator today. It was separated by a slatted partition from what we called the salting-house. There were large oval troughs for salting the sides of bacon, which were then hung on hooks. Mother also made sausages and hogs puddings. We used to make butter too. I remember a cousin from Bondleigh going away for the week once and I was asked to make their butter as well. I made over 100lb of butter that week, all by hand, using one of the big wooden churns on a stand. We sold it at the Saturday market in Okehampton. We made cream and Eleanor [Irene's sister] also made cheese during the First World War. To make cream, you first scalded the milk in a big pan on the stove, then left it to cool in the dairy overnight; the cream would come to the top and would be skimmed off the next morning. We always had cream on the table at mealtimes. We also sold eggs at Okehampton market at 6d. a dozen. We had two beautiful orchards at Solland with eating and cooking apples, some of which we sold at the market. We never

made cider; we were teetotal and all the family had signed the pledge.

Everyone was invited to Solland; it was always an open door. I can hardly remember ever being on our own. My parents were very hospitable people. We didn't go on the village outings; we had our own outings in the summer. Father would put seats across the wagon and take the farm workers and their wives and children on the outing. [The married farm workers lived in Solland cottages.] The older ones would perhaps cycle. Mother would take a joint of cooked beef and salads, etc. We would drive right out to Taw Marsh and let the two horses go. We would sit and have our meal and the young ones would go for a swim in the river. Or sometimes we went to the Moor and the older ones would walk up to Cosdon Beacon. We would get back to the others in time for tea. We would go round to collect odd sticks and gorse to boil the kettle. I remember the tea was very often smoky from the fire. It was a wonderful time. Then we had to go back of course to do the milking. Lizzie always stayed at home. Lizzie [whose maiden name was Piper] didn't marry until she was about 50 and went to live in Sandford near Crediton. I used to visit her there. I remember her husband saying 'Make Miss Hawkins a cup of tea Lizzie!'

We were self-sufficient for most food. We kept flour in wooden containers in the pantry, having taken corn to Newland Mill or Murrins at Monkokehampton to be ground. We took animals for slaughter to two butchers in Exbourne –

Above: *Harvest day at Solland, 1919. Lizzie Piper is in the front row on the left.*

Left: *The Hawkins family and friends picnicking on Dartmoor, 1919.*

Above: *The Hawkins sisters at Solland, 1914/5.*
Left to right: *Muriel, Kathleen, Irene, Eleanor.*

Top right: *Milkmaids, Muriel and Kathleen Hawkins at Solland, c.1915.*

Right: *Solland, 1919 – Clifford, Kathleen and Eleanor Hawkins with two visiting Methodist ministers.*

The Hawkins family ready for market, c.1920.

Glanville's and Chapple's. We bought in large quarters of beef, which didn't last long with all of us. On Christmas Eve we entertained the workmen and their families at an evening meal of roast sirloin of beef and suet pudding. Father and the boys would go to the quarry for a huge back log for the fire. We had a tennis-court and a swimming-pool at Solland. Father bought our first car in 1922, a 22 hp Chevrolet which cost £198. We were one of the first families in the parish to have a car.

I went to Sampford Courtenay School until I was 11 and then went to Okehampton Grammar until I was nearly 18. I passed my exams and could have gone into nursing or domestic science. However, because Eddie had died and Clifford was in the ministry, Father said 'There's work to be done here' and I had to help on the farm. I never felt farming was hard work; I enjoyed every minute of it. I didn't work outside so much in the winter, but we always milked the cows. There were two or three of us to milk about 20 cows in the shippen. It was a beautiful shippen; I don't know what's happened to it now. It was lovely and warm on a winter's night and we had paraffin lanterns. All the cows had names. On Sundays we just did the milking, but no other work, not even if it was going to rain the next day. I remember an occasion when my sisters and I had overslept one Sunday morning and consequently were late doing the milking. Father insisted the horses should have a day of rest on Sundays so the milk-cart had to be dragged up to the main road by hand, using a rope. Unfortunately the rope broke and Father lost his temper and said: 'You maidens will lie abed until seven stars become 14', or perhaps it was 14 become seven. He always called us maidens.

We weren't allowed to go to dances; Herbert and I met at school. We had a wind-up gramophone at home, but we played classical not modern music. In the evenings we did knitting and sewing or writing letters, or sometimes played cards. Every Sunday evening we spent in the sitting-room around the piano singing hymns. Each year we would have a harvest festival at Solland and it got bigger and bigger, so we eventually had to open up a barn. Clifford and I would cut branches to decorate it. We would borrow seating from Sampford Courtenay or Exbourne Sunday

Harvest festival at Solland, 1926.

schools. Mother was the brains behind all the catering. We had North Tawton Choir and a piano for the occasion. The building would be cleaned out and tables set up with white tablecloths for the luncheon. Father and the men would dig a pit just outside and put girders across for boilers to heat the water to make the tea and do the washing-up. Although it was really a Methodist celebration, Anglicans from all around used to come.

Myrtle Hunkin (née Hawking)

Myrtle's parents, William and Bessie Hawking, moved to Glebe Farm in Honeychurch in 1923 when Myrtle was four. She lived there until her marriage in 1948 and has many memories of her early life in Honeychurch.

We did a lot of cooking in the bread oven. We made saffron cake in it. The night before you had to chop up the saffron and put boiling water on it to get the flavour out and put all the fruit into a bowl. The next day you made your own yeast up and made the cake. We heated the oven with a faggot of wood. You had to break up the twigs small and keep on adding to it until the fire had been going for about three quarters of an hour. Then you scraped it all out into the hearth. The oven was then ready to cook your yeast buns first, then your dinner, then your bread, cakes, apple tarts and pasties. You knew, as it was cooling down, the different things to put in. When that was finished and the oven wasn't too hot, my mother used to stew fruit. She would put the fruit in jars and leave them in the oven probably for hours; it would come out lovely. The oven, which was made of fire bricks, would retain the heat for a long time. We had a cloam oven at first, but then we had a brick one when that wore away. Also, if you put paper in the oven first, you could use it to air your clothes. We also had an oil stove with an oven on the top and we sometimes cooked things in a pot over the fire too.

There was a wild pear tree growing on some rough ground near Glebe; the pears were called French Eagles, they were very small. There were whortleberries growing from Westacott Lane down to the bottom, and, on the moor to the left as you go towards Corstone, there were lots of orchids and cotton grass, which is now rare. We made rosehip syrup at home; there aren't many rosehips about now because they cut all the hedges down so much. We planted the orchard at Glebe. John Reddaway at Middleton had a cider press and we used to take our apples there. Valerie's dad [William Squire] at Slade used to take the jug round to Middleton for cider. It was nice but very strong and, as children, we were only allowed a small amount.

When I left school at 15, I worked on the farm. I had to work hard. I had to bring the cows back from the field for milking every day. I hated it when they used to go in the stream on the way and I couldn't get them out again. I didn't do any milking; Valerie would come down to help milk the cows if the men were harvesting. They were Red Devons and were well-behaved and quiet to milk. I also helped with the poultry, calves and pigs – feeding them and collecting the eggs. When the men were threshing, we had to do a lot of cooking – bread and cakes, etc. I went to poultry classes through the Young Farmers' Club and learnt how to kill chickens; I killed hundreds of chickens and I didn't get upset when the pig was killed. We were a cruel lot! The crooks and bars are still there at Glebe where we used to hang the pigs. The pig was fattened for six months with pig meal and household scraps. We made butter up until the time that Ambrosia took the milk. Before that we kept it all ourselves; we only had five or six cows. The calves would have some of it. We made butter and cream, but we didn't scald the milk, we used a separator. Shobbrooks from Okehampton would come round and buy our eggs and butter. I would help Father and my brother Roy to drive the bullocks to North Tawton market. I used to dread it because at a certain point the hedges were low and the bullocks would jump over them into the field. I remember it taking hours getting them out.

Freddie Johns

Freddie was born in Sampford Courtenay in 1931 and lived and worked in the parish for much of his life. He now lives just outside the boundary at Chichacott, but he continues to look after Sampford Courtenay churchyard. He also does some gardening work in the parish.

My father [William] married twice and had five children by his first wife. She died aged 36. He married again and had another five children, three girls and two boys [of which Freddie was one]. My mother Beatrice died when I was eight; she was only 38. My youngest sister Jean can't remember her. Granny looked after us then. My brother Bert and sisters Ivy and Patsie were born at Pound Cottage [now gone]. The family moved to Sampford Station, to one of the council-houses, and Jean and I were born there. My father was a farm worker; he worked for Frank Jury at Beerhill. Charlie Hodge (John's and Victor's father) worked for him too. Father was only earning a few shillings a week when he started, but he was also given some swedes, turnips and potatoes and the odd rabbit or two. He was very strict. He made us know what was right and what was wrong. You were never to touch what didn't belong to you. We had to go to bed on time. He would pick up the stick when we were naughty and it would just catch the door as we disappeared through it up the stairs.

We made our own fun; there was no money to buy toys and we made our own – out of a corned-beef tin

Pound Cottage, 1981 – last occupied (by the Johns family) in 1930.

or clay dolls. We also made something with cotton reels and a candle and rubber bands and it would go along on its own, and paper aeroplanes. Our spending money, when we were kids during the war, was from picking blackberries and rosehips for Billy Hearn. We walked to school from Sampford Station, all five of us with Bert in charge. We would meet up with other children on the way. I could take you back to every place where Mother would come to meet us with our dinner. Summer and winter, she would set off and we would meet her halfway, sometimes by the council-houses, sometimes near Cricket Farm, and, if we were a bit quicker than Mother, at the top of Hatherton Lane. We would always go to school clean and come home dirty, no matter what condition the road was in. Kids are always clean today.

I started work when I was 14 at Harry Cleverdon's at Higher Cliston. I lived in and I was earning £1 a week plus my lunch and dinner. I worked for Walter [Harry's son] for over 16 years. I was the last one to use horses at Cliston. Instead of having a drag harrow with spikes, we used to pull a large holly bush round with a horse to fluff up the ground after sowing grass seed, so as not to bury the seed too deep. I used to drive the horses between the teddie [potato] alleys and mangolds to cut the weed. Mr King next door [Great Cliston] had two teams of horses, one brown team and one white team. He ploughed with one team in the morning and the other in the afternoon. One acre a day was ploughed; it's 18 acres a day now.

After working for the Cleverdons, I went to work where the Bridgmans are now on the Winkleigh road for three or four years and I lodged with my sister-in-law Pearl on Hammett's Hill. [Pearl, who still lives in Sampford Courtenay, was married to Courtenay, Freddie's half-brother.] I didn't want to shift, but they had two sons leaving school and I had to move on. I then worked for Willie Weeks [at Hillside, Honeychurch], but when the two boys got older, I had to move on again. I worked for a chap in North Tawton and then in Hatherleigh. Farming was a beautiful life; I wouldn't have changed my life for the world.

Lorna Weeks

Bill and Lorna Weeks farmed Hillside in Honeychurch and Beerhill in Sampford Courtenay for many years; their sons Richard and Wilf run the farms at the time of writing. Lorna, who still lives at Beerhill, remembers threshing day in around 1940.

The sheaves of corn were all safely stacked in their ricks in August and September, carried from stooks in the fields on wagons with the cart-horse straining and sweating up the hills and helped by a younger second horse harnessed in front and led by the horseman. Each load was brought to the rick, where a base of faggot wood was already in place to keep the sheaves off the ground to keep dry. The ricks were thatched with good strong rushes.

When the thresher and steam engine were in the area, the farmer put in his order for one or more days' threshing, letting his neighbours know to send along one or two men to help, as eleven or twelve men were required, more if reed combing. Probably the men already had been threshing at a neighbouring farm. Threshing was a winter job so the days were short. I remember the excitement and anticipation as the children heard the steam engine drawing the thresher, chuffing along the lane and stopping at the stream to draw water. It drew up beside the rick; if the ground was sloping the machine would be made level by digging pits for one set of wheels and perhaps the other end would be on large wooden blocks. The two thresher men arrived before dawn the next morning to get up steam with plenty of steam coal, which the farmer had bought in for the purpose. They then came into the farm kitchen for a good breakfast of bacon and eggs. The farmer's wife had been busy baking pasties, tarts and

cakes, peeling large quantities of potatoes and soaking and boiling a salted ham from the home-killed pig. Her worst dread was the weather suddenly turning wet. Her food preparation would keep if threshing was delayed just one or two days, but one or two weeks would be a disaster with no freezer in the house. She would then have to prepare all over again.

The helpers arrived quite early; the thatch was stripped and threshing commenced. The hum of the machine could be heard until 10.30a.m., when the farmer's daughter or another helper carried out a large basket of food and kettles of steaming tea. After the food, everyone would be back to work. Two men pitched the sheaves from the rick onto the top of the thresher for another two men who worked by the dangerous opening, cutting the binder cord and feeding in the sheaves, ears first. A further two men attended to the corn bags; they would have to be strong as each hundredweight of corn had to be carried on their backs up a flight of steps to an upstairs room or 'granary'. Other men dealt with the trusses of straw relentlessly coming out of the other end of the thresher; these had to be moved clear. At about 1.00p.m., after the farmer had checked with his wife, all the workers filed into the kitchen and sat at the long table to enjoy the meal provided. After this, everyone went out again until the day's work was finished.

As they got nearer the bottom of the rick, rats would start running out; most would be caught by wire netting placed around to prevent them escaping. Much shouting and running to kill them would add to the excitement, with the farm dogs joining in the sport. The threshing machine then moved to the next farm and the farmer had much clearing up to do the following day. A huge pile of 'douse' (dusty waste from the ears of corn) would have to be cleared away before it got wet. It was either burned or used for animal bedding.

Bob Johnson

Bob Johnson was an evacuee from the Battersea area of London and arrived in the parish in 1940 when he was eight. His first few years in Sampford Courtenay proved quite an experience. Bob stayed in the parish and married local girl Barbara Sanders. He and Barbara subsequently kept bullocks near Cliston, where they built Sanders Park, and then bought Paize in 1981. After living at the Chapple Inn for a while, they moved to North Tawton.

I don't remember how I got here from Battersea. I got chickenpox or measles and was sent to Belstone with a lady. Then I moved to Solland with Hawkins Madge. I couldn't get on with the girl [Farmer Madge's daughter Margaret]. I was only there for an after-noon. I didn't stop crying, so they took me over to Great Cliston. Ronald King was there [about Bob's age] and I saw the ducks and wouldn't leave. My two brothers first of all went to someone in Northlew, but they were being locked in the pump-house for hours on end. They were taken away and came to stay at

Coronation bonfire, 1953. **Left to right, top:** *Fred Reynolds, Canon Arthur Squance;* **on ladder:** *Bob Johnson, George Sanders;* **on ground:** *Ron King, Archie Watts, Laddie the rector's dog, Will Reddaway, Ronnie West, Courtenay Sanders, Phil Reddaway.*

Cliston with me. Granny King looked after all three of us for a couple of years. My brothers would get home from school before me and I used to get into trouble because I'd be skulking around somewhere. I fell down the school steps once and hurt myself on the gate. My brothers went back to London.

Eventually, at the end of the war, I had to go back as well. They came for me several times. They wrote a letter to the old man and said they were coming to fetch me but I'd go and sit in Solland Quarry and wait till they'd gone. The attendance officer came and said 'You've got to go back' and even the old man said I had to go. Anyway, they got me as far as Reading and I jumped off the train and caught the next train back to Sampford Courtenay. The next time they took me I went handcuffed to a policeman. I was taken all the way to Mother's, but I was so upset she let me come back after two days.

I left North Tawton School to work on the farm at Cliston; that's all I wanted to do. Bill King never paid me until I was 21. He and Granny would buy my clothes. I liked the job so much I didn't mind. At first, I worked with horses. The last one was drowned in a swamp. He had broken down some wire and got into a boggy bit of ground where he got stuck. Nobody saw him, poor old devil, and we pulled him out with a digger but he was dead. I remember another horse we had that we'd tied up to have some corn. He was still in the shafts of a two-wheeled cart. We heard this choking sound and looked round and he was hanging in the air. The cart had been overloaded at the back with sacks of corn and had tipped up, taking the hames up in the air. The horse had to be cut down, but he was all right.

They made their own cider at Cliston. We used to climb up the trees and shake the apples down. It was good cider, which they used to sell. There was a huge corkscrew press for pressing the apples into a big stone trough and the liquid was poured through a funnel into large hogshead barrels. People used to come from miles around to buy King's cider. It used to put a few people away! The orchard is still there, but the trees are now lying on the ground. At Christmas we would have ash faggots on the open fire. These were large bundles of ash saplings, bound with twisted strips of hazel and every time one of the bindings burst open in the flames, we would pass round a mug of hot cider and each have a swig. [The burning of the ashen faggot on Christmas Eve was a local custom observed for many years and was remembered by Richard Pyke, c.1880.]

Lilian Loosemore

Lilian and Frank Loosemore, as a young couple, farmed Frankland from 1946 until 1955.

We had dairy cows, bullocks, sheep and pigs and some corn and potatoes. When we started we bought two beautiful Shire-horses but soon had a tractor. I helped round the farm. I did everything. My eldest son Tom was a little monkey. The men would be harvesting or haymaking and I would have to go and get the cows and milk them. I've sat and milked out 25 gallons by hand. I used to make Tom stand in an old heavy bottomed milk churn to watch me milk, because otherwise I couldn't keep my eye on him.

Frankland Farm, 1996.

Jane Reynolds from Sampford Chapple, planting a commemorative tree, 1935.

He was about four and his curly head was sticking out the top and he would kick with his feet. The yard wasn't concreted at that time [or drained] and there was always a big pond in the middle. My brother had had a drink or two one night; we'd had a game of cards, and he went out and fell in. We didn't have electricity; we had calor gas which ran lights downstairs, but we had candles for upstairs. There was no mains water, just the pump in the back yard and no bathroom and no inside toilet. There was just a horrible earth closet in the back yard.

I had this old sow. On one occasion, we went to Exeter on market day and brought home some young pigs. The young pigs got out and my old sow got out too when we were having our breakfast. There was a hell of a commotion in the yard and Frank rushed out and the sow had killed one of the young pigs. That was our profit gone! She killed a lamb on a second occasion, just another of our many disasters.

There was a ghost at Frankland; we had some frights there I can tell you. It was one particular bedroom that was worst, people couldn't sleep there because of the noises in the night. Doors would open and shut and windows too. Pots and pans would rattle in the larder. We had a sideboard in the dining-room on which there was a nice big bowl (a wedding present). It just came off one night and broke into pieces. We would also hear footsteps running about upstairs, but, if you went up to look, the children would be asleep in bed. Eventually we got Canon Squance to say a special prayer to exorcise the ghost and we didn't have any more trouble after that.

There are reports of other ghosts in the parish. Bob and Barbara Johnson saw a white female figure with a walking stick on the road from the Village Hall to Sampford Chapple and were convinced it was old Mrs Jane Reynolds who used to live at Sampford Chapple crossroads in one of the cottages that has now gone. There was supposedly a ghost at Great Cliston that used to sit on the water-pump and also one at South Town. Another ghost, at one of the village cottages, had to be exorcised. Interestingly, a well-known writer of ghost stories, M.R. James, set one of his tales in Sampford Courtenay. James was provost of King's College in 1905 and in this capacity would have visited the parish. The ghost was that of a young woman who had been murdered, and she haunted the New Inn. James claimed that all his stories were pure invention, but who knows?

David Bickerton

The following extracts are taken from Revd David Bickerton's diaries kept during the severe winters of 1962–63 and 1978.

> 31.12.1962 *Walked with the boys, Robert King, Terry Bridgeman, John Sanders and David Sercombe, along Honeychurch Lane – quite impassable beyond Oxenpark Barn until Red Post Cross. Arthur and Ralph Squire and Stewart Reddaway had come down from Honeychurch on tractors for bread and supplies... Rosemary Cleverdon and Jean Staddon had walked across fields from Clisson.*

3.1.1963 *It must have snowed quietly all night. This morning still snowing and so all day... the steady fall has given a cover of 12 to 18 inches everywhere. A most lovely sight... The church was surpassingly beautiful, every feature picked out in snow. The trees are magnificent. But the hardship on the Moor will be severe.*

8.1.1963 *Sometimes the sun comes through and we can see the wall of Dartmoor, a completely white mass. It seems more dangerous underfoot than ever after a near thaw. I avoid the trodden snow and walk in the deep snow on the road verges. To the village, I go across the meadow and down the 'Hop Way' as they call it. Visited old Mrs Taylor, 'Fla' or 'Coopy' as they call her.*

9.1.1963 *At 4p.m. there was a pink light suffusing the west and the iceberg shapes of the northern slopes of the Moor appeared through the grey-blue sky. Then in the north-east as I walked across the meadow to the Post Office there was an orange full moon actually throwing a glow on the snow-covered fields and hedges.*

10.1.1963 *Last night was perhaps the most wonderful I ever remember. The full moon lit up the snow-covered countryside and the roofs of the cottages and the New Inn below the rectory. I pulled back the curtains and put out the lights. I could not bear to leave the firelight within and the bright moonlight outside.*

12.1.1963 *Walked to Honeychurch... a wonderful walk in the sun – the wind has dropped. Had to stop frequently to wonder at the changing views. The boys had a wonderful sledge run on the slope of the East Town field. Their excited voices came across to the road – the three Aldred boys and the Weeks twins. All little boys at Honeychurch.*

13.1.1963 *Walked to Honeychurch with surplice and communion vessels in my rucksack. A lovely walk through the snow banks in sunshine.*

17.1.1963 *Walking up to the village, noticed that the runnel across the village street is completely frozen all round, while the water flows in an ice cave.*

18.1.1963 *Took the car out for the first time this morning. Stuck in the drive. Fortunately Phil Reddaway was coming up the hill in Mr Ash's lorry (taking him to Okehampton to the bank). He came and pushed me out.*

23.1.1963 *Last night the coldest we have had, so the reports say – nought degrees Fahrenheit, 32 degrees of frost – I would like to see the rivers frozen – many photographs in the papers.*

Revd David Bickerton's retirement party at the Village Hall, 1985. Left to right: *Phil Reddaway, Courtenay Ash, David Bickerton, Lorna Weeks, Jose Reddaway.*

24.1.1963 Saw old Mrs Taylor at the farmhouse. A wonderful talker, full of old Devon words: 'Draw up Sus and have a skriddle'. Sus = sister (I think) and skriddle is a warm at the open fire – piled against a great 'back stick'.

4.2.1963 Woke this morning to steady quiet snow – filling all the tracks under an even blanket. First waking impression – a lorry stuck on the hill outside.

6.2.1963 What a night of blizzard – said to be the worst in memory – 20 feet drifts on Dartmoor... Many vehicles were all night in the snow at Whiddon Down – stayed in a schoolroom without food – and the electricity failed as it did with us. Five trains in the snow between Exeter and Lydford. Okehampton is cut off by road and rail. The North Tawton road is completely blocked and Station Road; the only way out up to Exbourne and so to Hatherleigh.

7.2.1963 The news is that 70 people spent all night Tuesday in the schoolroom at Whiddon Down – yesterday got away to Exeter with the help of snow ploughs and Royal Marines. The railway is blocked between North Tawton and Sampford Courtenay. That accounts for the plaintive whistles from the railway yesterday.

14.2.1963 Steady rain and a southerly high wind... The fields are now green again.

Fifteen years later he recorded:

16.2.1978 All last night a fierce blizzard from the east... the A30 is blocked and cars abandoned.

17.2.1978 This afternoon walked down the hill. Bob Johnson and David Sercombe working with tractor and scoop and Robert Reddaway with his father Stewart from Honeychurch have come down with their tractor dragging a V-shaped improvised snow plough behind them... They were all busy clearing the deep snow at the New Inn junction.

19.2.1978 Last night the constant gale from the east and driving snow continued. Then the electric light and power failed... Not a road in Devon is passable.

20.2.1978 At 7a.m. a dull thud from the back of the house. Feared Mrs Coles [David Bickerton's housekeeper] had fallen down the stairs – but inspection showed that 30 feet of the guttering had fallen. The thin supports were not sufficient to hold the weight of snow... Okehampton and North Devon still completely isolated and the whole of Dartmoor... Dartmoor a disaster area... Power restored at 3.30p.m. Roy Hawking 'phoned from Honeychurch; they have no electricity there. He managed to scramble through drifts to his ewes. Also Arthur Squire and Raymond got to sheep at Venn. Ralph is digging out ewes at Frankland.

21.2.1978 Opposite the village shop there is a huge snow-drift in front of the church house, yesterday it covered the steps... The drift by Thornbury is enormous, roof high at the road junction. The men were digging out Barton sheep, dug out the last eight this afternoon, some 10 feet down. The Chapple to Okehampton road totally impassable.

22.2.1978 A definite thaw – quite warm and wind from the south... The Post Office has bread, a group of soldiers (cadets) led by Dartmoor Rescue people brought it from Exbourne – 50 loaves. The news is that the snow ploughs have got through to Exbourne and Jacobstowe... and Okehampton on the A30.

24.2.1978 Snow is going fast.

Picnic in the harvest field at South Town, 1950s – 'Coopy' and Fred Taylor are standing back right.

Sampford Courtenay crossroads, c.1915.
Note the New Inn outbuildings are thatched, including the linhay (centre).

Conclusion

I hope that this history has given readers an insight into life in Sampford Courtenay and Honeychurch over the last millennium. Until well into the twentieth century the inhabitants of the parish were almost entirely involved in agriculture; there were no resident gentry and the population mostly was made up of small tenant farmers and their labourers. In 1894 Revd Thomas Little commented to Charles Grant, the bursar of King's College: 'I cannot disguise that this neighbourhood is poor.' Examination of the old records reveals a close-knit community. There was a major influence from the college, but the parish was in most respects self-contained. The Manor Courts, although presided over by a representative of the college, were attended by local farmers who ensured that the land was properly managed. The farmers also acted, in rotation, as parish officers who arranged for the care of the poor, the sick and the elderly and organised the maintenance of the local roads and bridges. Food and clothes and children's education were provided within the parish. Farmers helped one other at busy times and most leisure hours were spent with fellow parishioners.

Remaining relatively unchanged over several centuries, this way of life has now disappeared. Far fewer people manage the land and farms operate independently. Responsibility for those in need has passed from the parish. The inhabitants are more diverse and, although many are in one way or another involved in agriculture, there is now a large number of commuters and retired inhabitants. Employment, education, shopping expeditions and leisure activities take people out of the parish and it is difficult to achieve the same community spirit. Nevertheless, there is still a sense of community as evidenced by the achievements in the Britain in Bloom campaign from the 1970s until the 1990s and more recently by the support received for the golden jubilee celebrations in 2002. Sampford Courtenay and Honeychurch so far have avoided any major commercial or housing development and the countryside, the village and the hamlets look much the same as they have for several centuries. The parish remains a beautiful and unspoilt place in which to live and it is hoped that this valuable heritage is preserved throughout the new millennium.

Millennium Stone dedicated by Revd Brian Ardill, New Year's Eve, 2000.

BIBLIOGRAPHY AND SOURCES

Books, Articles and Poems

Adams, Maxwell – 'Honeychurch', *Devon Notes & Queries Vol. 2* (1902/3).

Anderson, Anthony – *The Man who was H.M. Bateman* (Webb & Bower, 1982).

Bateman, H.M. – *H.M. Bateman by Himself* (Collins, 1937).

Bateman, H.M. – *The Man who drew the Twentieth Century* (Macdonald & Co. Ltd, 1969).

Bickerton, David – Diaries 1962/3 and 1978 (unpublished).

Caraman, Philip – *The Western Rising 1549 – The Prayer Book Rebellion* (Westcountry Books, 1994).

Charity Commissioners – *Reports on Parish Charities (1826) and (1912)*.

Cherry, Bridget, and Pevsner, Nikolaus – *The Buildings of England, Devon* (Penguin Books, 1991).

Copeland, G.W. – 'Devonshire Church Houses', *Transactions of the Devonshire Association (TDA) Vol. 92* (1960) and *Vol. 93* (1961).

Crabbe, George – 'Barnaby the Shopman' (1834).

Crabbe, George – 'The Village' (1783).

Cresswell, Beatrix – *Notes on Devon Churches* (1921).

Domesday Book, Devon (Phillimore, 1985).

Dredge, John Ingle – 'A Few Sheaves of Devon Bibliography', *TDA Vol. 31* (1899).

Edwards, Peter – *Farming: Sources for Local Historians* (B.T. Batsford Ltd, 1991).

Erskine, A.M. – *The Devonshire Lay Subsidy of 1332* (1969).

Express & Echo (*Western Times*) and *Western Morning News*.

Fox, Aileen – 'Archaeology and Early History – North Tawton', *TDA Vol. 85* (1953).

Friar, Stephen – *The Batsford Companion to Local History* (1991).

Goldsmith, Oliver – 'The Deserted Village' (1770).

Gover, J.E.B., Mawer, A., and Stenton, F.M. – *Place Names of Devon* (1931).

Gray, Thomas – 'Elegy Written in a Country Churchyard' (1751).

Hoskins, W.G. – *Devon* (David & Charles, 1954).

Hoskins, W.G. – *Devon and its People* (David & Charles, 1959).

Hoskins, W.G. – *Old Devon* (David & Charles, 1966).

Hoskins, W.G. – *St Mary's, Honeychurch* (unpublished).

Howard, A.J. – *Devon Protestation Returns, 1641* (1973).

Joce, T.J. – 'The Original Main Road West of Exeter', *TDA Vol. 50* (1918).

Lysons, D. – *Magna Britannia, Devon* (1822).

Maxwell, J.G. – *Sighs, Smiles and Sketches: Poems* (W. Kent, 1860).

May, Trevor – *The Victorian Schoolroom* (Shire Publications Ltd, 1999).

Mugford, W.E. – 'Honeychurch', *Devon Notes & Queries Vol. 3* (1904/5).

Nicholas, John, and Reeve, George – *The Okehampton Line* (Irwell Press Ltd, 2001).

North Devon Decorative and Fine Arts Society, The – *St Mary's, Honeychurch* (1993).

Oldham, D'Oyly W. – 'The Private Chapels of Devon Ancient and Modern', *TDA Vol. 38* (1906).

Owen, Wilfred – 'Anthem for Doomed Youth' (1917).

Phillips, E. Masson – 'The Ancient Stone Crosses of Devon', *TDA Vol. 69* (1937) and *Vol. 71* (1939).

Polwhele, Richard – *The History of Devonshire (1793–1806)*.

Prideaux, Edith – 'The Church of St James the Less, Honeychurch', *Transactions of the Exeter Architectural Society Third Series Vol. 3* (1913).

Pyke, Richard – *The Golden Chain*.

Pyke, Richard – *Men and Memories* (The Epworth Press, 1948).

Pyke, Richard – *The Story of Shebbear College* (Chudley, 1953).

Rawlence, E.A. – *Three Old Crosses at Sampford Courtenay*.

Richards, George P. – *A Memoir and Diary of Ann Palmer* (W. Roberts, 1838).
Rose-Troup, Frances – *The Western Rebellion of 1549* (Smith, Elder & Co., 1913)
St Leger-Gordon, D. – *Portrait of Devon* (Robert Hale Ltd, 1963).
St Leger-Gordon, D. – *Under Dartmoor Hills* (Robert Hale Ltd, 1954).
Sellman, R.R. – *Aspects of Devon History* (Devon Books, 1962).
Sellman, R.R. – *Devon Village Schools in the Nineteenth Century* (David & Charles, 1967).
Spurr, David – *Devon Churches Vol. 2* (Merlin Books Ltd, 1984).
Stanes, Robin – *A History of Devon* (Phillimore, 1986).
Stoate, T.L. – *The Devon Muster Roll for 1569* (1977).
Stoate, T.L. – *Devon Subsidy Rolls, 1524–7* (1979).
Stoate, T.L. – *Devon Subsidy Rolls, 1543–5* (1986).
Sturt, John – *Revolt in the West: The Western Rebellion of 1549* (Devon Books, 1987).
Tate, W.E. – *The Parish Chest* (Cambridge University Press, 1946).
Tilden, Philip – *True Remembrances: the Memoirs of an Architect* (Country Life Ltd, 1954).
Trade Directories – *Billing's, Harrod's, Kelly's, Morris's , Post Office* and *White's.*
Vancouver, Charles – *General View of the Agriculture of the County of Devon* (1808).
Vince, John – *Farms and Farming* (Ian Allan Ltd, 1971).
Webb, S. and B. – *The Story of the King's Highway* (1913).
Westcote, Thomas – *A View of Devonshire* (1845).
Westcott, Margaret – *The Estates of the Earls of Devon, 1485–1538* (unpublished 1958).
Whale, T.W. – 'The Tax Roll of "Testa de Nevill"', *TDA Vol. 30* (1898).
Williams, H. Fulford – 'The Rectors of Sampford Courtenay', *Devon & Cornwall Notes & Queries Vol. 26* (1954/5).
Williams, H. Fulford – 'Sampford Courtenay and Honeychurch', *TDA Vol. 89* (1957).

Other Sources

Ancient Order of Foresters: Foresters' Heritage Trust, Camberley.
Devon Record Office.
Exeter Diocesan Registry.
Heavitree Brewery Company, Exeter.
Humberts (formerly Rawlence & Squarey), Sherborne.
King's College Archive Library, Cambridge.
Okehampton Library.
Okehampton Museum of Dartmoor Life.
Postal Markings of Devon Study Group.
Shebbear College, Shebbear, Beaworthy.
Westcountry Studies Library.

Photographs

Beaford Photographic Archive, Beaford, Winkleigh.
Burnard, Robert.
Crediton Country Courier.
Express & Echo (Western Times) and *Western Morning News.*
Hall, Barrie – Braetor Studio, Okehampton.
Hewitson, John B. – Red Lion Studios, Okehampton.
Mills, Bernard – Buckland Monachorum.
RAF Museum, Hendon.

Maps

Rawlence & Squarey (now Humberts, Sherborne) reproduced from Ordnance Survey maps.

Sale Catalogues

Rawlence & Squarey (now Humberts, Sherborne).

SUBSCRIBERS

Angela Arathoon, Farnham, Surrey

Revd Brian Ardill (Rector) and Mrs Bridie Ardill

Mr Christopher Ash Miles, Yondhill, Sampford Courtenay

Mr Timothy Ash Miles, Yondhill, Sampford Courtenay

Mrs K. Askew, Woking, Surrey

Mrs A.B. Baker, Plymtree, Devon

George and Catherine Ball, Sampford Courtenay

Ross and Mary Barton, Prestwich, Manchester

Leslie G. Beer, Sampford Courtenay, Devon

Joan Bessell, Mangotsfield, Bristol

Betty Jean Bolt (née Johns)

Mrs Shirley Elizabeth Bourne (née Squire), formerly from Sampford Courtenay

Connie Brooker (née Snell), Orpington, Kent

Frances and Arthur Brookes, North Tawton

Mrs Sylvia Bundick, USA

Miss E. Burnaby, Farnham, Surrey

K.J. Burrow, Bucks Cross, Devon

Mark Butchers and Hilary Burr, Oxford

T.M. Caplin, Croydon

Grace Cardis (née Snell), Capetown, South Africa

Noel and Sheila Cartwright, Sampford Courtenay, Devon

K.V. and V.J. Christmas, Sampford Courtenay, Devon

Roy and Susan Churchill, Sampford Courtenay, Devon

Mrs Barbara Clark (née Tremlett)

Margery Clarke, Frinton, Essex

Philip and Rosemary Clarke, Bexley Heath, Kent

Nick and Karen Clayton

Mrs Emma, Mary Cleverdon (née Bolt), East Cliston

Tony and Ann Cloke, Honeycott, Sampford Courtenay

Patrick and Christine Cockwill, Sampford Courtenay

Colin and Annette Coleman, Sampford Courtenay

Rob Corlett, Sampford Courtenay, Devon

Maurice Cornelius, Saham Toney, Norfolk

Ron Cornelius, Fareham, Hampshire

The Courtenay Society

Sandra Coventry, Chagford

Simon and Rosalind Coy, Ruthernbridge, Cornwall

Malcolm and Nicky Craig, Sampford Courtenay, Devon

Pauline Curtis, Hayling Island, Hampshire

Edwina Dagger, Downend, Bristol

Robert and Kate Dean, Corscombe, Devon

Mike and Jenny Denison Smith, Sampford Courtenay

Richard Denot, Argentat, France

Gwyneth and John Dickinson

Mr and Mrs E.J. Dunn, Lower Underdown, Sampford Courtenay

Amanda Jane Dunn (née Hodge)

Teresa J. Dunster (née Bolt), North Tawton

S.M. Finch, Okehampton, Devon

Avril and Mike Flanagan, Sampford Courtenay

Alan and Jo George

Pamela Green (née Horn), Weymouth, Dorset

Peter and Ann Green, Okehampton, Devon

Daisy I. Griffiths, Fullaford Farm

D.J. Gundry, Okehampton, Devon

Olive and Brian Hall, Alton, Hampshire

Jill D. Hall (née Smallbone), late of Senderhills, North Tawton 1949–1955

John and Sarah Hanks, Great Cliston, Sampford Courtenay

Sandra and Tony Harper, Sampford Courtenay, Devon

Nancy Harrison (née Snell), Saffron Walden, Essex

Valerie E. Hawking, Honeychurch, Devon

David Henderson, Monksilver, Somerset

Shirley and Michael Hide, Brook Cottage, Sampford Courtenay

David and Ann Hoare, North Tawton

Victor Hodge, Sampford Courtenay

Ivan John Hodge, Bridge, near Chard, Somerset

The Hoggins Family, Sampford Courtenay

Raymond Honeychurch, Calgary, Alberta, Canada

John W. Horn, Sampford Courtenay, Devon

Pauline Houben, Wood Farm, Sampford Courtenay

Mrs Ingrid Howard-Taylor (née Snell), Brisbane, Australia

Mike and Pat Hunt, North Tawton, Devon

Brenda Jackson, Hanham, Bristol

J. Loveys Jervoise, Rowden, Sampford Courtenay

J. Loveys Jervoise, Rowden, Sampford Courtenay

Mr Freddie Johns, Chichacott Cross, Okehampton

R.R. Kelly, Belstone, Devon

Richard and Carolyn Knapman, Sampford Courtenay, Devon

Roman Kozlowski, Taw Green

Tom Lake, Lichfield, Staffordshire

John and Sue Lamming, Sampford Courtenay

Margaret and David Latham, Yelverton

R.V. Letheren, Exbourne

Mr S. Lew, Lamisell Ltd, Sampford Courtenay

Edward, John, Cleverdon Lowe, Higher Cliston Farm

Mr John and Mrs Rosemary Lowe (née Cleverdon)

Phil and Yvonne Maker (née Cockwill), Kingskerswell, South Devon

Christine Marsh, Okehampton, Devon

Mr and Mrs Donald Miles, Ridgeway, Sampford Courtenay

Harrison R.J. Montgomery, Honeychurch, Devon

Quentin and Helen Morgan Edwards, Glebe House, Sampford Courtenay

Anthony Morris, Sampford Courtenay

Rosalie Newman, Maldon, Essex

Northam, formerly ran Village Shop

Mr and Mrs C. Owen, Lower Middletown

Alison and Michael Palmer, Bideford, Devon

Janice Phillips, Sampford Courtenay, Devon

Jean Mary Pinwill (née Hornett), Chagford, Devon

Andrea and Christopher Piper, Sampford Chapple, Devon

Bert and Doris Piper, Sampford Chapple, Devon

Leonard and Doris Piper, Sampford Courtenay, Devon

Jerry and Maureen Pitts-Tucker, Forge House, Sampford Courtenay. 1984–2000

Yvonne R. Potter, South Tawton, Devon

Cyril Potter, Shobrooke, Devon

Mrs Catherine E. Powell (née Ash), Johannesburg, South Africa

Mrs Marjorie Pratt, Hertfordshire

Mr and Mrs D.W. Puttick, Eastbourne, Sussex

Marguerite Pye, Middleton Farmhouse, Sampford Courtenay

Mrs Gladys Pyke, North Tawton

Audrey and Phil Reddaway, North Tawton

John Reddaway, Taw Green, Sticklepath

Robert J. Reddaway, Reddaway Farm

Stewart and Jose Reddaway, Honeychurch

R.W.A. Rivett

Patrick and Amanda Roberts, Chapel Cottage, Sampford Courtenay, Devon

Linda Robertson and Richard Mellor, Molly and Harry. Yondhill, Sampford Courtenay

Jennifer and John Rogers, Middle Trecott, Sampford Courtenay

Michael and Barbara Sampson, Sticklepath, Devon

Clarice Sampson (née Green), Crediton, Devon

Mrs I. Sampson (née Hawkins), North Tawton

Hilary M. Semmons, Burston, Plymouth, Devonshire

The Sercombe Family, Sampford Courtenay, Devon

Jean M. Shields, North Tawton, Devon

Betty Sims, Buntingford, Hertfordshire

John and Joyce Slate, Exmouth

Margaret Slattery, Whitefield, Manchester

Mavis J. Sleeman, Sampford Courtenay

Ralph and Margaret Smith, Sampford Courtenay

Barbara H. Smith, Sampford Courtenay, Devon

Steve, Karen, Keeley and Tom Smith, Trecott

Margaret Snell, Okehampton, Devon

Joy Snell, Bury St Edmunds

Marie Snell, Bristol

Vivien South (née Hopper), late of North Tawton

Hugh and Thelma Spratt, Sampford Courtenay

Nick, Teela, Charlotte and Fraser Spratt, Part Haveys, Sampford Courtenay

Reggie Squire, Sampford Courtenay, Devon

R.R. Squire, Sampford Courtenay

Jim and Joyce Stacey, Sampford Courtenay

Joyce F. Stanley, Sampford Courtenay Station. Born 1936

William E. and Dorothy M. Stanley (deceased), Station View, Sampford Bridge

Mike Steward

Joe and Christine Stoneman, Ventown Farm, Sampford Courtenay

Mr Pat and Ruth Summers, Bude Farm, Honeychurch, Devon

Peter and Anne Tandy, Forge House, Sampford Courtenay

Deborah, Lionel and Caroline Taylor, Churchward, Sampford Courtenay

Mrs G.E.H. Taylor, Okehampton, Devon

Mr W.B. Taylor, Crediton, Devon

Chester Thomas and Christine Denniford, Maidenhead, Berkshire

Mrs B.A. Thorne, North Tawton, Devon

Mrs Alice Towell (Johns), New Inn 1931

Andrew Townsend Green

Tim and Gillian Townsend Green, Southey Farm, Sampford Courtenay

Dr Elspeth Veale and cousins

Dr John Veale, Sydney, Australia

John F.W. Walling, Newton Abbot, Devon

Dr Hugh Webb, North Tawton

Margaret Weeks, Exbourne, Devon

The Weeks Family, Honeychurch

Eric and Pauline Weldon, Torre Cottage, Sampford Courtenay

Ronald West, Whimple, near Exeter

Christopher H. Westaway, Belstone, Devon

Mr Charles Westlake, Okehampton

Douglas E. Whittall, Sampford Courtenay (evacuee)

Community Histories

The Book of Addiscombe • Canning and Clyde Road Residents Association and Friends
The Book of Addiscombe, Vol. II • Canning and Clyde Road Residents Association and Friends
The Book of Axminster with Kilmington • L. Berry and G. Gosling
The Book of Bampton • Caroline Seward
The Book of Barnstaple • Avril Stone
The Book of Barnstaple, Vol. II • Avril Stone
The Book of The Bedwyns • Bedwyn History Society
The Book of Bickington • Stuart Hands
Blandford Forum: A Millennium Portrait • Blandford Forum Town Council
The Book of Bramford • Bramford Local History Group
The Book of Breage & Germoe • Stephen Polglase
The Book of Bridestowe • D. Richard Cann
The Book of Bridport • Rodney Legg
The Book of Brixham • Frank Pearce
The Book of Buckfastleigh • Sandra Coleman
The Book of Buckland Monachorum & Yelverton • Pauline Hamilton-Leggett
The Book of Carharrack • Carharrack Old Cornwall Society
The Book of Carshalton • Stella Wilks and Gordon Rookledge
The Parish Book of Cerne Abbas • Vivian and Patricia Vale
The Book of Chagford • Iain Rice
The Book of Chapel-en-le-Frith • Mike Smith
The Book of Chittlehamholt with Warkleigh & Satterleigh • Richard Lethbridge
The Book of Chittlehampton • Various
The Book of Colney Heath • Bryan Lilley
The Book of Constantine • Moore and Trethowan
The Book of Cornwood & Lutton • Compiled by the People of the Parish
The Book of Creech St Michael • June Small
The Book of Cullompton • Compiled by the People of the Parish
The Book of Dawlish • Frank Pearce
The Book of Dulverton, Brushford, Bury & Exebridge • Dulverton and District Civic Society
The Book of Dunster • Hilary Binding
The Book of Edale • Gordon Miller
The Ellacombe Book • Sydney R. Langmead
The Book of Exmouth • W.H. Pascoe
The Book of Grampound with Creed • Bane and Oliver
The Book of Hayling Island & Langstone • Peter Rogers
The Book of Helston • Jenkin with Carter
The Book of Hemyock • Clist and Dracott
The Book of Herne Hill • Patricia Jenkyns
The Book of Hethersett • Hethersett Society Research Group
The Book of High Bickington • Avril Stone
The Book of Ilsington • Dick Wills
The Book of Kingskerswell • Carsewella Local History Group
The Book of Lamerton • Ann Cole and Friends
Lanner, A Cornish Mining Parish • Sharron Schwartz and Roger Parker
The Book of Leigh & Bransford • Malcolm Scott
The Book of Litcham with Lexham & Mileham • Litcham Historical and Amenity Society
The Book of Loddiswell • Loddiswell Parish History Group
The New Book of Lostwithiel • Barbara Fraser
The Book of Lulworth • Rodney Legg
The Book of Lustleigh • Joe Crowdy
The Book of Lyme Regis • Rodney Legg
The Book of Manaton • Compiled by the People of the Parish

The Book of Markyate • Markyate Local History Society
The Book of Mawnan • Mawnan Local History Group
The Book of Meavy • Pauline Hemery
The Book of Minehead with Alcombe • Binding and Stevens
The Book of Morchard Bishop • Jeff Kingaby
The Book of Newdigate • John Callcut
The Book of Nidderdale • Nidderdale Museum Society
The Book of Northlew with Ashbury • Northlew History Group
The Book of North Newton • J.C. and K.C. Robins
The Book of North Tawton • Baker, Hoare and Shields
The Book of Nynehead • Nynehead & District History Society
The Book of Okehampton • R. and U. Radford
The Book of Paignton • Frank Pearce
The Book of Penge, Anerley & Crystal Palace • Peter Abbott
The Book of Peter Tavy with Cudlipptown • Peter Tavy Heritage Group
The Book of Pimperne • Jean Coull
The Book of Plymtree • Tony Eames
The Book of Porlock • Dennis Corner
Postbridge – The Heart of Dartmoor • Reg Bellamy
The Book of Priddy • Albert Thompson
The Book of Princetown • Dr Gardner-Thorpe
The Book of Rattery • By the People of the Parish
The Book of St Day • Joseph Mills and Paul Annear
The Book of Sampford Courtenay with Honeychurch • Stephanie Pouya
The Book of Sculthorpe • Gary Windeler
The Book of Seaton • Ted Gosling
The Book of Sidmouth • Ted Gosling and Sheila Luxton
The Book of Silverton • Silverton Local History Society
The Book of South Molton • Jonathan Edmunds
The Book of South Stoke with Midford • Edited by Robert Parfitt
South Tawton & South Zeal with Sticklepath • R. and U. Radford
The Book of Sparkwell with Hemerdon & Lee Mill • Pam James
The Book of Staverton • Pete Lavis
The Book of Stithians • Stithians Parish History Group
The Book of Stogumber, Monksilver, Nettlecombe & Elworthy • Maurice and Joyce Chidgey
The Book of Studland • Rodney Legg
The Book of Swanage • Rodney Legg
The Book of Tavistock • Gerry Woodcock
The Book of Thorley • Sylvia McDonald and Bill Hardy
The Book of Torbay • Frank Pearce
The Book of Watchet • Compiled by David Banks
The Book of West Huntspill • By the People of the Parish
Widecombe-in-the-Moor • Stephen Woods
Widecombe – Uncle Tom Cobley & All • Stephen Woods
The Book of Williton • Michael Williams
The Book of Witheridge • Peter and Freda Tout and John Usmar
The Book of Withycombe • Chris Boyles
Woodbury: The Twentieth Century Revisited • Roger Stokes
The Book of Woolmer Green • Compiled by the People of the Parish

For details of any of the above titles or if you are interested in writing your own history, please contact: Commissioning Editor Community Histories, Halsgrove House, Lower Moor Way, Tiverton Business Park, Tiverton, Devon EX16 6SS, England; email: naomic@halsgrove.com

In order to include as many historical photographs as possible in this volume, a printed index is not included. However, the Devon titles in the Community History Series are indexed by Genuki. For further information and indexes to various volumes in the series, please visit: http://www.cs.ncl.ac.uk/genuki/DEV/indexingproject.html